Lawrenceville Press

A Guide to Programming the IBM® Personal Computers

SECOND EDITION

For the IBM PC and PC JR.

BRUCE PRESLEY

DISTRIBUTED BY

DELMAR Publishers Inc.

First edition published in 1982
Second edition published in 1985
Copyright © 1985
by

Second Edition
ISBN 0-931717-11-6

Lawrenceville Press books are distributed by Delmar Publishers. Educational orders may be placed by writing or calling them at:

By Mail
Delmar Publishers Inc.
2 Computer Drive, West
Box 15015
Albany, New York 12212-5105

By Phone
Delmar Publishers Inc.
Customer Service Dept.
1-800-833-3350
1-800-252-2550 (NYS)
(518) 459-1150

16 15 14 13 12 11 10 9 8 7 6 5 4 3

PREFACE

It is widely acknowledged that a familiarity with computers is a vital part of today's education. We believe that learning to program offers a student an invaluable opportunity to learn problem solving skills. The process of defining a problem, breaking it down into a series of smaller problems and finally writing a computer program is an exercise in learning to think logically. The student also becomes aware of the capabilities and limitations of the computer and soon realizes that the programmer—the human element—is more important than the machine.

The Lawrenceville Press series of programming texts, authored by Bruce Presley, focuses on the development of these problem-solving skills and emphasizes the value of good programming style and structure. The texts are written for a one- or two-term course for the high school or college student. No previous programming experience is required or assumed, although a background of one year of algebra is necessary.

Design and Features

The author of this text, Bruce Presley, has been teaching programming for the past 17 years, and was a founding member of the Advanced Placement Computer Science Committe of the College Entrance Examination Board. His years of experience as a teacher and an author are clearly reflected in this text. Some of the features of special interest are:

- **Format.** Each computer command is printed in red at the beginning of the section in which it is introduced. The command is given a clear definition, shown in a single program line, and then demonstrated in a program. Commands are also highlighted in red in the Table of Contents, making it easy to use this text as a reference guide.

- **Review Problems.** Numerous review problems are presented throughout each chapter, with solutions given at the back of the text. This provides immediate reinforcement of new concepts.

- **Exercises.** At the end of each chapter there is a large set of exercises of varying difficulty, making them appropriate for students with a wide range of abilities. Answers to odd-numbered exercises are found at the back of the text, enabling students to check their own solutions. Answers to even-numbered exercises are included in the Teacher's Guide.

- **Line-by-Line Program Analysis.** Whenever a major program is shown, it is followed with a line-by-line analysis. In addition to explaining the function of each program line, proper programming style is stressed.

- **Algorithmic Approach.** Beginning in Chapter 2, most chapters end with a problem requiring a carefully thought out algorithm. By analyzing and reviewing the techniques used, students learn valuable problem-solving skills.

- **Advanced Topics.** Two chapters have been included for higher-level students, one covering mathematical functions and the other searching and sorting algorithms.

- **Appendices.** A list of BASIC commands, a glossary, and Disk Operating System instructions are found at the back of the text.

Teacher's Guide

An extensive teacher's guide is available. Each chapter of the text is broken down into a series of lessons which contain: discussion topics; reading and problem assignments; transparency masters; worksheets; supplementary problems; chapter, mid-term and final tests; detailed answers to all problems in the Guide and answers to all text exercises. For the convenience of the instructor, all this material is contained in a loose-leaf binder so that pages may be removed for duplication and the instructor's own notes may be inserted. Note: The Guide is available only when ordered by an educational institution through our distributor, Delmar Publishers.

Acknowledgements

The author wishes to thank the following people whose talents contributed to the production of this text.

Michael Bidwell has authored and taken responsibility for specific areas of the manual. The clarity and accuracy of much of the material it contains are due to his efforts and expertise. Heidi Crane, Carol Tibbetts, Robert Bracalente and Michael Porter have all helped in editing and laying out the text. A special thanks is due Gregg Schwinn, who produced the imaginative graphic design, and the staffs at Browne Book Composition, Inc. and Heffernan Press, Inc.

TABLE OF CONTENTS

1

INTRODUCTION

PRINT

AUTO

RUN

LIST

HOME

NEW

CLS

REM

When discussing computers, it is convenient to divide the subject into two broad categories—hardware and software. Hardware refers to the computer itself and its peripheral devices—disk drives, printers, etc. whereas software refers to the programs or instructions which are entered into the computer to make it perform specific tasks. It is the purpose of this book to teach you how to program your computer. Therefore, it is a guide for producing software.

What is a computer?

A computer is a machine that accepts information, processes it according to specific instructions, and provides the results as new information. The computer differs from a simple calculator in several ways. It can store and move large quantities of data at very high speed and, even though it cannot think, it can make simple decisions and comparisons. For instance, the computer is capable of determining which of two numbers is larger or which of two names comes first alphabetically. Another major difference is that the computer can perform many varied tasks by having its instructions changed.

What is a program?

A program is a list of instructions written in a special code, or language, which direct the computer in performing its operations. The program instructs the computer in what operations it will perform and in what sequence it will perform them. While there are many different languages, such as FORTRAN, COBOL, Pascal, and LOGO, this manual will teach you to program in BASIC (Beginner's All-purpose Symbolic Instruction Code), which was originally developed by John Kemeny and Tom Kurtz at Dartmouth College.

Why learn to program?

The primary reason for learning to program is that you will be able to use the computer efficiently for your own purposes. While there are many programs available commercially, they are seldom written for an individual's specific needs. By learning to write your own programs, you can develop software designed to meet your requirements.

Secondly, and of equal importance, are skills you will acquire in developing problem-solving techniques. Learning how to define a problem, break it down into manageable parts and then design a series of operations to reach a solution are invaluable skills.

Thirdly, it is recognized that computers have become a major factor in our lives, affecting virtually every profession and business. By possessing even a limited knowledge of programming you will be aware of the capabilities and limitations of computers, which will enable you to deal with them both knowledgeably and confidently.

Finally, programming is fun. The intellectual challenge of controlling the operations of a computer is not only rewarding but an invaluable skill.

Developing problem solving skills

It is tempting when first beginning to program to sit down at the computer and type short programs without giving much thought to their structure or logic. This approach will only teach you poor habits and thus hinder the development of your problem solving skills. This text presents you with a series of carefully worked out examples: we urge you to study them carefully.

What is an algorithm?

By definition an algorithm is a set of well-defined rules and processes for solving a problem in a finite number of steps. Put more simply, an algorithm is a plan. Using this definition a computer program is, therefore, an algorithm. The following steps outline how an algorithm is developed for solving a problem on the computer.

1. State the problem to be solved so that it is clear and unambiguous.
2. Develop a solution by breaking the problem down into a series of separate parts.
3. Write a computer program that will follow the solution developed in step (2).

Notice that writing the program is the last step, performed only after the solution to the problem has been developed.

To illustrate how an algorithm is produced, let's take the simple every day problem of shopping for groceries and break it down into a series of steps.

1. Write a shopping list—
   Check through the kitchen cabinets and the refrigerator to determine what items are in low supply and list them.
2. Leave house—
   Turn off the lights and lock door.
3. Go to store—
   Get in the car, drive to the store and park the car.
4. Shop—
   Go through the aisles of the supermarket searching for each item on the shopping list and place found items in shopping cart. Go to check out counter and pay for items selected.
5. Go home—
   Get in the car, drive home and park the car.
6. Enter house—
   Unlock the door and turn on the lights.
7. Unpack groceries—
   Place each item purchased in its proper place in the kitchen cabinets and refrigerator.

Although this example may appear trivial, it illustrates the process employed in developing an algorithm. A large problem has been broken down into a series of smaller problems, each of which can be solved individually. One point that should be obvious is that a number of algorithms can be developed to solve the same problem, and the number of steps the algorithm contains will be determined by the person who is writing it.

Review

1. Write an algorithm for making a trip by airplane from your home to a hotel in Paris, France. Start by phoning your travel agent to make reservations.

2. Write an algorithm for holding a birthday party. Start by making a list of those who will be invited.

As we have already noted, it is necessary to use a special language to communicate with the computer. You should be aware that each language, in this case BASIC, varies slightly with the different brands of computers. This book describes BASIC as it is used on the IBM PC and PCjr. This chapter will instruct you in the procedures for doing simple mathematics and displaying messages on the screen. It will also explain how a program is written and errors are corrected.

The Cursor

When the computer is first turned on, a small blinking square appears which is called a cursor. The cursor can be moved around the screen by using the cursor control keys, which make the job of writing a program easier.

All the cursor keys are repeat keys, which means that they continue printing the same thing as long as they are held down. As long as a cursor key is held down, the cursor will continue to move over anything written on the screen without erasing it. To move the cursor down the screen use the key marked with a down arrow. Everytime this key is pressed the cursor moves down one line. Similarly, to move the cursor up, left or right, use the keys marked with arrows pointing in these directions.

Review

Try these exercises using the cursor control keys:

3. Turn the computer off and then on again and type the word BASIC. The computer's start up message will then appear. Use the cursor keys to move the cursor to the middle of the screen and then type your name.

4. Use the cursor keys to move the cursor to the first "I" in IBM and change IBM to International Business Machines.

5. Hit the ENTER (↵) key marked with a return arrow and note that the computer responds with the message SYNTAX ERROR. Hitting the ENTER (↵) key enters whatever has been typed into the computer's memory and since the computer does not understand what instructions you have given it, it responds with an error message.

Immediate Mode

A computer does nothing without first being given instructions. It is possible to have the computer follow an instruction immediately by typing a BASIC statement and then pressing ENTER (↩); this is called using the computer in immediate mode. It is also possible to give the computer instructions using a program, which will be explained later in this chapter.

PRINT

PRINT is the BASIC statement used to display numbers, characters and words on the screen. Using immediate mode, the following example prints the results of a math operation on the screen as soon as ENTER (↩) is pressed.

> PRINT 12 + 5 (↩)
> 17

PRINT followed by a math operation tells the computer to print the result of that operation. Notice that only the result and not the math statement is printed. In immediate mode the computer carries out this operation as soon as the ENTER (↩) key is pressed.

In BASIC the following symbols are used for each of the four math operations:

Operation	Sign
Addition	+
Subtraction	−
Multiplication	*
Division	/

The computer can use both numbers and words. To the computer a number is something that can be used in a mathematical calculation; something that can be added, subtracted, multiplied or divided. A word or character, on the other hand, cannot be used to do any of those things.

PRINT with Quotation Marks

PRINT followed by quotation marks tells the computer to print whatever appears between the quotation marks. Using immediate mode, the following example prints a message on the screen:

> PRINT "THE COMPUTER IS FAST" (↩)

As soon as ENTER (↩) is pressed, THE COMPUTER IS FAST is printed on the screen. The word PRINT and the quotation marks are not displayed.

SYNTAX ERROR

The computer will only act when it recognizes a command or instruction that is in its language. Anytime the computer does not recognize an instruction, it prints an error message and either stops what it is doing or waits until the programmer corrects the error.

One of the most common error message is the SYNTAX ERROR.

> PRUNT "THE COMPUTER IS FAST"
> SYNTAX ERROR

Since the computer cannot think for itself, it does not realize that the programmer meant PRINT. The BASIC language does not contain the word

PRUNT, so the computer displays an error message and halts its attempt to carry out the instruction it was given.

Most BASIC commands can be used in immediate mode. However, it is best to use immediate mode only for simple calculations and to use programs to perform most tasks.

Review

6. Enter each of the following statements in immediate mode. Predict what the computer will print when ENTER (←) is pressed.

>   PRINT 2 + 5
>   PRINT 6 − 3
>   PRINT 5 ∗ 3
>   PRINT 5 / 3

7. Enter the following in immediate mode and predict what the computer will print:

>   PRINT "I AM 6 FEET TALL."

8. What will the output of the following be:

>   PRLNT "LOOK MA! NO HANDS."

9. Correct the PRINT statement in number 8.

Writing a Program

As we have noted, immediate mode instructs the computer one command at a time. A program on the other hand, gives the computer a series of instructions written as numbered lines. These lines are stored in the computer's memory until it is given a command to execute the program. The computer then finds the lowest numbered line, executes the instructions on that line, and continues to read the lines and carry out the instructions until the highest numbered line is completed.

END

The END statement, which should be the last statement in a program, is used to halt the program's run. For example,

>   50 END

will cause the run of a program to stop when line 50 is reached. It is good programming practice to place an END statement on all programs since it helps ensure that the program will terminate properly. The following is an example of a program:

>   10 PRINT "THIS IS A PROGRAM."
>   20 PRINT "INSTRUCTIONS ARE WRITTEN"
>   30 PRINT "ON LINES. EACH LINE"
>   40 PRINT "HAS A LINE NUMBER."
>   50 END

Entering Program Lines

There are a few simple rules about program lines and line numbering which you should keep in mind when writing a program:

1. To enter a program line into the computer's memory, press the ENTER key when the line is completed.

   10 PRINT 2 + 2

2. When writing a program, you should use line numbers that are units of ten (10, 20, . . . 100, 110, 120, etc.). This leaves room to insert nine possible lines between any two lines in case it is necessary to add lines later.

3. It is not necessary to enter lines in order. Line 20 can be entered first, then line 10 and later line 30. The computer will automatically put the lines in numerical order. Any time a new instruction is to be added to a program, just type the line number, the instruction and press ENTER. The computer will then put the line into proper sequence.

   10 PRINT "MATHEMATICS"
   30 PRINT "2 + 2"
   20 PRINT "WITH A COMPUTER"
   40 PRINT 2 + 2
   50 END

4. Do not confuse the capital letter "O" with a zero "0". Use the zero (0) when a number is needed and the letter (O) when a letter is needed.

5. Any whole number from 0 to 65529 can be used as a line number.

6. Do not use the ENTER key or the space bar to move the cursor around the screen; instead use the cursor control keys to move up, down, left or right. Using ENTER to move down the screen can cause lines to be entered or erased by accident, and using the space bar will erase characters by printing a space over them.

AUTO

A useful feature of BASIC is the AUTO command which will automatically number the lines of your program by tens as you type them. Simply type AUTO and ENTER before you start typing your program. After the last program line has been typed and the ENTER key hit to store it in memory, the computer prints an additional line number. At this point, hit the "CTRL" and "C" keys at the same time to leave the AUTO mode. It is important to note that the line where the CTRL-C combination is typed will not be saved in the computer's memory.

RUN

The command RUN tells the computer to begin executing the program in its memory. Type the word RUN and press ENTER when you have completed your program. It is important to realize that the command RUN is not part of the program and is typed only after a program is complete.

Program 1.1   Type in this program and then RUN it. Be sure to copy it exactly, and do not forget to press ENTER after each line:

```
10 PRINT "HELLO"
20 PRINT "I AM A COMPUTER"
30 END

RUN
HELLO
I AM A COMPUTER
```

When RUN is typed and ENTER is pressed, the computer, beginning at line 10, executes the program lines that are stored in its memory. When a line is executed, PRINT works the same as it does in immediate mode. The message HELLO is printed because those characters are between quotation marks as is the message "I AM A COMPUTER" on line 20. Notice that the word PRINT and the quotation marks are not printed when the program is executed.

Program 1.2   This program uses the PRINT statement to print the results of four mathematical operations:

```
10 PRINT 5 + 3
20 PRINT 5 - 3
30 PRINT 5 * 3
40 PRINT 15 / 3
50 END

RUN
 8
 2
 15
 5
```

When line 10 is executed, the computer prints the sum of 5 and 3. Line 20 tells the computer to print the difference between 5 and 3. Line 30 tells the computer to print the product of 5 and 3, while line 40 prints the result of 15 divided by 3. It is not necessary to use an equal sign since the computer performs the operation and prints the result without it. The command RUN, which is not part of the program, was typed after line 50 was entered to tell the computer to begin executing the instructions of the program.

Review   10. What will a RUN of the following program print on the screen?

```
10 PRINT "MY COMPUTER IS"
20 PRINT "A CHIP OFF THE OLD"
30 PRINT "BLOCK!"
40 END
```

11. Predict the results of the following program:

```
10 PRINT 123 + 456 + 789
20 PRINT 27 * 13
30 END
```

It is possible to use PRINT on one line both to display the result of a math operation and to print a message. The rules for doing this are simple. Whatever words, numbers or characters are to be printed must be typed within quotation marks while any math operations that are to be carried out must be typed outside the quotation marks.

Program 1.3   This program shows how to print numbers, words and characters at the same time.

```
10  PRINT "MATHEMATICS"
20  PRINT "5 * 3"
30  PRINT 5 * 3
40  PRINT "5 * 3 =" 5 * 3
50  END

RUN
MATHEMATICS
5 * 3
 15
5 * 3 = 15
```

- **Line 10:** Prints the word MATHEMATICS since it is enclosed in quotation marks.
- **Line 20:** Prints 5 * 3 on the screen. It does not print the product of 5 and 3 because the computer understands the 5, * and 3 to be characters when they are inside quotation marks.
- **Line 30:** Since the 5, * and 3 are not inside quotation marks, the computer prints the product, 15.
- **Line 40:** Combines the printing of words and numbers in one PRINT statement. 5 * 3 = appears on the screen because it is inside the quotation marks and the product 15 is printed because 5 * 3 is outside the quotation marks.

Review   12. What will be the exact output of the following line?

10 PRINT 4 * 3 "COOKIES MAKE A DOZEN."

13. Predict what this program will print on the screen when it is RUN:

10 PRINT 5 + 3 "EQUALS" 4 * 2
20 PRINT "40 + " 5 * 4 "=" 50 + 10

LIST   The LIST command is used to display the program currently in the computer's memory. For instance, when an error is made and needs to be corrected, LIST shows the program lines enabling, the programmer to see where the mistake is and correct it. Program 1.3 helps demonstrate two ways that LIST can be used:

1. List by itself:

> LIST
> 10 PRINT "MATHEMATICS"
> 20 PRINT "5 * 3"
> 30 PRINT 5 * 3
> 40 PRINT "5 * 3 = " 5 * 3
> 50 END

Typing LIST and then pressing the ENTER key displays the entire program. It is also possible to LIST a single line of a program by typing LIST followed by the line number of the desired line.

2. LIST a single line:

> LIST 10
> 10 PRINT "MATHEMATICS"

NEW

The NEW command is used to erase the computer's memory. Before entering a program into the computer's memory it is good programming practice to type NEW. This will ensure that program lines from any previous program will not affect the new program:

> LIST
> 10 PRINT "MATHEMATICS"
> 20 PRINT "5 * 3"
> 30 PRINT 5 * 3
> 40 PRINT "5 * 3 = " 5 * 3
> 50 END
>
> Ok
>
> NEW
>
> Ok
>
> LIST
>
> Ok

After the NEW command is entered by typing NEW and pressing ENTER, the LIST command shows that there is no program in the computer's memory. Be sure that you really want your program erased from the computer's memory when you type NEW. Once it is erased it is lost forever unless it has been saved on a diskette (See Appendix A for disk operations).

Review

14. Write a program that prints your name on the screen and then RUN it.

        RUN
        BRUCE PRESLEY

15. LIST the program and add a line to the program that says "THE COM-PUTER IS FAST". RUN the program and then use the NEW command to clear the computer's memory.

        RUN
        BRUCE PRESLEY
        THE COMPUTER IS FAST

Correcting Errors

Typing errors or other mistakes in a program can be corrected in several ways. The following examples use Program 1.3:

1. RETYPING A LINE: A program line can be changed by simply retyping it using the same line number.

        LIST 10
        10 PRINT "MATHEMATICS"

        10 PRINT "MATH MAGIC"
        RUN
        MATH MAGIC
        5 * 3
         15
        5 * 3 = 15

Notice that only the output of line 10 is changed. Instead of MATHEMATICS, the program now outputs MATH MAGIC.

2. DELETING A CHARACTER: The DEL key is used to erase one character at a time. Each time the DEL key is pressed the space above the cursor will be erased. Note: the DEL key is a repeat key. The following example shows how to use the DEL key to delete the word MAGIC from line 10 of Program 1.3:

   A. First LIST line 10 and then use the cursor keys to move the cursor to the space between MATH and MAGIC in "MATH MAGIC".

           LIST 10
           10 PRINT "MATH MAGIC"

   B. With the cursor under the space, press the DEL key six times which will delete the last six characters leaving only the word MATH.

   C. Press ENTER to enter the changed line into the computer's memory and then RUN the program.

```
10 PRINT "MATH"

RUN
MATH
5 * 3
 15
5 * 3
```

3. INSERTING CHARACTERS: INS is the abbreviation for insert. The INSert key is used to open spaces so that changes can be typed in. To insert spaces between characters, move the cursor to the location where the insertion is to be made and press the INS key. Each character now typed will be inserted into the text. When you have completed the insertion, press the INS key again to halt the insertion and then enter the corrected line into the computer's memory by pressing ENTER. The following example uses the INS key to replace the word MAGIC in line 10.

   A. First LIST line 10 and then use the cursor keys to move the cursor to the M in MATH.

   ```
   LIST 10
   10 PRINT "MATH"
   ```

   B. Press the INS key and then type MAGIC and a space.

   ```
   10 PRINT "MAGIC MATH"
   ```

   C. Press the INS key again to halt the insertion and then press ENTER.

   ```
   10 PRINT "MAGIC MATH"

   RUN
   MAGIC MATH
   5 * 3
    15
   5 * 3 = 15
   ```

4. ERASING A WHOLE LINE: An entire line of a program can be erased by typing the line number and pressing ENTER. Using Program 1.3 type:

   ```
   20
   30

   RUN
   MAGIC MATH
   5 * 3 = 15
   ```

Notice that the output of lines 20 and 30 of the original program does not appear since these lines have now been erased from the computer's memory.

5. ADDING A NEW LINE: To add a line between other lines of a program, type the new line and press ENTER. The computer will then put the line in its proper place. A new line can be added to Program 1.3 as shown below:

```
25 PRINT "PRESTO!"

RUN
MAGIC MATH
PRESTO!
5 * 3 = 15
```

Review

Type this program into the computer exactly as it is written. After it is typed, correct the errors by using the methods mentioned above:

```
10 PRUNT "SCREEN EDITING"
20 PRINT "CAN BE USFUL"
30 PRINT "IT SAVES WORK."
40 END
```

16. Use the cursor control keys to change the "U" in PRUNT to an "I".

17. The "E" is missing from the word USEFUL in line 20. Use the INS key to insert the "E" so that the program looks like this when it is RUN:

```
RUN
SCREEN EDITING
CAN BE USEFUL
IT SAVES WORK.
```

18. Add a new line between lines 20 and 30 so that the program now looks like this when RUN:

```
RUN
SCREEN EDITING
CAN BE USEFUL
AND
IT SAVES WORK.
```

19. Delete lines 10 and 20 so that a RUN produces the following output:

```
RUN
AND
IT SAVES WORK
```

---

*Clearing
Things Up*

After a program has been used for a while, the screen can become filled with program lines, error messages, numbers and other "old" output. In fact, this "old" output can begin to get in the way as a programmer tries to make changes, correct errors or RUN the program. The following are methods which may be used to clear the screen.

HOME

The HOME key allows a programmer either to erase the screen completely or to put the cursor in the upper left corner of the screen, which is its home position. To move the cursor to the home position press the HOME key. To clear everything off the screen, hold down the CTRL key and press the HOME key, which will also return the cursor to the home position. Clearing the screen has no effect on the computer's memory. All program lines that have been entered will remain in the memory of the computer; only the screen is erased. To illustrate this, type in this program:

```
10 PRINT "I CONTROL MY"
20 PRINT "COMPUTER."
30 END

RUN
I CONTROL MY
COMPUTER.
```

Now clear the screen using the CTRL-HOME keys and then LIST the program:

```
LIST
10 PRINT "I CONTROL MY"
20 PRINT "COMPUTER."
30 END
```

LIST prints the program on the screen, which shows that the memory of the computer was not erased.

CLS

The CLS statement is used to clear the entire display screen except for the function key display line during the execution of a program. CLS may also be used in immediate mode. It is important to remember that only the screen is being erased, not the contents of the computer's memory. CLS performs the same function as the CRTL-HOME keys except that it may be used within a program.

Review

20. Use the CTRL-HOME keys to clear the screen and NEW to clear the computer's memory. Then write a program that prints your name on the screen and RUN it.

```
RUN
BRUCE PRESLEY
```

21. LIST the program. Add a line to the program that says "THE COMPUTER IS POWERFUL" and RUN it.

```
RUN
BRUCE PRESLEY
THE COMPUTER IS POWERFUL
```

22. LIST the program again. Using the CLS statement to clear the screen, LIST the program again to prove that it is still in the computer's memory. Now clear the computer's memory using the NEW command so that it is ready for a new program.

23. Write a new program that adds the numbers 25 and 15 and prints their sum and then RUN it:

    ```
    RUN
    25 + 15 = 40
    ```

REM

The REM statement is used in the body of a program to explain what the program is doing. These REMarks are ignored by the computer when the program is RUN. For example, the line

$$30 \text{ REM } ** \text{ Calculate the Area of a Rectangle } **$$

will be displayed only when the program is LISTed. It is good programming style to use REM statements throughout a program to explain what different parts of the program do so that another programmer would be able to read and understand the program without difficulty. To identify REM statements, you should type them in upper and lower case.

Program 1.4

This program illustrates a variety of uses of the PRINT statement. Review it carefully:

```
10 REM THIS PROGRAM ILLUSTRATES THE PRINT STATEMENT
20 PRINT "A COMPUTER IS A USEFUL TOOL"
30 PRINT "IT CAN ADD:       2 + 2 =" 2 + 2
40 PRINT "IT CAN SUBTRACT: 4 - 2 =" 4 - 2
50 PRINT "IT CAN MULTIPLY: 2 * 2 =" 2 * 2
60 PRINT "IT CAN DIVIDE:    4 / 2 =" 4 / 2
70 END

RUN
A COMPUTER IS A USEFUL TOOL
IT CAN ADD:       2 + 2 = 4
IT CAN SUBTRACT: 4 - 2 = 2
IT CAN MULTIPLY: 2 * 2 = 4
IT CAN DIVIDE:    4 / 2 = 2
```

Note that line 10 is not printed when Program 1.4 is RUN since the computer ignores REM statements.

EXERCISES

1. Perform each of the following computations on paper. Check your answers using immediate mode:

   a. 5 + 16   b. 33 − 16
   c. 13 ∗ 3   d. 239 ∗ 27
   e. 250 / 5   f. 999 / 11

2. Write a program that displays the following:

   ```
   RUN
   A
     B
       C
         D
   ABCD
   ```

3. Write a program that draws a rectangle using the "∗" symbol:

   ```
   RUN
   ************
   *          *
   *          *
   *          *
   ************
   ```

4. Write a program that first clears the screen and then draws a triangle using the "/", "\" and "_" symbols:

   RUN

5. Write a program that first clears the screen and then draws the following face on the screen:

   RUN

6. Write a program that will add the numbers 3, 5 and 7:

   ```
   RUN
    3 + 5 + 7 = 15
   ```

7. Write a program that first multiplies 275 times 39, and then divides 275 by 39. A run of the program should look like this:

   ```
   RUN
    275 * 39 = 10725
    275 / 39 = 7.051282
   ```

8. In the first week of the season, the jogging club ran the following number of miles each day: 2, 3, 5, 3, 5. Write a program to calculate and print the total mileage for the week:

   ```
   RUN
   MILEAGE FOR THE FIRST WEEK IS 18
   ```

9. There are 5 gerbils, 6 mice and 3 birds in the biology lab. Write a program that lists these animals:

   ```
   RUN
   BIOLOGY LAB
   GERBILS: 5
   MICE: 6
   BIRDS: 3
   ```

10. Change the biology lab program so that it also prints how many animals there are in all:

    ```
    RUN
    BIOLOGY LAB
    GERBILS: 5
    MICE: 6
    BIRDS: 3
    TOTAL ANIMALS = 14
    ```

11. Orange juice is $1.99 a half gallon on sale this week. Milk is $.89 a quart. Write a program that displays the following sign:

    ```
    RUN
    **************************
    *                        *
    *          BIG SALE       *
    *                        *
    *    ORANGE JUICE  $1.99  *
    *    MILK / QUART  $ .89  *
    *                        *
    **************************
    ```

12. Write a program to calculate the cost of 2 half gallons of orange juice and 2 quarts of milk. The program's output should look like this:

    ```
    RUN
    ORANGE JUICE $ 3.98
    MILK $ 1.78
    ```

2

USING VARIABLES

INPUT

GOTO

READ

DATA

INPUT

GOTO

READ

DATA

As we have noted, a computer is a data processing machine which accepts data in the form of numbers, words, letters and symbols, which are called "input". When the input has been entered into the program, the result is then displayed on the screen, saved on a disk, or printed on paper. This information is known as "output."

There are many different ways in which data is used. The same information may be used repeatedly in a program or it may change each time the program is run. To cover these different situations, BASIC uses "variables". This chapter will explain what variables are and how they are used within a program.

Variables

A variable is a name which is used to represent a value. For example,

$$A = 5$$

The number 5 is given the variable name A, which can then be used in place of the number 5. Because variables stand for a value, they are one of the most useful ways to bring data into a program.

To the computer there are two kinds of data: numbers and characters. Therefore, in order to use variables, the computer must be told both the name of the variable and the type of data, either number or character, that the variable stands for.

Assigning a Numeric Variable

An assignment statement is one way of assigning a variable name its value. For example,

$$10\ A = 5$$

tells the computer to set aside a place in its memory called A where the number 5 is stored. The computer's memory is like a post office with its memory divided into many boxes with a variable name used to represent the address of a single box. When the computer reads the above assignment statement, it sets aside a box in its memory, names it A and puts 5 in it.

A

5

Whenever the computer is told to use A, it will look in the box named A and use the value that A represents, in this case 5.

Variables can change in value as the name itself implies; however, it is important to realize that a variable can hold only one value at a time. Suppose a later statement such as

50 A = 7

is entered. Then at line 50 the value A will change from 5 to 7.

Thus, the value in the box named A is now 7:

A

7

The old value of A is lost and may not be retrieved again.

Variable names can be any single letter, a letter and a single digit or two letters. A, D, A1, D1, AA or DD are all legal variable names. When any legal variable name is used, the computer expects a number to be assigned to the variable name.

```
10 N = 27
20 PRINT N
30 END

RUN
 27
```

The computer will not accept placing the value before the variable name since the "=" sign really means "is given the value". Therefore, it is not possible to have "value = variable".

```
10 5 = A
20 PRINT A
30 END

RUN
?SYNTAX ERROR IN 10
10 5 = A
```

Statements must be written in exactly the way the computer has been programmed to understand them. If a statement is not in the correct form, the computer stops the program and prints the SYNTAX ERROR message. The computer indicates in which line the error can be found and then automatically lists that line, placing the cursor at the beginning so that the line may be edited.

___

Program 2.1

This program shows how variable names are used in a program:

```
10 A = 5
20 B = 3
30 PRINT A * B
40 END

RUN
 15
```

Line 10 puts a 5 in a box named A, and line 20 puts a 3 into a box named B. Line 30 tells the computer to print the product of A times B and does this by using the values stored in A and B.

A variable box can only hold one value at a time. If a different number is put in the box, then the first number is erased and lost.

___

Program 2.2

This program shows how a variable's value is changed when a new value is assigned during a program:

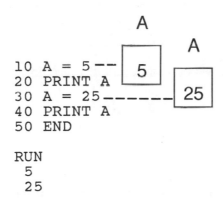

```
10 A = 5
20 PRINT A
30 A = 25
40 PRINT A
50 END

RUN
 5
 25
```

When the computer reads line 10, a 5 is stored in the box named A. On line 30, A is changed to 25 and the first value of A is erased from the computer's memory. Therefore, when the computer prints A for the second time on line 40, it prints 25.

A variable is used the same way that a number is used, which means that one variable can be used to give another variable its value.

Program 2.3

Here one variable is used to give another variable its value:

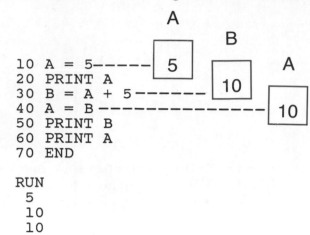

```
10  A = 5
20  PRINT A
30  B = A + 5
40  A = B
50  PRINT B
60  PRINT A
70  END

RUN
 5
 10
 10
```

- **Line 10:** Variable name A is assigned the value 5.
- **Line 20:** Prints the value of A, 5.
- **Line 30:** B is assigned the value of A + 5, which equals 10.
- **Line 40:** Changes the value of A, 5, to the value of B.
- **Line 50:** Prints the value of B,10.
- **Line 60:** Prints the value of A, which is now 10.

Review

1. Write a program that assigns a variable named B a value of 45 and a variable named C a value of 15. Write a program that will produce their difference:

   ```
   RUN
    30
   ```

2. What will be the output of the following program?

   ```
   10 A = 20
   20 B = A + 10
   30 PRINT B
   40 END
   ```

3. Find the errors in the following program. When you have found them, type the corrected program and run it.

   ```
   10 64 = B
   20 32 = A
   30 C = A + B
   40 PRINT C
   50 END
   ```

Assigning a
String Variable

A character is any letter, number, punctuation mark or mathematical sign which can be found on the computer's keyboard. For example, A, *, and 5 are all characters. Even a blank space is a character. A string is a single character or series of characters that are strung together to form a word, number or sequence of symbols.

When a string variable is given a name, the variable name must be followed by a dollar sign ($). A letter, a letter and single digit, or two letters followed by a dollar sign ($) tell the computer that the variable is a string variable. A$, D$, A1$, D5$, AA$ and DD$, are all legal string variable names.

When a string variable is given its value by an assignment statement, the characters that make up the string must be enclosed by quotation marks:

    10 A$ = "HARRY"

This statement assigns the string HARRY to the variable name A$.

If we think of mailboxes again, the computer will name one of its boxes A$ and place the string HARRY in that box when line 10 is executed.

A$

HARRY

As with numeric variables, it is possible to change the characters that have been assigned to the variable name A$. For example,

    50 A$ = "SHERRY"

changes the value of A$ from HARRY to SHERRY when line 50 is executed by the computer.

A$

SHERRY

Program 2.4   This program shows a string variable being assigned and then changed:

```
10 B$ = "JUDY"
20 PRINT B$
30 B$ = "GEORGE"
40 PRINT B$
50 END

RUN
JUDY
GEORGE
```

- **Line 10:** Variable name B$ is assigned the value JUDY.
- **Line 20:** Prints the value of B$, JUDY.
- **Line 30:** Reassigns the variable name B$ the value GEORGE and erases JUDY.
- **Line 40:** Prints the new value of B$, GEORGE.

Program 2.5

This program shows what kind of characters can be part of a string:

```
10 A$ = "ALPHABET LAND"
20 B$ = "+,-;*:/ SYMBOL CENTER"
30 C$ = "123456789 NUMBERS TOO"
40 PRINT "WHAT GOES IN A STRING?"
50 PRINT A$
60 PRINT B$
70 PRINT C$
80 END

RUN
WHAT GOES IN A STRING?
ALPHABET LAND
+,-;*:/ SYMBOL CENTER
123456789 NUMBERS TOO
```

Lines 10, 20 and 30 show letters, spaces, numbers and various symbols being assigned to variable names A$, B$ and C$. The strings are then printed in lines 50, 60 and 70.

When numbers are used as part of a string, they cannot be used mathematically because the computer sees them only as characters. Remember, numbers and numeric variables can be used to perform math operations, but characters and string variables cannot.

Program 2.6

This program demonstrates the difference between numbers assigned to a string variable name and numbers assigned to a numeric variable name:

```
10 A$ = "5"
20 B$ = "10"
30 C = 5
40 D = 10
50 PRINT A$ + B$
60 PRINT C + D
70 PRINT B$ + A$
80 PRINT D + C
90 END

RUN
510
 15
105
 15
```

In line 50 the plus sign tells the computer to add A$ to B$. The dollar sign ($) tells the machine that they are not numeric variable names but character strings, so it attaches B$ to A$. This causes the machine to print 510 on the screen. In line 60, C and D are numbers so they can be added mathematically, and 15 is printed on the screen. Line 70 puts B$ first and then attaches A$ to it so that 105 is printed. Adding 10 and 5 gives the same answer as adding 5 and 10, so 15 is printed by line 80.

Review

4. What will be the output of the following program?

```
10 M2$ = "BROKE"
20 M1$ = "GO FOR "
30 PRINT M1$ + M2$
40 END
```

Note the blank space at the end of "GO FOR " is needed to place a space before "BROKE" when it is printed.

5. Find the errors in the following program. What will the corrected program print on the screen?

```
10 A$ = COMPUTER
20 64 = B
30 PRINT A$
40 PRINT B
50 END
```

PRINT Messages and Variables

Variable names can be combined with PRINT messages. This allows a programmer to display both the value of a variable name and a message.

It is important to note that in printing variables the computer places a space before and after a numeric variable, whereas a string variable has no leading or trailing spaces. Any spaces that are needed to keep the characters of a string variable separated from the characters of a PRINT message must be provided by the programmer. This is illustrated in Program 2.7.

Program 2.7

Look at the way spacing is done when a PRINT message and a variable are printed together:

```
10 A = 5
20 A$ = "FIVE"
30 PRINT "GIVE ME" A
40 PRINT "GIVE ME " A$
50 PRINT A "IS ALIVE"
60 PRINT A$ " IS ALIVE"
70 PRINT "JOHN IS" A "YEARS OLD"
80 PRINT "JOHN IS " A$ " YEARS OLD"
90 END

RUN
GIVE ME 5
GIVE ME FIVE
 5 IS ALIVE
FIVE IS ALIVE
JOHN IS 5 YEARS OLD
JOHN IS FIVE YEARS OLD
```

- **Line 10:** Assigns variable name A the value 5.
- **Line 20:** Assigns string variable name A$ the value FIVE.
- **Line 30:** Notice that a leading space is automatically placed before the 5.
- **Line 40:** Since a string is printed, a space must be left before the closing quotation marks.
- **Line 50:** A trailing space is automatically placed after the 5.
- **Line 60:** A space is included inside the quotes since a string is being printed.
- **Line 70:** No extra spaces are needed since a numeric variable is printed.
- **Line 80:** Spaces before and after A$ are included inside the quotation marks.

Review

6. Write a program that has two variables, X and Y. Assign X the value 25 and Y the value 50 and have the program produce the following output:

```
RUN
THE PRODUCT OF 25 AND 50 IS 1250.
25 * 50 = 1250
```

INPUT: a number

Often the data that a program will use to accomplish its task will be different each time the program is run. The INPUT statement is a good way to assign a variable name its value in such a situation. The assignment statement, on the other hand, is best used when data will remain the same each time the program is run. A savings account provides a good example of these two situations. Each time money is deposited or withdrawn from the account the amount is likely to be different, but the amount of interest that the bank pays its depositors will change infrequently. Therefore, the rate of interest is best brought into the program with an assignment statement while a deposit or withdrawal is best entered with an INPUT statement.

To use an INPUT statement, type the word INPUT and the variable name that will be assigned a value:

```
10 INPUT A
```

When the computer reads the INPUT statement, it will print a question mark on the screen and then wait for data to be typed in on the keyboard. When the ENTER key is pressed, the computer reads the data and assigns it to a variable name.

```
10 INPUT A
20 PRINT A
30 END

RUN
?45
 45
```

Until ENTER is pressed, the computer waits for more data. When ENTER is pressed, the computer sets aside a box in its memory,

A

```
┌─────┐
│ 45  │
└─────┘
```

names the box A and puts a 45 in the box as the value of the variable named A.

Program 2.8   The following program shows how a number is assigned to a variable name with an INPUT statement.

```
10 INPUT N
20 PRINT "5 *" N
30 PRINT 5 * N
40 END

RUN
? 5
5 * 5
 25
```

When the computer reads the INPUT in line 10, it prints a question mark and waits for the data to be typed and the ENTER key to be pressed. When the 5 is typed and ENTER pressed, the computer sets aside a box in its memory, names it N, and places a 5 in it.

N

```
┌─────┐
│  5  │
└─────┘
```

Therefore, when lines 20 and 30 are read, the computer uses 5 as the value of variable name N.

Do not use commas when entering large numbers since commas will cause the computer to print a REDO FROM START error:

```
10 INPUT A
20 PRINT A
30 END

RUN
? 4,500
?Redo from start
? 4500
 4500
```

INPUT: a string

An INPUT statement can also be used to assign a string of characters a variable name, for example:

    10 INPUT A$

Letters, symbols or numbers can be used to give the variable name A$ a value because a string can have any character in it that can be typed in from the keyboard. Numbers can be made part of a string, but they cannot be used as numbers in a mathematical operation since the computer thinks of them as symbols rather than numbers.

Program 2.9

This program waits for a string variable name to be given its value when the characters are typed in from the keyboard:

```
10 INPUT A$
20 PRINT "THIS IS WHAT YOU TYPED"
30 PRINT A$
40 END

RUN
? COMPUTERS ARE FAST
THIS IS WHAT YOU TYPED
COMPUTERS ARE FAST
```

Line 10 tells the computer to set aside a box in its memory named A$. The computer then waits for data to be typed in from the keyboard, and when ENTER is pressed, the characters that have been typed are put in the box and the box given the variable name A$.

A$

```
┌─────────────────────┐
│ COMPUTERS ARE FAST  │
└─────────────────────┘
```

Since the characters typed are COMPUTERS ARE FAST, the variable name A$ is assigned those characters, and when line 30 is executed, they are printed.

Review

7. Write a program that will use INPUT to assign values to two variables named A and B. After assigning the variables their values, have the computer calculate their sum and product. A RUN of the program should look like this:

```
RUN
? 45
? 10
  45 + 10 = 55
  45 * 10 = 450
```

8. Write a program that uses INPUT to enter your name as a variable named N$. The program should then say HELLO to you.

```
RUN
? BARBARA
HELLO BARBARA
```

**REDO
FROM START**

If a letter or word is typed when the computer is expecting a number, the computer will print a REDO FROM START error message:

```
10 INPUT N
20 PRINT "5 *" N "=" 5 * N
30 END

RUN
? FIVE
?Redo from start
? 5
5 * 5 = 25
```

The REDO FROM START message does not mean that the program must be restarted. The computer had been expecting data in the form of a number, and when it was given a symbol instead, the REDO FROM START error message is printed and the computer waits for the proper input. When the computer is expecting a value for a string variable the error message will *not* appear, since the computer can accept characters as part of a string.

To prevent the REDO FROM START error, a message indicating the kind of data expected should be given. The message can be made part of an INPUT statement by combining the INPUT with a message enclosed in quotation marks:

```
10 INPUT "TYPE YOUR NAME"; N$
```

A semicolon (;) must follow the quotation marks that end the message. If a semicolon does not separate the quotation marks and variable name, a SYNTAX ERROR will halt the program.

Program 2.10

This program shows how a message can be made part of an INPUT statement:

```
10 INPUT "TYPE A NUMBER"; N
20 PRINT "THE NUMBER IS" N
30 END

RUN
TYPE A NUMBER? 250
THE NUMBER IS 250
```

An INPUT statement like the one in line 10 is less likely to cause a REDO FROM START warning because the user is told what type of input the computer is expecting. It is possible to enter the values for a number of variable names using a single INPUT statement by separating the variable names with commas. For example, the statement

10 INPUT A, B, C, D

assigns the variable names A, B, C, D their values.

Program 2.11

This program asks the user for a student's name and four grades, then prints the name and the student's average:

```
10  INPUT "Students Name"; N$
20  INPUT "Enter four grades"; A, B, C, D
30  PRINT
40  X = (A + B + C + D) / 4
50  PRINT "The average for " N$ " is" X
60  END

RUN
Students Name? MIKE
Enter four grades? 85, 87, 67, 98

The average for MIKE is 84.25
```

- **Line 10:** Allows the user to input the student's name.
- **Line 20:** Allows the user to input the student's four grades separated by commas.
- **Line 30:** A blank PRINT statement causes the computer to skip a line.
- **Line 40:** Calculates the average and assigns it to variable name X.
- **Line 50:** Prints the student's name and average.

Review

9. Write a program that allows you to input your name and a friend's name. The output should look like this:

```
RUN
WHAT IS YOUR NAME? TED
WHAT IS YOUR FRIEND'S NAME? BRIAN
BRIAN IS A FRIEND OF TED
```

GOTO

Computers are able to peform repetitive tasks quickly and accurately. Looping statements which allow program lines to be executed numerous times are a good example of this. The simplest example is the GOTO statement, which tells the computer to go to a specific line in a program just as if it had come to that line by following the normal sequence of line numbers.

The correct form of the GOTO statement is the word GOTO followed by the line number that the computer is to go to.

40 GOTO 10

will send the program from line 40 back to line 10. If there is no line with this number specified in the program, the computer will halt and print an UNDEFINED STATEMENT ERROR message, which means the computer has not been given the necessary information.

Program 2.12   The GOTO statement in this program tells the computer to continue printing the same message on the screen until the program is interrupted by a technique explained below:

```
10 PRINT "COMPUTERS ARE FAST"
20 GOTO 10
30 END

RUN
COMPUTERS ARE FAST
COMPUTERS ARE FAST
COMPUTERS ARE FAST
COMPUTERS ARE FAST
COMPUTERS ARE FAST
COMPUTERS ARE FAST
COMPUTERS ARE FAST
COMPUTERS ARE FAST
COMPUTERS ARE FAST
COMPUTERS ARE FAST
COMPUTERS ARE FAST

Break in 10
```

The GOTO statement in line 20 creates a loop with the program continually going from line 20 back to line 10 again and again. Each time line 10 is repeated, the computer prints the message COMPUTERS ARE FAST.

The computer will continue to repeat this loop until interrupted by the user. On the PC this is done by hitting the CTRL and BREAK keys; on the PC-jr, the FN and BREAK keys.

When the computer finishes a PRINT statement, the cursor is moved down to the next line and over to the left margin. Using a semicolon (;) as the last character of a PRINT statement tells the computer to keep the cursor where it is and to print in the next space to the right. For example, changing line 10 in Program 2.12 to read

```
10 PRINT "COMPUTERS ARE FAST" ;
```

will continuously print COMPUTERS ARE FAST on the same line until interrupted by the user.

```
RUN
COMPUTERS ARE FAST COMPUTERS ARE FAST
COMPUTERS ARE FAST ^C
BREAK IN 20
```

Program 2.13   The addition of a GOTO statement to Program 2.11 allows the program to continue to calculate student averages until interrupted by the user.

```
10 INPUT "Students Name"; N$
20 INPUT "Enter four grades"; A, B, C, D
30 X = (A + B + C + D) / 4
40 PRINT "The average for " N$ " is" X
50 PRINT
60 GOTO 10
70 END

RUN
Students Name? MIKE
Enter four grades? 76, 78, 87, 90
The average for MIKE is 82.75

Students Name? HEIDI
Enter four grades? 87, 98, 78, 99
The average for HEIDI is 90.5

Students Name? PAM
Enter four grades? 100, 76, 50, 99
The average for PAM is 81.25

Students Name?
^C
Break in 10
```

Both Programs 2.12 and 2.13 are examples of very poor programming style. In the definition of an algorithm given in Chapter 1 we stated that an algorithm should have a finite number of steps, but these two programs continue on endlessly until interrupted by the user. What is needed is a statement which will stop the program automatically when the desired results have been achieved. A number of such possible statements will be covered later in this text. It should also be noted that the indiscriminate use of GOTO statements within a program should be avoided since they interrupt the sequential flow of the program. If possible it is best to have a program move sequentially line by line without jumping around.

Review   10. Write a program that will print your name over and over down the left side of the screen until the program is interrupted.

11. Predict the output of the following program and then type it in and RUN it:

```
10 PRINT "*****";
20 GOTO 10
30 END
```

12. Write a program in which you input a value for a variable named N. Have the computer calculate the value of variable N plus 12 and variable N times 12. The output should look like this:

```
RUN
WHAT IS N? 12
12 + 12 = 24
12 * 12 = 144
WHAT IS N? 5
12 + 5 = 17
12 * 5 = 60
WHAT IS N?
```

13. Write a program which allows you to input your name and a friend's name. The output should look like this:

```
RUN
WHAT IS YOUR NAME? TED
WHAT IS YOUR FRIEND'S NAME? BRIAN
TED IS A FRIEND OF BRIAN
WHAT IS YOUR NAME? BILL
WHAT IS YOUR FRIEND'S NAME? JUDY
BILL IS A FRIEND OF JUDY
WHAT IS YOUR NAME?
```

READ & DATA

Another way to assign a value to a variable is to use the READ and DATA statements. These two statements work together as a team to assign data; one of them cannot be used without the other.

READ and DATA are useful because they store data within a program. The data need not be re-entered each time a program is run, which means that an INPUT statement or assignment statement is not needed to enter the data. The data is entered once in a data statement and then stored as part of the program.

Program 2.14

This program shows how to use READ to assign a value to a variable name:

```
10 READ A
20 PRINT "The number is" A
30 DATA 125
40 END

RUN
The number is 125
```

READ A in line 10 tells the computer to set aside a box in its memory for a variable named A. The computer then assigns the variable A the first value it finds in a DATA statement which is the number 125 on line 30.

When a READ is used to name a numeric variable, the computer will only accept numbers. Any symbols used with the numbers will cause an error message that will halt the program. Therefore, data like $2.75, or 2′6″ for 2 feet 6 inches will not work as numeric variables. Dollar signs, letters of the alphabet and any other characters can be read using READ and DATA if the computer is told instead to read a string variable. For example,

```
10 READ A$
```

will assign variable name A$ the value of a string stored in a DATA statement.

Program 2.15

This program assigns strings a value by using READ and DATA:

```
10 READ A$, B$
20 PRINT "The FORCE is with " A$ "."
30 PRINT "The evil " B$ " wants him."
40 DATA LUKE SKYWALKER, DARTH VADER
50 END

RUN
The FORCE is with LUKE SKYWALKER.
The evil DARTH VADER wants him.
```

The force is with LUKE SKYWALKER because his name is in the first DATA statement that the computer found. The computer begins looking for data at the lowest line number and then uses the data that it finds first. Once a piece of data has been read, the computer goes on to the next piece of data. When line 10 reads B$, it is assigned the second string of characters DARTH VADER.

DATA statements can be placed anywhere in a program, but it is good programming style to put them together in one place, usually at the end of a program.

When more than one variable in a program is assigned a value by READ and DATA statements, the data must be separated by commas as illustrated by line 40. The comma tells the computer that the first piece of data to be read is LUKE SKYWALKER, and the second piece of data is DARTH VADER. It is possible to have many pieces of data in one DATA statement as long as they are separated by commas.

Review

14. Write a program that READs two numbers, variable names X and Y, from DATA statements. The program should set variable X = 5 and variable Y = 3 and then print their difference.

```
RUN
5 - 3 = 2
```

15. Write a program that READs the name of your favorite snack and your favorite drink from DATA statements. The output of the program should look like this:

```
RUN
A HAMBURGER IS MY FAVORITE SNACK.
A COKE IS MY FAVORITE DRINK.
```

GOTO and READ/DATA

The GOTO statement is useful when it is used in conjunction with READ and DATA statements since the GOTO can be used to make a loop that reads data piece by piece until all the data in the program has been read. However, when the computer is told to READ data and all the data in the DATA statements has been read, the computer will print an OUT OF DATA ERROR and halt the program. The computer will not go back to the first DATA statement by itself and start over again.

It is important that the data be kept in the proper sequence by the use of commas so that the data matches the variable names that will read it. If the computer is told to READ a numeric variable and the next piece of data is a string, the computer will halt the program with a SYNTAX ERROR message:

```
10 READ N, A$
20 DATA HELLO, 007
30 END

RUN
SYNTAX ERROR IN 20
```

Line 20 does not appear to have an error in it, but the error is still there. The error is caused by READ in line 10. The variable name N is telling the computer to look for a number as the next piece of data, but the computer finds a string instead. This confuses the computer, so it prints a SYNTAX ERROR IN 20 message and halts the program. To correct the error, change either the order of the data in the DATA statement

```
10 READ N, A$
20 DATA 007, HELLO
```

or the order in which the variables are read in the READ statement

```
10 READ A$, N
20 DATA HELLO, 007
```

Program 2.16

This program reads a list of candies and their prices from data statements:

```
10 READ C$, P
20 PRINT "Candy: " C$
30 PRINT "Price: $" P
40 PRINT
50 GOTO 10
60 DATA HUBBA BUBBA, .35, HERSHEY BAR, .45
70 END

RUN
Candy: HUBBA BUBBA
Price: $ .35

Candy: HERSHEY BAR
Price: $ .45

Out of DATA in 10
```

- **Line 10:** Two variables are read using one READ statement by separating the two variables with a comma. Line 10 reads data from the DATA statement at line 60. The first piece of data read, HUBBA BUBBA, is assigned to variable name C$, and variable name P is assigned .35 as its value.
- **Line 20:** Prints the name of the candy that was just read.
- **Line 30:** The dollar sign ($) in the PRINT statement tells the program user that the numbers displayed are money figures. The DATA statements cannot contain a dollar sign as part of a number, but they can contain a decimal point.
- **Line 40:** The PRINT puts a blank line on the screen for easier reading.
- **Line 50:** GOTO 10 sends the computer back to line 10 where it reads a new value for variable name C$, HERSHEY BAR, and a new value for variable name P, .45.

These new values are then printed by lines 20 and 30. When the GOTO sends the computer back to 10 for a third time, there is no more data to read so the computer prints an OUT OF DATA ERROR message and halts the program.

Review

16. Write a program that reads a list of favorite sports teams and outputs that list to the screen.

```
RUN
MY FAVORITE TEAMS:
BOSTON RED SOX
NEW ENGLAND PATRIOTS
NEW YORK GIANTS

?OUT OF DATA ERROR IN 10
```

17. Write a program that reads the numbers from 1 to 10 from a DATA statement and then prints only the even numbers on the screen.

```
RUN
 2
 4
 6
 8
 10

?OUT OF DATA IN 10
```

18. Predict the output of the following program: (Hint: are there any errors?)

```
10 PRINT "SECRET AGENT FILE"
20 PRINT
30 READ N, N$
40 PRINT N, N$
50 GOTO 30
60 DATA JAMES BOND, 007, MAXWELL SMART, 86,
   MRS. SMART, 99
70 END
```

PRINT Formatting

The way in which data is displayed on the screen is an important part of good programming style. One way to tell the computer how to print data on the screen is to use commas and semicolons. When used as part of PRINT statements and outside of quotations marks, these punctuation marks give the computer special instructions about where data should be printed on the screen.

Commas are used in PRINT statements to tell the computer to move the cursor to one of the five print zones that divide the screen. Since the computer can print 80 characters on a single line, a line is divided into four print zones of 14 characters each and a fifth zone of 24.

```
10 A$ = "*"
20 PRINT A$, A$, A$, A$, A$
30 END

RUN
    *         *         *         *         *
```

Each time the computer reads a comma on line 20, the cursor is moved to the first space of the next print zone before it prints the next asterisk (*) character on the screen.

The semicolon, on the other hand, is used to tell the computer to print in the next space to the right of the screen:

```
10 A$ = "*"
20 PRINT A$; A$; A$; A$; A$
30 END

RUN
*****
```

Program 2.17

This program shows where the print zones are on the screen. It also shows the differences between commas and semicolons in a PRINT statement:

```
10 PRINT "*", "*", "*", "*", "*"
20 A$ = "*"
30 PRINT A$, A$, A$, A$
40 PRINT A$; A$; A$; A$
50 B = 25
60 PRINT A$; B
70 PRINT A$, B
80 PRINT B; A$
90 END

RUN
*              *              *              *              *
*              *              *              *
****
* 25
*              25
  25 *
```

- **Line 10:** Uses a comma to print an asterisk (∗) at the beginning of each of the five print zones.
- **Line 30:** Prints variable A$, an asterisk, in the first space of each zone because of the comma that follows each variable.
- **Line 40:** Prints four asterisks in a row because the semicolons that separate the variables tell the computer to print in the next available space.
- **Line 60:** Prints the asterisk and then 25 because these are the values that the variables A$ and B represent. There is a space between the asterisk and 25 because the computer puts a space before and after each numeric value.
- **Line 70:** The asterisk and 25 are separated by 10 spaces because of the comma between variable name A$ and variable name B.
- **Line 80:** Prints the 25 with spaces before and after followed by the value of A$.

Extended Variable Names

Up to this point, the text has covered only simple variable names of a single character. The computer is, however, capable of understanding variable names up to 40 characters in length. These longer names add valuable clarity to the program, since they give a more complete identification of what the variable represents.

End of Chapter Problems

From this point on, most chapters will end by solving a problem which requires a carefully thought out algorithm. A problem will be stated and then broken down into a series of smaller problems upon which the program will be based. As part of the algorithm, the data to be input and output will be given along with the variable names assigned for each. You are urged to carefully study and analyze the techniques which are used.

A teacher wants to write a program that will calculate and print the name of each of her students, their quiz and exam grades, and their term grades. Each student has three quiz grades and two exam grades. Each exam grade is to be given twice the weight of a quiz grade.

Algorithm:
1. Input student's name, quiz grades, and exam grades.
2. Compute the student's term grade by adding the exam grades multiplied by 2, to the sum of the quiz grades and then dividing the total by 7 to produce the properly weighted average.
3. Print each student's name and term average.

Input:

Student Name	: STUDENT$
Quiz Grades	: QUIZ 1, QUIZ 2, QUIZ 3
Exam Grades	: EXAM 1, EXAM 2

Output:

Student Name	: STUDENT$
Term Average	: TERM

Program 2.18

```
10 PRINT "NAME", "TERM AVERAGE"
20 PRINT
30 READ STUDENT$, QUIZ1, QUIZ2, QUIZ3, EXAM1, EXAM2
40 TOTAL = (2 * (EXAM1 + EXAM2) + (QUIZ1 + QUIZ2 + QUIZ3))
50 AVG = TOTAL / 7
60 PRINT STUDENT$, AVG
70 GOTO 30
80 DATA C. TIBBETS, 82, 71, 60, 90, 85
90 DATA M. PORTER, 85, 40, 75, 80, 70
100 DATA M. BIDWELL, 70, 65, 63, 71, 65
110 DATA H. CRANE, 80, 85, 90, 82, 80
120 END

RUN
NAME                 TERM AVERAGE

C. TIBBETS           80.42858
M. PORTER            71.42858
M. BIDWELL           67.14285
H. CRANE             82.71429
Out of DATA in 30
```

- **Line 10:** Prints the heading for the table. Note that if the header were placed elsewhere in the program, it would be printed more than once.
- **Line 30:** Reads each student's name and grades
- **Line 40:** Computes the weighted total of each student's grades. Notice how parentheses are used.
- **Line 50:** Calculates each student's term grade by dividing the weighted total by 7.
- **Line 60:** Prints the student's name and term grade.
- **Line 70:** Forms the loop required to read the name and grades for each of the four students. (How would the program work if line 70 read GOTO 10?)
- **Line 80-110:** Data statements containing students names and grades.

EXERCISES

1. What is the exact output of the following program?

   ```
   10 A = 3
   20 PRINT "The value of B"
   30 B = 4 * 4 + A
   40 PRINT B
   50 END
   ```

2. How many lines of output does the following program produce before an Out of DATA error message appears?

   ```
   10 READ A, B, C
   20 PRINT (A + B + C) / 3
   30 GOTO 10
   40 DATA 11, 32, 42, 14, 25, 36, 47
   50 DATA 58, 39, 50, 61, 22, 83, 94
   60 END
   ```

3. Here is a program which "mysteriously does not work". Correct it so that the output looks like the following:

   ```
   RUN
   The sum is 20
   The sum is 14
   Out of Data in 10
   ```

   ```
   10 READ AB
   20 PRINT The sum is A + B
   30 GOTO 12
   40 DATA 12, 8, 3*5 − 1
   50 END
   ```

4. Write the output produced by this program:

   ```
   10 READ A$
   20 PRINT A$
   30 GOTO 10
   40 DATA S, I, X!, " 6", 6
   50 END
   ```

5. Write a program in which the price (P) of a loaf of bread and the number (N) of loaves bought are INPUT from the keyboard. The total spent for the bread is to be printed in dollars and cents.

6. Write a program in which you input your weight (W) in pounds and height (H) in inches. Then print the quotient W/H followed by the phrase "Pounds per Inch."

7. Using the INPUT statement, write a program which produces the following output:

```
RUN
? 2,4
X = 2          Y = 4          X * Y = 8
?-8,70
X = -8         Y = 70         X * Y = -560
?
```

8. Predict the output of the following program:

```
10 P$ = "Total price"
20 P = .89
30 PRINT P$; " = $0";P
40 END
```

9. Predict the output of this program:

```
10 READ A, B, C, D
20 PRINT A, B
30 PRINT C; " "; D
40 DATA 123, 234, 435, 456765
50 END
```

10. Have the computer produce the following output:
```
RUN
12345678901234567890123456789012345678901234567890
*                 9*                oh      bye
```

11. What is the exact output of the following program?

```
10 A$ = "abcd"
20 B$ = "xyz"
30 F = 7
40 G = -4
50 PRINT A$; B$
60 PRINT A$; F
70 PRINT F; B$
80 PRINT G; B$
90 END
```

12. A piece of pizza normally contains about 375 calories. A man jogging one mile uses about 100 calories. Write a program that asks the user how many pieces of pizza he wishes to eat and then tells him how far he must jog to burn up the calories he will consume.

```
RUN
How many pieces do you want? 4
You must run 15 miles.
```

13. Write a program to have the computer evaluate the expression 12x + 7y for the following values:

X	3	7	12
Y	2	9	−4

14. Write a program that allows a string to be entered. Then, have the computer print the string followed by " keeps the doctor away".

15. Using an INPUT statement, write a program that will compute the volume of a room given its length, width and height.

16. Write a program to compute the areas (in cm^2) of circles with radii of 5.0, 3.0 and 8.0 cm. Have the output in the form "Area of circle =", with two spaces between each printed line.

17. Just as three-dimensional objects are measured by volume, so four-dimensional objects are measured by tesseracts. Have your program ask for the dimensions of a four-dimensional object (height, width, length and "presence") and print the object's tesseract (in cm^4).

        RUN
        Enter height, width, length and presence <in cm>? 1, 3, 9, 27
        The tesseract is 729 cm^4.

18. With the equation E = MC^2, Einstein predicted that energy could be produced from matter. If the average human hair weighs a tenth of a gram and the town of Woodsylvania uses 2×10^{11} units of energy per day, find out how many hairs from Einstein's head would be required to supply the town with energy for a day (C = 3×10^{10}).

19. Use the computer to calculate your library fines. Enter the number of books you have borrowed and how many days late they are. Have the computer print the amount of your fine if you are charged .10 per day per book.

20. The perimeter of a triangle is equal to the sum of the lengths of the three sides of the triangle. The semiperimeter is one-half of the perimeter. A triangle has sides of lengths 13, 8 and 11 cm. A second triangle has sides of 21, 16 and 12 ft. Write a program that reads these measurements from DATA statements and then prints the semiperimeter of each triangle, showing the correct units. The output should look like this:

        RUN
        Semiperimeter of first triangle: 16 cm.
        Semiperimeter of second triangle: 24.5 ft.

21. Professional athletes have succeeded in making staggering sums of money through careful negotiations. Of course, the real winner is Uncle Sam, who does not negotiate at all. Write a program which asks for a player's name and salary and then prints the player's name, take-home pay and taxes if the tax rate for his or her income bracket is 44%:

    ```
    RUN
    What is the player's name? TIMMY CONNORS
    What is TIMMY CONNORS wage? $150000
    TIMMY CONNORS would keep $84000
    TIMMY CONNORS would pay $66000 in taxes

    What is the player's name? TRISH EVERT
    What is TRISH EVERT'S wage? $420000
    TRISH EVERT would keep $235200
    TRISH EVERT would pay $184800 in taxes
    ```

22. Sale prices are often deceptive. Write a program to determine the original price of an item, given the sale price and the discount rate(%):

    ```
    RUN
    Sale price? 3.78
    Discount rate (%)? 10
    The original price was $4.20
    ```

23. The area of a triangle can be found by multiplying one-half times the base times the height (A = .5 * base * height). Write a program that allows the user to enter the base and altitude of a triangle and then skips a line before printing the area of the triangle.

    ```
    RUN
    What is the base? 10
    What is the height? 5

    The area is 25
    ```

24. A state has a 7% sales tax. Write a program which allows you to INPUT the names and prices (before taxes) of different items found in a department store and then prints the item, tax and the price of the item including tax.

    ```
    RUN
    Item's name? COAT
    What is the price? 65
    COAT has a tax of $ 4.55 and costs $ 69.55

    Item's name? TENNIS RACKET
    What is the price? $ 23
    TENNIS RACKET has a tax of $ 1.61 and costs $ 24.61
    ```

25. In an election in Grime City, candidate Smith ran against candidate Jones for mayor. Below is a listing of the number of votes each candidate received in each ward. How many and what percentage of the total votes did each candidate receive?

Candidate Ward	Smith	Jones
1	528	210
2	313	721
3	1003	822
4	413	1107
5	516	1700

26. Given the assumption that you sleep a healthy eight hours a night, have the computer print the number of hours in your life which you will have spent sleeping. Input the date of your birth and today's date in numeric form (e.g. 9,27,61). Use 365 days in each year and 30 days in a month to simplify your calculations.

27. Using an INPUT statement, write a program which averages each of the following sets of numbers. Note that each set does not contain the same numbers of elements.

(2, 7, 15, 13)
(8, 5, 2, 3)
(12, 19, 4)
(15, 7, 19, 24, 37)

3

MAKING DECISIONS

*T*he first two chapters introduced statements that allow the computer to accept data and carry out routine calculations. Though useful, these statements do not take advantage of the computer's ability to make decisions and produce loops with terminating values. This chapter will introduce two new statements that will perform these functions: the IF...THEN and FOR...NEXT statements.

IF...THEN

The IF...THEN statement is called a conditional statement. When a condition is met, a specified response is carried out; when the condition is not met, the statement is ignored. This is in contrast to the statements introduced so far (PRINT, GOTO, INPUT, etc.) which are executed whenever they are read by the computer.

The easiest way to describe a condition to a computer is to have it make a comparison using an IF...THEN statement in the form:

IF <condition> THEN <line number>

In the condition part of the statement a comparison is made. If the comparison is true, then the computer will go to the named line number; if false, it will ignore that line and go on to the next. By using one of the symbols shown below, two quantities can be compared:

Symbol	Meaning
=	equal to
>	greater than
<	less than
>=	greater than or equal to
<=	less than or equal to
<>	not equal to

An example of an IF...THEN statement is:

20 IF X > 5 THEN 60

When the condition in line 20, X is greater than 5, is true, the computer goes to line 60. When the condition is false, (X is less than or equal to 5), the computer goes on to the next line.

Program 3.1   This program determines whether the value entered as a variable named X is the solution to the equation $2 * X = 6$, and then decides which of two messages should be printed.

```
10 INPUT "Type a number"; X
20 IF 2 * X = 6 THEN 50
30 PRINT X; "is not the solution"
40 GOTO 10
50 PRINT X; "is the solution"
60 END

RUN
Type a number? 2
 2 is not the solution
Type a number? 4
 4 is not the solution
Type a number? 3
 3 is the solution
```

The computer makes its decision on line 20. When the condition true, it jumps to line 50 and prints "IS THE SOLUTION", but when condition is false, the computer moves on to line 30 and prints "IS N THE SOLUTION". Note the necessity of line 40. Without it the progra would print "IS THE SOLUTION" even when the value of variable X is the solution. When the value of variable X is the solution, the order in whi the line numbers are executed is 10, 20, 50, 60. When variable X is the solution, the sequence of line numbers is 10, 20, 30, 40, 10.

The IF...THEN statement can also compare letters of the alphabet strings. When using strings, the greater than ($>$), less than ($<$) and eq to ($=$) symbols are used to refer to alphabetical order rather than numeri order. Strings can be compared using variable names, letters or characte The following examples illustrate this:

```
10 IF A$ < B$ THEN 50
20 IF A$ > "M" THEN 50
30 IF N$ = "SUPERMAN" THEN 100
```

Program 3.2   The following program decides whether variable A$ is alphabetica before, the same, or after variable B$:

```
10  PRINT
20  INPUT "Type a word"; A$
30  INPUT "Type another word"; B$
40  IF A$ = B$ THEN 80
50  IF A$ > B$ THEN 100
60  PRINT A$; " is before "; B$
70  GOTO 10
80  PRINT A$; " equals "; B$
90  GOTO 10
100 PRINT  A$; " is after "; B$
110 GOTO 10
```

```
RUN

Type a word? SKY
Type another word? BLUE
SKY is after BLUE

Type a word? RAT
Type another word? SNAKE
RAT is before SNAKE

Type a word? COMPUTER
Type another word? COMPUTER
COMPUTER equals COMPUTER

Type a word?
Break in 20
```

If variable names A$ and B$ are equal, line 40 sends the computer to line 80. Line 50 causes a jump to line 100 if variable name A$ comes after variable name B$ in the alphabet. Line 60 is reached only when variable name A$ is before variable name B$. Since all the other possibilities have been checked in lines 40 and 50, an IF...THEN is not necessary. The PRINT in line 10 keeps a blank line between sets of comparisons to make them easier to read.

Program 3.2 is an example of a poorly written program. The combination of IF...THEN and GOTO statements causes the program to jump around destroying the logical, sequential flow. In addition, the program must be interrupted by the user to stop its running. To rectify these faults we need additional statements which will be presented later in this chapter.

Review

1. Write a program that allows a string to be entered as input. If the string is the password, "AVIATRIX", have the computer print "YOU'RE THE BOSS". Otherwise, have it print "SORRY CHARLIE".

```
RUN
ENTER PASSWORD PLEASE? DUMBO
SORRY CHARLIE

ENTER PASSWORD PLEASE? AVIATRIX
YOU'RE THE BOSS
```

2. Allow a number with the variable name N to be entered as input. When the value of variable N is greater than 25, have the computer print "TOO LARGE". When the value is less than 25 have it print "TOO SMALL" and when it equals 25 have the program print "JUST RIGHT".

```
RUN
TYPE A NUMBER? 17
TOO SMALL

TYPE A NUMBER? 47
TOO LARGE

TYPE A NUMBER? 25
JUST RIGHT
```

Extended Use of IF...THEN

The simplest form of the IF...THEN statement has been given as:

IF <condition> THEN <line number>

The IF...THEN statement may also be used with a BASIC instruction following THEN so that the statement after THEN will be executed by the computer only when the condition is true. This makes the statement more flexible and is particularly useful in reducing the number of GOTOs. As mentioned earlier, using too many GOTOs is not good programming style, making a program difficult to read and correct. The following examples show how IF...THEN may be used with other BASIC statements:

```
10 IF X <> 0 THEN PRINT X
30 IF N > 1 THEN PRINT "IT IS LARGER THAN ONE"
50 IF R <= 0 THEN R = X + 2
```

Program 3.3

This program is a re-write of program 3.2. Notice how the program flows sequentially now that all but one GOTO statement have been eliminated.

```
10 PRINT
20 INPUT "Type a word"; A$
30 INPUT "Type another word"; B$
40 IF A$ = B$ THEN PRINT A$; " equals "; B$
50 IF A$ > B$ THEN PRINT A$; " is after "; B$
60 IF A$ < B$ THEN PRINT A$; " is before "; B$
70 GOTO 10
80 END

RUN

Type a word? SKY
Type another word? BLUE
SKY is after BLUE

Type a word? RAT
Type another word? SNAKE
RAT is before SNAKE

Type a word? COMPUTER
Type another word? COMPUTER
COMPUTER equals COMPUTER

Type a word?

Break in 20
```

The program can be further refined by adding the lines:

```
70 INPUT "Do you wish to check another set of words"; X$
80 IF X$ = "YES" THEN 10
90 END
```

```
RUN

Type a word? SKY
Type another word? BLUE
SKY is after BLUE
Do you wish to check another set of words? YES

Type a word? RAT
Type another word? SNAKE
RAT is before SNAKE
Do you wish to check another set of words? YES

Type a word? COMPUTER
Type another word? COMPUTER
COMPUTER equals COMPUTER
Do you wish to check another set of words? NO
```

Now the user is asked whether the program should continue or end. This results in better programming style, since the program will stop automatically.

Review

3. Write a program that allows the user to enter two numbers and then prints the numbers in descending order:

```
RUN
ENTER FIRST NUMBER? 27
ENTER SECOND NUMBER? 32
32
27
```

4. Write a program that allows two names to be entered and then outputs them in alphabetical order. The program should then ask if the user wants to enter two more names. If the user does not want to continue, the program should show that it is no longer running:

```
RUN
ENTER A LAST NAME? SMITH
ENTER ANOTHER NAME? JONES
JONES
SMITH

TWO MORE NAMES TO COMPARE? NO
BYE.
```

Making IF...THEN Smarter: AND & OR

AND and OR are used with an IF...THEN statement to join two or more comparisons together as one condition. AND and OR combine comparisons differently to decide whether a condition is true or false. Because of this, the decisions that a program makes can be more complex.

AND: When AND is used to join comparisons, all comparisons must be true for the entire condition to be true. For example,

```
20 IF X > 5 AND Y = 3 THEN PRINT "BOTH ARE TRUE"
```

will print BOTH ARE TRUE only when this is so. That is, the value of X must be greater than 5 and the value of Y must also equal 3.

OR: When OR is used to join comparisons, the condition will be true when any of the comparisons is true. The condition is false only when all comparisons are false. For example,

20 IF X > 5 OR Y = 3 THEN PRINT "ONE OR BOTH IS TRUE"

will print ONE OR BOTH IS TRUE if either of the comparisons is true. When both comparisons are false, the message will not be printed.

Program 3.4   A problem for spies is that they have to remember so many code words. This program uses OR to help James Bond get the message that is meant only for him. The use of OR allows the computer to decide whether the names or words entered from the keyboard are acceptable before the user is allowed to go on with the program:

```
10  INPUT "Who are you"; N$
20  IF N$ = "JAMES BOND" OR N$ = "007" OR N$ = "BOND" THEN 60
30  PRINT "This mission is not for you!"
40  PRINT
50  GOTO 10
60  PRINT "These orders are for your eyes only!"
70  INPUT "Are you alone"; A$
80  IF A$ = "YES" OR A$ = "TRUE" THEN 120
90  PRINT "Try later!"
100 PRINT
110 GOTO 10
120 PRINT "Doctor Zhivago has escaped!"
130 PRINT "Your mission is to return him to prison."
140 END
```

```
RUN
Who are you? MAXWELL SMART
This mission is not for you!

Who are you? JAMES BOND
These orders are for your eyes only!
Are you alone? NO
Try later!

Who are you? JAMES BOND
These orders are for your eyes only!
Are you alone? YES
Doctor Zhivago has escaped!
Your mission is to return him to prison.
```

- **Line 10:** A name is assigned to variable name N$.
- **Line 20:** The name entered as variable N$ is compared to the three code words: "JAMES BOND", "007", or "BOND". If variable N$ is the same as one of them, the condition is true, so the program branches to line 60.
- **Line 30:** When the condition in line 20 is false, THIS MESSAGE IS NOT FOR YOU is printed.

- **Lines 40-50:** A blank line is printed and then the computer returns to line 10 to input a new name.
- **Line 60:** Prints a warning message.
- **Line 70:** Inputs a response to the question ARE YOU ALONE?
- **Line 80:** The OR connecting the comparisons on line 80 allows an answer of either YES or TRUE to send the program to line 120.
- **Lines 90-110:** When the condition on line 80 is false, a warning message is printed, and the program returns to line 10 to begin the questioning again.
- **Lines 120-130:** The mission is revealed.

Multiple Statement Lines

The computer allows a series of statements to be entered on a single program line if they are separated from each other by colons (:). Colons are especially useful when used with IF...THEN. When multiple statement lines are used, all statements following THEN will be executed when the condition is true. For example,

$$60 \text{ IF } X = 5 \text{ THEN PRINT "GOOD": GOTO } 80$$

has two statements on one line. If the condition X = 5 is true, then "GOOD" will be printed and program control will be passed to line 80. If the condition is false, neither of these actions is taken. Instead, the program will continue on to the line following line 60. This means either both the PRINT "GOOD" and the GOTO 80 statements are executed, or neither is executed.

IF...THEN...ELSE

The IF...THEN statement can be extended by the use of the modifier ELSE to include an alternate statement if the condition of the IF...THEN is false. When the IF condition is true, the statement following THEN is executed; otherwise, the statement following ELSE is executed. The general form of the IF...THEN...ELSE statement is

$$\text{IF <condition> THEN <statement> ELSE <statement>}$$

When the following statement is executed, "LARGER" is printed if X > 50; otherwise, the program will print "SMALLER OR EQUAL":

$$40 \text{ IF } X > 50 \text{ THEN PRINT "LARGER"}$$
$$\text{ELSE PRINT "SMALLER OR EQUAL"}$$

A line number is also valid following ELSE:

$$40 \text{ IF } X > 50 \text{ THEN PRINT "LARGER" ELSE } 100$$

When IF...THEN...ELSE is used, more than one statement may appear between THEN and ELSE; therefore, the following line is valid:

$$70 \text{ IF } Y = 3 \text{ THEN PRINT "DONE": GOTO } 200 \text{ ELSE } 30$$

Also, more than one statement may appear after the ELSE. When the statement

$$80 \text{ IF } Z <> 5 \text{ THEN } 200 \text{ ELSE PRINT "RIGHT": GOTO } 20$$

is executed, the program will jump to line 200 if Z <> 5; otherwise, "RIGHT" is printed and the program jumps to line 20.

It is possible to use multiple IF...THEN...ELSE statements all on a single program line. The following line uses three IF...THEN...ELSE statements to determine if N is lower, higher, or equal to 35 and then prints the appropriate message:

```
30 IF N < 35 THEN PRINT "LOW"
          ELSE IF N > 35 THEN PRINT "HIGH"
                      ELSE PRINT "CORRECT"
```

Notice how the line is structured; this is most important. Each new ELSE statement is lined up under the corresponding THEN, which clarifies the structure of the line by showing how each decision will branch.

If N < 35, then LOW will be printed and the rest of the line ignored, but if N >= 35, the ELSE portion of the line will be executed. We say that the THEN and ELSE portions of the statement have equal "weight" and therefore appear lined up under each other.

To the computer such structure makes no difference, but to a person reading the program it is extremely helpful. The only restriction on the use of multiple IF...THEN...ELSE statements is that the total length of a single programming line may not exceed 255 characters. It is also important in structuring an IF...THEN...ELSE statement to hit the ENTER key only after the whole structured line has been typed since the computer expects a new line number after an ENTER. Therefore, the cursor keys must be used to format the line.

The tremendous flexibility of the IF...THEN statement with its extensions and modifiers should now be apparent. Using this statement properly can substantially reduce both the size and complexity of a program.

Program 3.5   This program uses the previous IF...THEN...ELSE statement as part of a number guessing game where the user enters a number between 1 and 1000, inclusive, and is told whether the guess is low, high or correct. The game continues until the correct number (35) is input.

```
10 INPUT "What is your guess"; N
20 IF N <= 1 OR N >= 1000 THEN PRINT"Out of range": GOTO 10
30 IF N < 35 THEN PRINT "Low"
          ELSE IF N > 35 THEN PRINT "High"
                      ELSE PRINT "Correct" : GOTO 999
40 GOTO 10
999 END

RUN
What is your guess? 1001
Out of range
What is your guess? 100
High
What is your guess? 25
Low
What is your guess? 35
Correct
```

This short program illustrates a number of important programming concepts and should therefore be carefully analyzed.

- **Line 10:** Allows the user to guess the number.
- **Line 20:** Checks to make sure that the guess is in the correct range, between 1 and 1000, inclusive. Checking to make sure that a user has entered proper input is called "input protection" and is a very good programming practice.
- **Line 30:** This one line performs the function of a number of single statement lines. It is identical to the multiple IF...THEN...ELSE statement described previously except for the GOTO 999 used to terminate the program when the correct numer is entered.

Using a high line number like 999 for the END statement allows the programmer to know its location while the program is being written. It is possible to END a program at an IF...THEN statement. For example:

        20 IF X > 5 THEN END

This is considered poor programming style. It is better to send the program to the highest numbered line and END there instead.

        20 IF X > 5 THEN 999
        •
        •
        •
        •
        999 END

Counting in a Loop

If the programmer decides to keep score in the number guessing game of Program 3.5, some technique will have to be devised to keep count of the number of guesses taken. One way is to use the ability of variables to change their values and have the computer count with a statement called a "counter." A counter looks like this

        10 C = C + 1

Algebraically this statement makes little sense. But, when a variable name is assigned its value by the computer, the equal sign really means "is given the value" rather than "equals". Therefore, this statement means "C is given the value $C + 1$." Each time the computer reads line 10, the value of C will be increased by one.

Program 3.6

In this program a "counter" increases its value by one each time a loop is repeated:

```
10 C = C + 1
20 IF C > 5 THEN 999
30 PRINT C
40 GOTO 10
999 END

RUN
 1
 2
 3
 4
 5
```

Whenever a program is RUN, all variables have a value of 0 until they are assigned a value. Therefore, on line 10 variable C becomes 1 because $0 + 1 = 1$. When the loop repeats line 10 for a second time, variable C becomes 2. Each time the loop is repeated variable C equals its current value plus 1.

A counter does not have to count by 1. If line 10 were replaced by

$$10 \ C = C + 2$$

the program would count by twos.

```
RUN
 2
 4
```

Program 3.7   This program is a rewrite of Program 3.5, which now keeps score. The user starts with a score of 100 and loses 10 points for each guess taken.

```
5 C = 100
10 INPUT "What is your guess"; N
20 IF N <= 1 OR N >= 1000 THEN PRINT"Out of range": GOTO 10
30 IF N < 35 THEN PRINT "Low"
           ELSE IF N > 35 THEN PRINT"High"
                          ELSE PRINT"Score =";C: GOTO 999
40 C = C - 10
50 GOTO 10
999 END

RUN
What is your guess? 20
Low
What is your guess? 40
High
What is your guess? 35
Score = 80
```

Note that line 5 is needed to initialize the counter C to 100. Line 30 has been amended so that it will print the score when the correct number is chosen and line 40 subtracts 10 points from C for every wrong guess. What would happen if line 50 were changed to GOTO 5?

**Accumulating
a Total**   Often, a problem requires some sort of running total to produce the required output. One way of calculating this is through the use of a special type of counter known as an accumulator. An accumulator adds an amount that may vary each time the statement is executed. For example,

$$10 \ A = A + N$$

is an accumulator, where N is a changing value added to the total stored in A.

Program 3.8

This program incorporates both a counter and an accumulator to calculate the compounded interest on an Individual Retirement Account (IRA) in which $2000 is invested each year for 30 years. The annual interest rate is 10%.

```
10 IRA = 2000
20 C = C + 1
30 IF C > 30 THEN 60
40 TOTAL = (TOTAL + IRA) * 1.1
50 GOTO 20
60 PRINT "After 30 years, your IRA is worth $"; TOTAL
70 END

RUN
After 30 years, your IRA is worth $ 361887
```

- **Line 10:** Sets the value of the IRA to $2,000 per year.
- **Line 20:** Adds a 1 to the counter which will keep track of the number of years the TOTAL has been calculated.
- **Line 30:** Makes sure that the loop from lines 20-50 is executed only 30 times.
- **Line 40:** Calculates the total value of the IRA by adding each year's deposit ($2000) to the current total and multiplying the sum by 1.1 to account for the interest.
- **Line 50:** Sends the program back to line 20 to calculate the IRA value for the next year.
- **Line 60:** Prints out the final value of the IRA after 30 years.

Review

5. Write a program which asks for a student's grade average and then prints the message HIGH HONORS if the average is 90 or above, HONORS if above 80, PASSING if above or equal to 60 and FAILING if below 60. Use a properly structured IF...THEN...ELSE statement to print the message.

```
RUN
WHAT IS YOUR AVERAGE? 75
PASSING
```

6. Write a program which asks a user to enter 5 numbers and then prints the sum of the numbers. You can use only a single input variable N.

```
RUN
ENTER NUMBER 1? 12
ENTER NUMBER 2? 28
ENTER NUMBER 3? 32
ENTER NUMBER 4? 15
ENTER NUMBER 5? 71
THE SUM OF THE FIVE NUMBERS IS 158
```

FOR...TO... STEP, NEXT

So far we have used only the GOTO statement to produce simple loops. For many applications the FOR...TO...STEP, NEXT statements provide a superior method for producing a loop in which a sequence of numbers is produced with each number in the sequence differing from its predecessor by a constant amount. The general form of the FOR...TO...STEP, NEXT statements is:

FOR <variable> = <starting value> TO <ending value> STEP <increment>
   •
   •
   •
NEXT <variable>

Note that the variable after FOR and NEXT must be the same and that a string variable cannot be used. The STEP value determines how much the loop variable is incremented. If omitted the increment equals +1. The following are examples of valid FOR...NEXT loops:

```
 ┌─ 10 FOR X = 2 TO 6
 │      •
 │      •
 │      •
 └─ 40 NEXT X

 ┌─ 70 FOR H1 = (N * 2) TO 26 STEP 2
 │      •
 │      •
 │      •
 └─ 100 NEXT H1

 ┌─ 120 FOR T = 10 TO 0 STEP –1
 │      •
 │      •
 │      •
 └─ 180 NEXT T

 ┌─ 30 FOR N = 3 TO 11 STEP 2
 │      •
 │      •
 │      •
 └─ 80 NEXT N
```

In the last example variable N starts at line 30 with a value of 3. N retains this value until the NEXT N statement is encountered at line 80. At this point N is increased by the STEP value, changing 3 to 5. All the statements in the lines occurring between lines 30 and 80 are executed in sequence during each consecutive pass through the loop. The program continues to return from line 80 to the line immediately following line 30 until N exceeds the specified limit of 11. At this point the program exits from the loop and moves to the line following 80.

Program 3.9

Here a FOR...NEXT loop is used to calculate and print the 5 times table from 0 to 10:

```
10 FOR J = 0 TO 10
20    PRINT J; " * 5 ="; J * 5
30 NEXT J
40 PRINT  "Finished the loop"
50 END

RUN
 0  * 5 = 0
 1  * 5 = 5
 2  * 5 = 10
 3  * 5 = 15
 4  * 5 = 20
 5  * 5 = 25
 6  * 5 = 30
 7  * 5 = 35
 8  * 5 = 40
 9  * 5 = 45
10   * 5 = 50
Finished the loop
```

In line 10, J is initialized to 0 and increased by 1 each time the loop is repeated. Line 20 displays the multiplication table. The NEXT J on line 30 tells the computer to increase the value of J by 1. If its value is less than or equal to 10, the computer repeats lines 20 and 30; otherwise, the computer exits the loop and goes on to line 40.

Line 20 is indented. Indenting the lines between the FOR... and NEXT statements is a good practice to follow because it gives a program a shape or structure. The indentation shows anyone reading the program where a loop begins, which lines are inside the loop and where the loop ends.

Program 3.10

This program finds solutions to the compound condition $5 * X + 3 < 100$ and $2 * X \char94 2 - 1 > 50$ and tests all odd integers from 1 to 25:

```
10 FOR X = 1 TO 25 STEP 2
20    IF (5*X)+3 < 100 AND (2*X^2)-1 > 50 THEN PRINT X;
30 NEXT X
40 PRINT "Done"
50 END

RUN
 7  9  11  13  15  17  19 Done
```

Note that on the Model 4, the symbol (^) is used to denote "raised to the power" (e.g., $X \char94 2$ means $X * X$). The (^) symbol does not appear on the keyboard, but is available by typing the CLEAR and semicolon (;) keys. The Models I and III use the symbol ([) which is available by typing the ↑ key. Lines 10 and 30 create a loop for testing the conditions located at line 20. The loop starts at line 10 with $X = 1$ and each time the program reaches the NEXT X statement at line 30, X is incremented by a STEP value of 2. The program then returns to line 20 unless the value of X has exceeded 25, at which time the loop is exited and DONE printed.

FOR...NEXT loops should not be interrupted by a GOTO or IF...THEN statement which sends the program outside of the loop since this may cause a memory overflow. The loop should be allowed to complete itself before exiting to the program lines which follow. If a loop is needed where the number of passes through it will be determined while it is being executed, WHILE...WEND should be used rather than FOR...NEXT. This method is explained later in this chapter.

Review

7. Write a program that prints the sum of the integers between 1 and 25, inclusive.

8. Using a FOR...NEXT loop, have the computer print the following:

   RUN
    20   18   16   14   12   10

9. Write a program that will allow a number N to be entered and then using N as a STEP value, print numbers between 8 and 20.

   RUN
   STEP VALUE? 2
    8   10   12   14   16   18   20

RESTORE

At times it is desirable to employ a set of data more than once. The RESTORE statement makes it possible to return to read the data again from the beginning. For example,

   40 RESTORE

causes the next READ statement encountered to go back to the first item in the first DATA statement.

Computer Flags

A computer flag uses an IF...THEN statement to look for a signal that a certain condition has been met. For instance, a flag can be used to keep the computer from halting a program with an OUT OF DATA ERROR or to END a program.

Program 3.11

This program demonstrates how the RESTORE statement allows a list of names to be searched repeatedly starting each time from the beginning of the list. A flag is used to determine whether a name has been found or not:

```
10 A$ = "NO FLAG"
20 PRINT
30 INPUT "Name to be searched";B$
40 RESTORE
50 FOR P = 1 TO 20
60    READ N$
70    IF N$ = B$ THEN PRINT N$; " HAS BEEN FOUND" : A$ = "FLAG"
80 NEXT P
90 IF A$ <> "FLAG" THEN PRINT "NOT ON LIST"
100 INPUT "Do you want to search for another name";X$
110 IF X$ = "Y" OR X$ = "YES" THEN 10
                                ELSE 999
120 DATA SMITH, JONES, BIDWELL, PRESLEY, DECKLE, PORTER
130 DATA CRANE, TIBBETTS, ROBBINS, GRAHAM, BOCZKOWSKI
140 DATA HAVENS, STETLER, CHAMBERS, COLE, JAMES, TOLAND
150 DATA HARRIS, MCCLELLAN, END OF LIST
999 END


RUN

Name to be searched? MANTLE
NOT ON LIST
Do you want to search for another name? Y

Name to be searched? BIDWELL
BIDWELL HAS BEEN FOUND
Do you want to search for another name? N
```

- **Line 10:** Sets the flag A$ to NO FLAG.
- **Line 40:** Ensures that each time the list is searched the search starts from the beginning of the list.
- **Line 70:** If the name being searched for (B$) is found, then HAS BEEN FOUND is printed and the flag (A$) is set to FLAG.
- **Line 80:** Completes the loop.
- **Line 90:** If the flag has not been reset to FLAG, the name must not be on the list and NOT ON LIST is printed.

Review this program carefully to make sure that you understand how the flag A$ is used. What would happen if line 110 sent the program to line 20 rather than line 10?

WHILE...WEND

The FOR...NEXT statements allow a loop to be established so that every statement within the loop is executed a predetermined number of times. Sometimes it may be desirable to execute one or more statements only as long as a given condition is true. This may be done by using the WHILE...WEND statements whose general form is:

```
WHILE <condition>
   •
   •
   •
WEND
```

When the WHILE statement is encountered, the "condition" is evaluated and if true, the statements between WHILE and WEND are executed. The computer then returns to the WHILE statement and re-evaluates the "condition" again. If the condition is still true, the process is repeated; otherwise, execution resumes with the statement immediately following WEND.

Program 3.12   This program is a rewrite of Program 3.11 except that the FOR...NEXT loop has been replaced by a WHILE...WEND loop. Note that the loop is executed only the number of times necessary to find the desired name:

```
10 A$ = "NO FLAG"
20 PRINT
30 INPUT "Name to be searched";B$
40 RESTORE
50 WHILE A$ <> "FLAG"
60      READ N$
70      IF N$ = "END OF LIST" THEN A$ = "FLAG"
80      IF N$ = B$ THEN PRINT N$; " has been found" : A$ = "FLAG"
90 WEND
100 IF N$ = "END OF LIST" THEN PRINT "Name not on list"
110 INPUT "Do you want to search for another name";X$
120 IF X$ = "Y" OR X$ = "YES" THEN 10
                              ELSE 999
130 DATA SMITH, JONES, BIDWELL, PRESLEY, DECKLE, PORTER
140 DATA CRANE, TIBBETTS, ROBBINS, GRAHAM, BOCZKOWSKI
150 DATA HAVENS, STETLER, CHAMBERS, COLE, JAMES, TOLAND
160 DATA HARRIS, MCCLELLAN, END OF LIST
999 END

RUN

Name to be searched? MANTLE
Name not on list
Do you want to search for another name? Y

Name to be searched? BIDWELL
BIDWELL has been found
Do you want to search for another name? N
```

Review   10. Write a program which will read in an employee's name, hours worked and pay rate from DATA statements. Then, compute and print the weekly salary. Use a WHILE...WEND loop to control the processing with the terminating condition being the data NAME = "ZZZ", which will be placed in the last DATA statements. Hint: Remember not to print the last set of data.

PRINT TAB   The PRINT TAB statement, which works similarly to the TAB key on a typewriter, provides an easy way to format output and allows the programmer to begin portions of the printout at specified locations. The left edge of the screen is located at TAB(1), while the right edge of the screen is located at TAB(80). For example, the following statement would print information beginning at screen positions 13, 25 and 32:

```
10 PRINT TAB(13) ; "This"; TAB(25) ; "is"; TAB(32); "TAB"
RUN
              This                    is                    Tab
```

It is necessary to include the semicolon (;) after each TAB.

Program 3.13   The substitution of variables for the numbers in the TAB parentheses is permissible provided these variables have assigned values:

```
10 READ X, Y, Z
20 PRINT TAB(X); "This"; TAB(Y); "is"; TAB(Z); "TAB"
30 DATA 13, 25, 32
40 END

RUN
              This              is        TAB
```

- **Line 10:** Reads in values for X, Y and Z
- **Line 20:** Incorporates the information read in line 10 with the TAB( ) function to achieve the same results as in the previous example.
- **Line 30:** Data used for the READ statement in line 10.

Program 3.14   This program uses TAB to draw a triangle on the display screen:

```
10 PRINT TAB(10); "*******"
20 FOR X = 1 TO 5
30     PRINT TAB(X + 10); "*"; TAB(16); "*"
40 NEXT X
50 PRINT TAB(16); "*"
60 END

RUN
              *******
             *       *
              *      *
               *     *
                *   *
                 * *
                  **
                   *
```

- **Line 10:** Prints the top side of the triangle starting at position 10.
- **Line 20:** Initiates the loop which will print the two other sides of the triangle.
- **Line 30:** Prints two points on the screen. Notice how X is incorporated with the TAB( ) function to draw a diagonal line.
- **Line 40:** Completes the loop which was started in line 20.
- **Line 50:** Completes the triangle by plotting the final point at position 16.

The PRINT TAB statement does not move the cursor to the left but only to the right. If a TAB position is specified which is to the left of the current position, printing will continue on the next line:

```
10 PRINT TAB(10) ; "##"; TAB(15) ; "##"
20 PRINT TAB(15) ; "##"; TAB(10) ; "##"

RUN
    ##    ##
          ##
    ##
```

- **Line 10:** Prints 2 sets of pound signs beginning at positions 10 and 15, respectively.
- **Line 20:** Prints a set of pound signs at position 15 and since position 10 is to the left of the TAB(15), the second set is printed on the next line.

Review

11. Using the TAB function, draw the following triangle on a clear screen.

RUN

12. Write a program which will read a music store's inventory from the following DATA statements. Print out a chart showing all the information plus the value of each item:

```
100 REM Name Quantity Price
110 DATA Grand Piano, 4, 12795.95
120 DATA Bass Fiddle, 7, 784.95
130 DATA Electronic Guitar, 15, 398.95
140 DATA Mandolin, 6, 235.95
```

RUN

ITEM	QUANTITY	PRICE	TOTAL VALUE
Grand Piano	4	12795.95	51183.80
Bass Fiddle	7	784.95	5494.65
Electric Guitar	15	398.95	5985.25
Mandolin	6	235.95	1415.70

LOCATE

The video display can hold 25 lines of 40 or 80 characters each. The LOCATE statement allows output to begin at any of these positions. The simplest form of LOCATE is:

LOCATE <row>, <column>

where "row" can have values from 1 to 25, and "column" from 1 to 40 or 80. For example,

```
10 LOCATE 1,1
20 PRINT "HERE"
```

will print "HERE" in the upper left hand corner, while

```
10 LOCATE 12,40
20 PRINT A$
```

will print the contents of the string variable A$ in the middle of the screen.

The "row" and "column" can be numeric variables. For instance, if X = 24 and Y = 10 then,

```
10 LOCATE X,Y
20 PRINT "CARROTS";
```

will place the word CARROTS at row 24, column 10. The trailing semicolon leaves the cursor positioned immediately after CARROTS so that a subsequent PRINT statement will begin output at that point on the screen.

Program 3.15   The following program will print M*A*S*H and 4077 fifteen times in diagonals on the screen using the LOCATE statement.

```
10 CLS
20 FOR I = 0 TO 14
30     LOCATE I+1, (4*I)+1 : PRINT "M*A*S*H"
40     LOCATE I+1, 57-(I*4) : PRINT "4 0 7 7"
50 NEXT I
60 END

RUN
```

```
M*A*S*H                                                              4 0 7 7
    M*A*S*H                                                      4 0 7 7
        M*A*S*H                                              4 0 7 7
            M*A*S*H                                      4 0 7 7
                M*A*S*H                              4 0 7 7
                    M*A*S*H                      4 0 7 7
                        M*A*S*H 4 0 7 7
                          4 0 7 7
                    4 0 7 7 M*A*S*H
                4 0 7 7              M*A*S*H
            4 0 7 7                      M*A*S*H
        4 0 7 7                              M*A*S*H
    4 0 7 7                                      M*A*S*H
  4 0 7 7                                          M*A*S*H
4 0 7 7                                                M*A*S*H
```

- **Line 30:** Positions the cursor at a location on the screen based upon the value of the loop variable, I, in order to print the word M*A*S*H.
- **Line 40:** Positions the cursor on the same line as the previous LOCATE but at a different horizontal location, where it will print 4 0 7 7.

Review

13. Write a program which will clear the screen and print an asterisk in each corner. Use LOCATE and store the screen positions in a DATA statement.

End of Chapter Problem

To review the material covered in this chapter we are going to design a program that allows a school to enter the name of a student and determine the student's extra-curricular activities. Each student in the school is a member of an athletic team, a musical group, a club and a school publication. To shorten the DATA statements that store the student names and activities, the following codes are used:

Athletic Teams	**Musical Groups**
1. Football	1. Band
2. Soccer	2. Glee Club
3. Swimming	3. Orchestra
Clubs	**School Publications**
1. Photography	1. Newspaper
2. Electronics	2. Year Book
3. Computer	3. Literary Magazine

Algorithm:

1. Enter student name.
2. Search through data to find student.
3. If student is found, convert codes to names of activities and print out a message; if not found, print NOT FOUND.
4. Ask if a search for another name is desired. If yes, "Y", then repeat steps 1 through 4; if not, end program.

Input:

Student Name	: STUDENT$
Repeat Search	: RESPONSE$

Output:

Student Name	: NAME$
Four Activities	: A1$, A2$, A3$, A4$

Program 3.16

```
10 FLAG = 0
20 PRINT
30 INPUT "NAME"; STUDENT$
40 RESTORE
50 WHILE FLAG = 0
60      READ N$, A1, A2, A3, A4
70      IF N$ = "END OF DATA" THEN FLAG = -1
80      IF STUDENT$ <> N$ THEN 170
90      IF A1 = 1 THEN A1$ = "FOOTBALL"
                ELSE IF A1 = 2 THEN A1$ = "SOCCER"
                              ELSE A1$ = "SWIMMING"
100     IF A2 = 1 THEN A2$ = "BAND"
                ELSE IF A2 = 2 THEN A2$ = "GLEE CLUB"
                              ELSE A2$ = "ORCHESTRA"
110     IF A3 = 1 THEN A3$ = "PHOTOGRAPHY"
                ELSE IF A3 = 2 THEN A3$ = "ELECTRONICS"
                              ELSE A3$ = "COMPUTER"
120     IF A4 = 1 THEN A4$ = "NEWSPAPER"
                ELSE IF A4 = 2 THEN A4$ = "YEAR BOOK"
                              ELSE A4$ = "LITERARY MAGAZINE"
```

```
130      PRINT TAB(5);"NAME"; TAB(15);"SPORT"; TAB(25);"MUSIC";
140      PRINT TAB(35); "CLUB"; TAB(48); "PUBLICATION" : PRINT
150      PRINT TAB(5);N$;TAB(15);A1$;TAB(25);A2$;TAB(35);A3$;
              TAB(48);A4$
160      FLAG = -1
170 WEND
180 IF N$ = "END OF DATA" THEN PRINT STUDENT$; " NOT FOUND"
190 INPUT "ANOTHER Y/N"; A$
200 IF A$ = "Y" OR A$ = "YES" THEN 10
210 DATA JIM,1,1,1,1, MARK,1,1,2,2, MIKE,1,1,3,3, JOE,1,2,1,2
220 DATA TOM,1,2,3,1, MARY,2,1,1,2, CAROL,2,1,2,3, HEIDI,2,1,3,2
230 DATA LISA,2,3,3,1, EILEEN,3,2,3,2, BRUCE,3,1,3,3, TED,3,2,2,2
240 DATA SUE,3,3,3,1, MARTHA,3,2,1,2, FRED,3,3,3,3, PATTI,2,3,2,2
250 DATA LARRY,1,2,2,1, PAM,2,3,1,1, BART,1,3,2,1, BETH,1,2,3,1
260 DATA END OF DATA, 999, 999, 999, 999
999 END

RUN

NAME? BOB
BOB NOT FOUND
ANOTHER Y/N? Y

NAME? HEIDI
     NAME           SPORT       MUSIC       CLUB            PUBLICATION

     HEIDI          SOCCER      BAND        COMPUTER        YEAR BOOK
ANOTHER Y/N? Y

NAME? BRUCE
     NAME           SPORT       MUSIC       CLUB            PUBLICATION

     BRUCE          SWIMMING    BAND        COMPUTER        LITERARY MAGAZINE
ANOTHER Y/N? N
```

- **Line 10:** Sets the variable FLAG to zero. FLAG will be used to test if a student had been found.
- **Line 30:** Asks the user to input the name of the student whose activities are desired.
- **Line 40:** Ensures that each time the list is searched, it will start from the beginning of the data list.
- **Line 50:** Starts the loop which will search through the list of students.
- **Line 60:** Reads in the student names and activity codes.
- **Line 70:** If the end-of-data has been reached, the FLAG is set to –1.
- **Line 80:** If the student name does not match the name input, the computer advances to the next student.
- **Lines 90-120:** When a student has been found, the activity codes are converted to the appropriate names.
- **Lines 130-150:** Print out headings and student information in table form using PRINT TAB.
- **Line 170:** Ends the loop initiated by line 50.
- **Line 180:** Tests N$ to check if the student name input in line 20 was found.
- **Line 190:** Asks the user whether or not to continue and search for another student.
- **Line 200:** If the user inputs an answer of "Y" or "YES", then the program continues from the beginning; otherwise, it ends.
- **Lines 210-260:** Contain the student data.

EXERCISES

1. Write a program that allows two numbers (A and B) to be entered. Have the computer compare them and print a message stating whether A is less than, equal to, or greater than B.

        RUN
        ? 23, 45
         23 is less than 45

2. Write a program which allows three names to be entered as A$, B$ and C$. Have the computer print the name which is alphabetically last.

3. Write a program which prints six exclamation marks if BIGWOW is entered but which otherwise prints six question marks. The program is run until the letters ZZZ are typed:

        RUN
        ? COMPUTER
        ??????
        ? BIGWOW
        !!!!!!
        ? ZZZ

4. Use LOCATE to draw a straight diagonal line (composed of asterisks) starting at the upper left hand corner and moving one space down and one space to the right until the line hits the bottom of the screen.

5. Determine the output of the following program:

        10 FOR Z = 1 TO 4
        20   PRINT TAB(Z);Z
        30 NEXT Z
        40 FOR Y = 1 TO 4
        50   PRINT TAB(Y),Y
        60 NEXT Y

6. Use a FOR...NEXT loop and CLS to display a sign on the screen which advertises Uncle Bill's Whamburgers for $0.59:

   RUN

   ```
   ! _____ !
   !                               !
   !    TODAY ONLY!                !
   !       UNCLE BILL'S            !
   !       WHAMBURGERS             !
   !            ONLY $0.59         !
   !                               !
   ! _____ !
   ```

7. Allow a number (X) to be entered. Print the message "NOT BETWEEN" if X is either less than –24 or greater than 17. Only one IF...THEN statement is permitted.

8. Allow a string (A$) to be entered. Print the message "A$ IS BETWEEN" if A$ comes between "DOWN" and "UP" alphabetically. Only one IF...THEN statement is permitted.

9. Write a program in which the user inputs a number (X). Print "IN THE INTERVAL" if X satisfies the inequality $25 < X < 75$, but otherwise print "NOT IN THE INTERVAL". Only one AND and one IF...THEN statement are to be used.

10. Rewrite exercise 9, using OR instead of AND.

11. Use only one PRINT statement to produce the following rectangle:

    RUN
    ```
    ************
    ************
    ************
    ```

12. Print the cubes of the odd integers from 11 to –11, inclusive, in descending order.

13. Print all the integers which end in 4 from 4 to 84, inclusive.

14. Use a loop to print a horizontal line of 40 asterisks.

15. Print all the integers in the set 10, 13, 16, 19, ..., 94, 97.

16. Using a loop, have the computer print a letter I using asterisks as follows:

    RUN
    ```
    *****
     ***
     ***
     ***
     ***
     ***
     ***
    *****
    ```

17. Below is a list of various creatures and the weapon necessary to destroy each:

Creature	**Weapon**
Lich	Fire Ball
Mummy	Flaming Torch
Werewolf	Silver Bullet
Vampire	Wooden Stake
Medusa	Sharp Sword
Triffid	Fire Hose

Using READ and DATA, have the computer state what weapon is to be used to destroy a given creature. For example:

RUN
Monster? King Kong
King Kong not found
RUN
Monster? Vampire
Vampire can be killed with a wooden stake

18. State the exact order in which the lines of the following program are to be executed:

```
10 READ A,B,C
20 S = A + B * C
30 IF S = 10 THEN RESTORE: READ S
40 PRINT S,
50 IF S = 14 THEN END
60 GOTO 10
70 DATA 4, 2, 3, 6, 0, 2, 7
```

10. Write a program which asks for a person's age. If the person is 16 years or older, have the computer print "You are old enough to drive a car!". Otherwise, have the computer indicate how many years the person must wait before being able to drive.

RUN
How old are you? 16
You are old enough to drive a car!

20. The Happy Holiday Motel has 10 rooms. Have the computer print a label for each room's door indicating the room number. For example:

RUN

```
********************
Happy Holiday Motel
Room 1
********************
```

21. As candidate for mayor, you are very busy. Use the computer to print thank-you letters to 10 people who have contributed money to your election campaign. Be sure to mention the exact amount each person has contributed.

    RUN

    Dear Rich Bryburry,
        Thank you for your generous contribution
    of 25000 dollars to my election campaign. Maybe
    next year we will have better luck!

    Sincerely,
    Smiley R. Politico

22. Write a program which will produce the following table:

    RUN

X	X^2	X^3
2	4	8
4	16	64
6	36	216
8	64	512
10	100	1000

23. The Bored Auto Company has done it again! Some models of their cars may be difficult to drive because their wheels are not exactly round. Cars with model numbers 102, 780, 119, 229, 189 and 195 have been found to have a defect. Write a computer program that allows 10 of their customers to enter the model number of their car to find out whether or not it is defective.

24. Using only two print statements, write a program to print a triangle that is N lines high and N columns wide. For example:

    RUN
    ? 5
    *
    **
    ***
    ****
    *****

25. Write a program that will produce the following triangle. The figure is centered on TAB(10):

RUN

```
        *
      *   *
     *     *
    *       *
   *         *
  *           *
 *             *
 *************
```

26. The following table contains employee performance data for the Tippecanoe Typing Company:

Employee	Performance
Oakley	69%
Howe	92%
Anderson	96%
Wolley	88%
Goerz	74%

Tippecanoe Typing is suffering from financial difficulties and needs to cut back on its staff. Using READ, DATA and a loop, have the computer print notices of dismissal for any employee whose production is below 75%.

    RUN
    Dear Oakley,
       I am sorry that I must fire you.
    You have been such a fine employee
    with a performance rating of 69%.
    I'm sure you'll have no trouble
    finding another job.
                    Sincerely,
                    George Schwabb

    Dear Goerz,
       I am sorry that I must fire you.
    You have been such a fine employee
    with a performance rating of 74%.
    I'm sure you'll have no trouble
    finding another job.
                    Sincerely,
                    George Schwabb

27. Wayne Peber bought stock two years ago and wants to use the computer to calculate his profit or loss. He bought 200 shares of Consolidated Technologies at $85.58 per share and 400 shares of American Amalgamated Securites at $35.60 per share. Today C.T. is worth $70.82 a share and A.A.S. is worth $47.32 a share. What is his profit or loss?

28. The Crude Oil Company uses the computer to determine the weekly wages of its employees. If an employee works over 40 hours, he or she is paid one and a half times the hourly rate for each additional hour.

    > RUN
    > Hours worked? 45
    > Hourly wage? 10.00
    > The wage for the week is $475

29. You have $200.00 to spend on a buying spree. Write a program that, as you buy merchandise, subtracts the cost and the appropriate sales tax (5%) from your remaining money and shows your present total. The program should prevent you from buying items that cost more than you have. Entering 0 terminates the program.

    > RUN
    > How much does the item cost? 10.00
    > Your total is now $189.50
    >
    > How much does the item cost? 250.00
    > You don't have enough money.
    > How much does the item cost? 25.00
    > Your total is now $163.25
    >
    > How much does the item cost? 0

30. Have the computer find all odd integers from 5 to 25 which are simultaneous solutions of the inequalities $X^3 > 500$ and $X^2 + 3X + 2 < 700$. Print only the solutions.

31. The Lawrenceville National Bank needs a program to assist its customers with mortgage calculations. It wants the customer to be able to walk up to a terminal, enter the loan amount, interest rate and length of the loan, and have the monthly payment displayed. The formula for a monthly payment is:

$$\text{Payment} = \frac{A * I}{1 - (I + 1)^{-M}}$$

Write a program that displays the monthly payment when A, M and I are input.

32. A factorial (written N!) is a number which is the product of all integers from 1 to N. Therefore, If N = 4, then N! = $1 * 2 * 3 * 4 = 24$.

    > RUN
    > Enter a Number? 5
    >   5! = 120
    >
    > Do you want another (Y/N)? Y
    >
    > Enter a Number? 3
    >   3! = 6
    >
    > Do you want another (Y/N)? N

Advanced Exercises

The following exercises require the development of a detailed algorithm. The program should not be written until all details of the algorithm have been worked out.

33. A car dealer orders cars by entering the name of the car, followed by a list of options from 4 categories: body style, seat type, sound system and engine. These options are simplified by using the following number codes:

Body Style	**Seat Type**
1) 2 door	1) bench
2) 4 door	2) bucket
3) hatchback	3) split bench
4) convertible	4) reclining

Sound System	**Engine**
1) AM radio	1) 4 cylinder
2) AM/FM mono	2) 6 cylinder
3) AM/FM/tape	3) 8 cylinder
4) AM/FM/disk	4) diesel

Write a program to accept the orders from a dealer and display the list of options based on the codes entered:

```
RUN
Enter car and options? Capri, 4, 2, 4, 3

Model: Capri
Options: Convertible
         Bucket Seats
         AM/FM/disk
         8 cylinder engine
```

4

COMPUTER ARITHMETIC

INT

RND

RANDOMIZE TIMER

INT

RND

RANDOMIZE TIMER

INT

RND

RANDOMIZE TIMER

*O*ne of the first things that comes to mind when people think of a computer is mathematics. The word compute means to calculate or figure mathematically, and computers are excellent "number crunchers". This chapter will describe how the computer carries out mathematical operations, and how it uses both very large and very small numbers. The chapter will also explain how the computer can be made to pick a random number, and some situations where the computer's calculations are not accurate.

Order of Operations	What value will be assigned to A when the computer calculates the following expression?

$$A = 3 + 12 / 3$$

Will the computer add 3 and 12 and then divide by 3? If it does, the answer will be 5. Or will the computer first divide 12 by 3 and then add 3 resulting in an answer of 7. Entering the expression in immediate mode,

    PRINT 3 + 12 / 3
     7

the answer is 7. The computer divided first and then added 3 to the result because it follows a specific order of operations. The computer will always carry out mathematical calculations in the same way. As a programmer you must know in what order math operations will be executed.

    The computer uses the following order of priority when it reads a mathematical expression:

FIRST
Exponents: Any number raised to a power, i.e. 2 ^ 2, are calculated first.

    PRINT 2 + 2 ^ 2
     6

The computer first calculated 2^2, which is 4, even though 2 + 2 appears first when reading from left to right. Then the computer reads through the statement again and adds 2 to the 4 to get 6.

SECOND
Multiplication and Division: Next, the computer looks for multiplication or division signs which are of equal priority:

    PRINT 2 + 5 * 4 / 2
12

First the computer reads through this statement looking for an exponent. Since there is none, it re-reads the statement. On its second reading, the computer looks for multiplication and division signs. Since these signs have a higher priority, the computer ignores the plus sign between 2 and 5. When the computer reads the multiplication sign between 5 and 4, it executes that multiplication with 20 as the result. The computer then reads the division sign and divides 20 by 2 with a result of 10. Only after all the multiplications and divisions are completed does the computer read the statement again and add 2 to 10 to get the final result of 12. Remember, when there is more than one operation of the same priority being performed in a statement, the computer does them in order from left to right.

THIRD
Addition and Subtraction: The third time the computer reads an expression it looks for addition and subtraction signs which are of equal priority:

PRINT 3 * 2 + 6
12

Since multiplication and division are done before addition, the computer first calculates the product of 3 and 2, which is 6. To get the final result, 6 is added to 6 , which is 12.

When parentheses, "(" and ")", are used, the computer does whatever operations are within the parentheses first. By using parentheses, a programmer can tell the computer to change the order of operations. If a programmer wants 3 added to 12 and the result divided by 3, parentheses tell the computer to follow that order:

PRINT (3 + 12) / 3
5

If parentheses are used within parentheses, the computer will execute the operation within the inner-most parentheses first:

PRINT (5 * ((3 + 12) / 3))
25

First the computer adds 3 and 12 and then divides by 3. Finally the computer multiplies that by 5. What would the result of this expression be if all parentheses were removed?

When the number of left parentheses "(" do not match the number of right parentheses ")", the computer will print a ?SYNTAX ERROR message and halt the program:

10 PRINT 5 * ((5 + 2) * (16 / 4 + 12)
RUN
?SYNTAX ERROR IN 10

Review

1. Solve the following by hand using the computer's order of operations and then check your answers by using immediate mode:

a. $6 - 9/3$	b. $5 * 15 - 5$
c. $3 \wedge 2 + 1$	d. $3 * (5 + 6)$
e. $25/5 + 3 * 12$	f. $(13 - 3)/(10/2)$
g. $(2 + 1) \wedge (8/4)$	h. $3 * (2 + (5 - 2))$

2. Find the error in the following program:

```
10 INPUT "TYPE A NUMBER"; A
20 INPUT "TYPE ANOTHER NUMBER"; B
30 C = (A + B) * 2)
40 PRINT C
```

Computer Numbers

The computer displays all numbers as decimals, including fractions and mixed numbers. It's use of decimal numbers is most obvious with division, since any result other than a whole number will be expressed as a decimal fraction:

```
PRINT 5/2
2.5
```

The computer expresses the answer as a mixed decimal 2.5. Often, the result of a division continues to have a remainder and so the process of division could be repeated continually:

```
PRINT 10 / 3
3.333333
```

This is called a repeating decimal because 3 will continue to be the result each time the division is repeated. The computer can only store numbers that have up to 7 digits plus a decimal point. Therefore, it stopped dividing when the number of digits reached 7.

If the value of a repeating decimal is equal to or greater than 5, the computer will round the last digit up to the next highest digit:

```
PRINT 10 / 6
1.666667
```

Since 6 is greater than 5, the computer rounded the 6 up to a 7 when it reached the eighth digit.

Review

3. Use immediate mode to have the computer execute the following operations. Can you predict how the computer will print the results?

    a. 100 / 8
    b. 22 / 7
    c. 5/6 − 1/8
    d. 37 / 2
    e. 11 / 3

INTegerizing

An integer is a whole number; therefore, the numbers 1, 2, 10 and 100 are all integers. Often, only the integer part of a number is important. For instance, if you have 30 golf balls and you need to know how many full dozen you have, only the whole number part of your division is used:

```
PRINT 30 / 12
2.5
```

By using the INTeger function, the computer can be told to use only the whole number part of any value:

INT(X)

X can be a number, a variable or a mathematical expression like 10 / 3. The computer looks at the value within the parentheses and then uses only the whole number portion:

PRINT INT(10 / 3)
3

INT(X) does not round off the number; instead, it drops any fractional part. For example:

$$INT(4.769) = 4 \qquad INT(5.9) = 5$$
$$INT(.63) = 0 \qquad INT(12.098) = 12$$

The value that the integer function returns is always equal to or smaller than the original value. Therefore, when INT(X) is used with negative numbers, the value returned is always one less than the whole number portion of a mixed number.

$$INT(-4.769) = -5 \qquad INT(-5.9) = -6$$
$$INT(-.63) = -1 \qquad INT(-12.098) = -13$$

Program 4.1

The Skyhook International Company wants to pack 3 left handed skyhooks in a box. They have written this program to tell them how many boxes are needed and how many skyhooks will be left over:

```
10 N = 3
20 INPUT "Enter the number of skyhooks"; H
30 B = INT(H / N)
40 L = H - (N * B)
50 PRINT "Boxes needed:"; B
60 PRINT "Skyhooks left over:"; L
70 END

RUN
Enter the number of skyhooks? 14
Boxes needed: 4
Skyhooks left over: 2
```

In the example shown, the value of H is 14 and the value of N is 3. Therefore, the result of 14/3 is 4.666667 and B is assigned a value of 4.

Review

4. Predict the outcome of the following and then use immediate mode to check your prediction:

a. INT(199.99999)   b. INT(22 / 7)
c. INT(-3.001)   d. INT(.005)
e. INT(-.999)

Random Numbers—RND   We can pick random numbers in many ways such as rolling dice, drawing a card from a deck or picking numbers from a hat. The computer can also be told to pick a random number. The statement

$$X = RND$$

will assign X a random number that has a value greater than 0 but less than 1.

Program 4.2   This program will print 5 random numbers. It is run twice. Note that it produces the same set of random numbers each time.

```
10 FOR I = 1 TO 5
20    PRINT RND,
30 NEXT I
40 END
```

```
RUN
 .629126        .1948297       .6305799       .8625746       .9363531

RUN
 .629126        .1948297       .6305799       .8625746       .9363531
```

In many cases, a value that is less than 1 is not very helpful. Therefore, the computer can be told to pick a number that is greater than 1 by using multiplication:

20 PRINT 10 ∗ RND,

This statement tells the computer to pick a number that is greater than 0 and less than 1 and to multiply that number by 10. When line 20 of Program 4.2 is changed and the program RUN it produces the following results:

```
RUN
 6.29126    1.948297    6.305799    8.625746    9.363531
```

There are several things to notice about these numbers. First, the numbers are all decimal fractions, which can be a problem when a programmer would prefer whole numbers. Second, the computer never picked 10 as one of the numbers. 10 will never be picked because the computer only chooses a number less than 1; only 10 ∗ 1 will cause the computer to output 10 in line 20.

More Useful Random Numbers   By using the integer function, a programmer can tell the computer to pick only whole numbers. When line 20 of Program 4.2 is replaced by

20 PRINT INT(10 ∗ RND),

it produces the following results:

```
RUN
 6        1        6        8        9
```

The value of each of these integers is between 0 and 9. The computer did what it was told. It picked one of 10 integers, but it still could not pick 10 because RND picks a fraction that is greater than 0 and less than 1.

By adding 1 to whatever number the computer picks on line 20, the computer can be told to pick any whole number from 1 to 10:

```
20 PRINT INT(10 * RND + 1)
```

If 0 is the integer picked, adding 1 will give us a 1. If 9 is the integer picked, adding 1 will give 10. Now when the program is run again, it may pick 10 but it will never pick 0:

```
RUN
 7        2        7        9        10
```

Review

5. Write a program that picks ten random integers between 1 and 100:

```
RUN
27        42        89        68        17
17        75        5         53        34
```

6. Write a program that picks two random integers from 1 to 25 and then adds them.

```
RUN
 17 + 3 = 20
```

Choosing Numbers from a Range

The computer can also be told to pick random numbers that are within a specific range. For example, picking numbers that are between 5 and 10, 10 and 20 or 100 and 200 is done by using the following formula. In this formula, the letter A stands for the lowest number in the range, and B for the highest number in the range:

```
INT((B − A + 1) * RND + A)
```

To pick a number that is greater than or equal to 10 and less than or equal to 20, the formula used is:

```
X = INT(11 * RND + 10)
```

To give X its value the computer does four things. First, it picks a number that is greater than 0 but less than 1. Then, that number is multiplied by 11 (20 − 10 + 1). Third, 10 is added to that number, and finally X is assigned the integer value of the number.

Program 4.3

This program creates 3 addition problems by picking two random numbers for addends. The computer waits for the program user to enter a correct answer:

```
10  PRINT
20  FOR J = 1 TO 3
30     A = INT(400 * RND + 100)
40     B = INT(100 * RND + 1)
50     C = A + B
60     PRINT A; "+"; B; "=";
70     INPUT D
80     IF D = C THEN PRINT "GOOD SHOW"
                ELSE PRINT "SORRY TRY AGAIN" : GOTO 60
90     PRINT
100 NEXT J
110 END
RUN

 148 + 66 =? 214
GOOD SHOW

 447 + 73 =? 520
GOOD SHOW

 419 + 8 =? 417
SORRY TRY AGAIN
 419 + 8 =? 427
GOOD SHOW
```

On line 30 the computer assigns A the integer value of a number chosen from within the range 100 to 499. On line 40 the computer assigns B the integer value of a number from within the range 1 to 100. The IF...THEN...ELSE statement on line 80 tells the computer whether the input answer is right or wrong and prints the appropriate message.

Review

7. Write a program that will output 15 random integers from 10 to 20.

8. Write a program that selects one random integer from 25 to 50 and another from 1 to 25 and outputs their difference:

```
RUN
37 - 17 = 20
```

RANDOMIZE TIMER

Numbers which the computer picks may still not be as random as a programmer would like. Since the computer will choose the same numbers in the same order each time it is turned on, game players will quickly figure out the pattern. To eliminate this problem, the following statement should be added to any program using random numbers:

RANDOMIZE TIMER

This statement "randomizes" the numbers that are picked so that they will be different each time the computer is turned on. The statement can be placed anywhere in a program, but it must be executed before the program begins choosing random numbers. Therefore, it is best to place the statement near the beginning of the program.

Program 4.4   This game program selects a random integer from 1 to 100 and then gives the player unlimited chances to guess the number. After each guess the computer tells the player whether the guess was too high, too low or correct:

```
10 RANDOMIZE TIMER
20 PRINT "I'm thinking of a number between 1 and 100"
30 NUMBER = INT(100 * RND + 1)
40 PRINT
50 INPUT "Type your guess"; GUESS
60 IF GUESS < NUMBER THEN PRINT "Low... try again" : GOTO 40
70 IF GUESS > NUMBER THEN PRINT "High... try again" : GOTO 40
80 PRINT "You are correct"
90 END

RUN
I'm thinking of a number between 1 and 100

Type your guess? 50
Too low... guess again

Type your guess? 75
Too high... guess again

Type your guess? 62
Too low... guess again

Type your guess? 70
Too low... guess again

Type your guess? 73
You are correct
```

- **Line 10:** Makes sure that the random numbers chosen will be different each time the program is run.
- **Line 30:** Picks a number between 1 and 100 using the formula ((B − A + 1) ∗ RND + A) where A = 1 and B = 100.
- **Lines 60-70:** Compare GUESS to the number picked by the computer, N, and print the appropriate message.
- **Line 80:** Prints the appropriate message and ends the program when GUESS is correct.

Rounding Errors   Computers are limited in some of the things they can do. One of these limitations causes the computer to make a slight error in some of its calculations, called a rounding error. For example,

PRINT 1/3
.3333334

produces an inaccurate result. Dividing 1 by 3 should give .3333333, not, 3333334. The error is small and usually will not cause any difficulty. However, a problem can arise when the computer is told to compare values in an IF...THEN statement:

10 IF 1/3 = .3333333 THEN PRINT "THEY ARE EQUAL"

The computer will not consider that these two statements equivalent and therefore, THEY ARE EQUAL will not be printed. To overcome this problem the numbers being compared should be rounded off to less than 7 places before the IF...THEN comparison. This technique is explained later in the chapter.

Scientific Notation/ E Notation

The computer is also limited in the size of a number which can be stored in its memory.

PRINT 1234567 * 1234567
1.524156E + 12

The computer can store numbers that have up to 7 digits plus a decimal point. To work with numbers that have more than seven digits, the computer rounds off the number and uses scientific notation. Scientific notation uses the letter E followed by a sign and a number as in 2.934E + 7. If the E is followed by a plus sign, the number must be multiplied by 10 that number of times.

1.524156E + 12 = 1,524,156,000,000.
_____
12 places to the right

A minus sign means multiplying by 1/10 that many times:

3.5678788E − 4 = .00035678788.
_____
4 places to the left

The computer will accept E notation in any situation where a number can be used, including DATA statements. The E in DATA 5.8943E + 6 will not cause an error message.

Review

9. Change the following from E notation to standard notation:

   a. 1.42E − 2   b. 4.321E + 5
   c. 4.56231E + 8 d. 5E − 3
   e. 6.7087E + 6   f. 6.7896E − 5

10. What will be the output of the following program? Make your prediction, then type it in to see if you were correct:

```
10 FOR J = 1 TO 3
20      READ A
30      PRINT A
40 NEXT J
50 PRINT "ALL DATA READ"
60 DATA .5E − 2, 1.234E + 5, 1.984E − 5
```

**Rounding
Fractions Off**

There are many situations where a programmer does not need or want numbers that are carried out to seven places. For example, dollar-and-cents calculations make little sense when they are carried out to the thousandth of a cent. Since the computer automatically calculates to seven places, it must be given specific instructions to round numbers.

In order to explain the proper method of rounding fractions, we will round 5.4356 to the nearest hundredth. The result should leave us with 5.44. The first step of the rounding process is to multiply the number by 10 for each decimal place required. For example, to round to two decimal places (i.e. the nearest hundredth), we should multiply by 100:

$$X = 100 * 5.4356 = 543.56$$

Once this is done, the last required digit is rounded to its proper value by adding .5:

$$X = 543.56 + .5 = 544.06$$

Now, to attain the desired number of digits, INT is used to "chop off" the part of the number that is unwanted:

$$X = INT(544.06) = 544$$

Finally, the decimal point is moved back where it belongs, by dividing by the number that was multiplied originally. For example, since we multiplied by 100 at the beginning of the process, we must now divide by 100. This yields

$$X = 544 / 100 = 5.44$$

which is the desired result. All of these steps can be incorporated into one line:

$$X = INT(100 * 5.4356 + .5) / 100$$

Or, to round a number N to Z decimal places, the general formula is:

$$X = INT(10 \char`\^ Z * N + .5) / 10 \char`\^ Z$$

If numbers are to be rounded off to the nearest hundred or ten, the Z in the formula should be negative. For example, to round to the nearest thousand (i.e. 5845 rounded to 6000), use the statement:

$$X = INT(10 \char`\^ (-3) * N + .5) / 10 \char`\^ (-3)$$

or

$$X = INT(.001 * N + .5) / .001$$

Program 4.5   This simple program asks the user to INPUT a number and state how many places it should be rounded to.

```
10 PRINT
20 INPUT "Number to be rounded"; N
30 INPUT "To how many decimal places"; Z
40 X = INT(10^Z * N + .5) / 10^Z
50 PRINT "The answer is:"; X
60 INPUT "Do you want to round another number (Y?N)"; Y$
70 IF Y$ = "Y" THEN 10
80 END

RUN

Number to be rounded? 29.4592
To how many decimal places? 1
The answer is: 29.5
Do you want to round another number (Y?N)? Y

Number to be rounded? 376.344
To how many decimal places? -2
The answer is: 400
Do you want to round another number (Y?N)? N
```

Note how the second number is rounded to the nearest hundred by instructing the computer to round to –2 decimal places.

Program 4.6   This program rounds off baseball batting averages to the nearest thousandth:

```
10 PRINT "BATTING AVERAGE CALCULATOR"
20 INPUT "Enter times at bat"; B
30 INPUT "Enter number of hits"; H
40 T = H / B
50 AVG = INT(1000 * T + .5) / 1000
60 PRINT
70 PRINT "Average is:"; AVG
80 END

RUN
BATTING AVERAGE CALCULATOR
Enter times at bat? 12
Enter number of hits? 4

Average is: .333
```

Line 40 calculates the batting average, and line 50 rounds it off to the thousandth place. Variable T is the average before it is rounded. In line 50, T is first multiplied by 1000 (10 ^ 3) because multiplication has a higher priority in the computer's order of operations. Then .5 is added and the result is INTegerized. To complete the process, the number is divided by 1000 to move the decimal place back to the correct position. The variable AVG now contains the properly rounded answer, which is printed at line 70.

Review

11. Write a program that accepts a number and rounds it off to the nearest tenth.

RUN
WHAT NUMBER IS TO BE ROUNDED? 25.92
25.92 TO THE NEAREST TENTH is 25.9

End of Chapter Problem

Since frogs are in short supply, the Calaveras County Frog Jumping Race has decided to computer-simulate this year's race. They want to have three championship frogs run a series of ten races to determine the winner. Past year's races have proven that when a frog wins a race, it is more likely to win future races. Therefore, we must provide a simulation where the three frogs have the same chance of winning, initially, but on each successive race, the odds should favor previous winners.

Each frog will start out with the ability to jump 4 feet forward at best and 2 feet backward at worst. When a frog wins a race; however, his worst possible jump is decreased by .05 feet. The finish line is 100 feet away. Since each frog will take many jumps in each race, a table should be printed of each frog's distance from the starting line only after one has crossed the finish line. The frog with the most number of wins after 10 races is the champion.

Algorithm:
1. Set the maximum and minimum jump variables for each frog.
2. Begin the races.
   a. Let each of the three frogs jump.
   b. Add the jump to the total distance the frog has travelled.
   c. Check if the finish line has been crossed.
   d. If not, go to step (a).
3. Find out which frog won, increment his win total, and increase his minimum jump limit by .05.
4. Go back to step (2) and race again until 10 races have been run.
5. Print out a table of the final results.

Input:

Delay loop response   : DUMMY$

Output:

Current race number   : I
Distance travelled   : D1, D2, D3
Winner of current race   : W
Number of wins for each   : WIN1, WIN2, WIN3

Other (Constants, etc.)

Maximum jump distance   : MAXJUMP
Amount LOWJUMP is
   incremented in case of win   : INC
Minimum jump for each frog   : LOWJUMP1, LOWJUMP2, LOWJUMP3
Length of jump   : JUMP1, JUMP2, JUMP3

Program 4.7

```
10 CLS
20 RANDOMIZE TIMER
30 MAXJUMP=6: INC=.05: LOWJUMP1=-2: LOWJUMP2=-2: LOWJUMP3=-2
40 PRINT: PRINT "Welcome to the Calaveras County Frog Race": PRINT
50 PRINT "The course is 100 feet long.  There will be 10 races."
60 PRINT "May the best frog win!": PRINT
70 FOR I=1 TO 10
80    PRINT: INPUT "Hit <Return> to start the race";DUMMY$
90    D1=0: D2=0: D3=0
100   JUMP1 = INT(MAXJUMP * RND + LOWJUMP1 + .5)
110   JUMP2 = INT(MAXJUMP * RND + LOWJUMP2 + .5)
120   JUMP3 = INT(MAXJUMP * RND + LOWJUMP3 + .5)
130   D1=D1+JUMP1: D2=D2+JUMP2: D3=D3+JUMP3
140   IF D1<100 AND D2<100 AND D3<100 THEN 100
150   PRINT: PRINT "The final results of race #";I;":"
160   PRINT "Frog #1 -";D1;"feet"
170   PRINT "Frog #2 -";D2;"feet"
180   PRINT "Frog #3 -";D3;"feet"
190   PRINT
200   IF D3>D2 AND D3>D1 THEN 230
                     ELSE IF D2>D1 THEN 220
210   W=1: WIN1=WIN1+1: LOWJUMP1=LOWJUMP1+INC: GOTO 240
220   W=2: WIN2=WIN2+1: LOWJUMP2=LOWJUMP2+INC: GOTO 240
230   W=3: WIN3=WIN3+1: LOWJUMP3=LOWJUMP3+INC: GOTO 240
240   PRINT "Frog #";W;"is the winner."
250   PRINT "The score is now (";WIN1;"-";WIN2;"-";WIN3;")"
260 NEXT I
270 PRINT : PRINT "----- Final Results -----"
280 PRINT "Frog #1 had";WIN1;"wins."
290 PRINT "Frog #2 had";WIN2;"wins."
300 PRINT "Frog #3 had";WIN3;"wins."
310 END

RUN


Welcome to the Calaveras County Frog Race

The course is 100 feet long.  There will be 10 races.
May the best frog win!


Hit <Return> to start the race?

The final results of race # 1 :
Frog #1 - 71 feet
Frog #2 - 80 feet
Frog #3 - 102 feet

Frog # 3 is the winner.
The score is now ( 0 - 0 - 1 )

Hit <Return> to start the race?
```

```
.
.          [Races 2-9 not shown]
.


The final results of race # 10 :
Frog #1 - 61 feet
Frog #2 - 87 feet
Frog #3 - 100 feet

Frog # 3 is the winner.
The score is now ( 2 - 2 - 6 )

----- Final Results -----
Frog #1 had 2 wins.
Frog #2 had 2 wins.
Frog #3 had 6 wins.
```

- **Line 10:** Clears the screen.
- **Line 20:** Makes sure a different sequence of random numbers is chosen each time the program is run.
- **Line 30:** The variables MAXJUMP, INC, LOWJUMP1, LOWJUMP2, and LOWJUMP3 are assigned their proper starting values.
- **Lines 40-60:** Prints out a message.
- **Line 70:** Initiates the FOR...NEXT loop to keep track of the number of races. It ends on line 260. Note how all the lines inbetween have been indented for clarity.
- **Line 80:** Prompts the user to start the race.
- **Line 90:** Each frog's distance is set to zero at the beginning of each race.
- **Lines 100-120:** Each frog's leap is calculated using a random statement, and stored in the variables JUMP1, JUMP2, and JUMP3.
- **Line 130:** Each frog's distance from the starting line is increased (or decreased) by the frog's latest jump.
- **Line 140:** This compound IF...THEN statement checks to see whether the finish line has been crossed. If it has not, the program branches back to line 100, where all the frogs take another jump. Once the finish line has been crossed, the program drops to line 150.
- **Lines 150-190:** Prints out a summary of each race when it is over.
- **Line 200:** A multiple IF...THEN statement is used to determine the winner of the race, and sends the program to the proper lines.
- **Line 210:** Is executed only when Frog #1 wins. The variable W is set to 1, its win total, and its worst jump are updated before the program branches to line 240.
- **Line 220:** Alters the proper variables if Frog #2 wins.
- **Line 230:** Alters the proper variables if Frog # 3 wins.
- **Line 240-250:** Prints the winner and the running score of the race.
- **Line 260:** This NEXT completes the loop started on line 70.
- **Lines 270-300:** Prints the final results of the race.

EXERCISES

1. Generate ten random numbers between 0 and 1, but print only those which are greater than 0.5.

2. Generate three random numbers between 0 and 1, and print their sum.

3. Input a number (N). Print it only if it is an integer. (Hint: compare N with INT(N)).

4. Allow a user to guess a random integer between -3 and 4, inclusive. Print whether the guess is correct or not. If the guess is wrong, print the correct value.

5. Determine randomly how many coins you find on the street. You are to find from 2 to 5 nickels, 1 to 4 dimes and 0 to 3 quarters. Lunch costs 99 cents. The program is to report the amount that you found and whether you are able to buy lunch with it.

   ```
   RUN
   You found $ .45
   Sorry, you can't buy lunch

   RUN
   You found $ 1.25
   You can buy lunch
   ```

6. Input an integer (N), and print the sum of N random numbers between 0 and 1.

7. A child puts pennies into a piggy bank once each week for four weeks. The bank initially contains 11 pennies. Write a program to allow pennies to be added each week and to print the dollar value of the bank's contents after each addition.

8. Write a program that will print ten random integers from −10 to 10, inclusive.

9. Perform each of the following computations on paper. Check your results using immediate mode.

(a) 3^2^3   (b) 5 − 4^2
(c) 3 * (5 + 16)   (d) 5 + 3 * 6 / 2
(e) 640 / 10 / 2 * 5   (f) 5 + 3 * 4 − 1
(g) 2^3^2   (h) 2^ (3^2)
(i) 64 / 4 * 0.5 + ((1 + 5) * 2^3) * 1 / (2 * 4)

10. Write a program to flip a coin 50 times and print the total number of heads and tails. Run the program ten times to get a comparison among the runs.

11. Write a program that generates 10 random integers between 8 and 25, inclusive, and prints them on the same line. The output should be

```
RUN
17    12    22    25    8    17    19    11    21    23
```

12. Make a chart showing in order the values taken by the variables X and Y. Circle those values that are printed by the computer. Check by running the program:

```
10 FOR X = 1 TO 3
20     READ Y
30     IF Y > 0 THEN 35
40     Y = Y + X
50     IF X = 2 THEN Y = Y − 1: GOTO 40
60     PRINT X,Y
70 NEXT X
80 DATA 5, 0, −1
90 END
```

13. The following program is designed to test a student on multiplication.

(a) Rewrite the program so that the message LEARN THE MULTIPLICATION TABLE is printed if three wrong answers are given.

(b) Rewrite the program so that five different questions are asked and the message NICE GOING is printed if all five questions are answered correctly:

```
5 RANDOMIZE TIMER
10 CLS: LOCATE 1,10
20 A = INT(10 * RND + 1)
30 B = INT(10 * RND + 1)
40 PRINT TAB(12); A; "*"; B; "=";
50 INPUT C
60 IF C = A * B THEN 90
70 PRINT "You are wrong. Try again."
80 GOTO 40
90 PRINT TAB(12)
100 PRINT "CORRECT"
```

14. This program allows the user to enter any integer greater than 1 then tells the user whether the integer is prime. A prime number is any integer that is evenly divisible only by itself or 1. For example, the numbers 2, 3, 5 and 7 are prime. The computer tests an integer by repeatedly dividing it by integers smaller than itself but larger than 1 and checking whether the quotient is whole. If so, the integer is not prime. This program contains errors. Find them, rewrite the program and run it. The output should look like this:

```
RUN
Integer > 2 please? 12
That integer is not prime.
RUN
Integer > 2 please? 17
That integer is prime.

20 READ "Integer > 2 please "; N
30 FOR X = 2 TO N − 1
40    IF N / X = INT(N / X) THEN 70
50 NEXT N
60 PRINT "That integer is prime." : END
70 PRINT "That integer is not prime."
```

15. Generate 1000 random integers between 1 and 9, inclusive, and print how many are even and how many are odd. The output should be similar to the following:

```
RUN
There are 577 odd integers.
There are 423 even integers.
```

16. Write a program that allows the user and computer to alternately select integers between 3 and 12, inclusive, keeps a sum of all the integers selected and declares the winner to be the one who selects that integer which makes the sum greater than 100. Have the program ask the user if he or she would like to proceed first or second.

17. A bank pays interest once a year at a yearly rate of 5%. A man deposits $1000 on January 1, 1985 and wishes to leave it there to accrue interest until the balance is at least $2000. Compute the balance on Jan. 1 of each year, starting with 1986 and ending in the year when the balance exceeds $2000. The output should resemble the following:

Date	Balance
Jan 1, 1986	$1050
Jan 1, 1987	$1102.5
. . .	. . .
. . .	. . .
. . .	$1979.93
. . .	$2078.93

18. Input a positive integer N, and print all positive integers that are factors of N. The output should resemble the following:

    RUN
    A positive integer, please? 1.4
    Your number is not a positive integer.
    A positive integer, please? 12
    1   2   3   4   6   12

19. (a) Print twenty random integers between 0 and 100, inclusive.

    (b) Change the program so that sixty percent of the twenty integers printed will be less than 25.

20. Write a program that will pick 20 random integers from 1 to 100, inclusive, and print only those numbers that are prime. A prime number is one that can only be divided exactly (i.e., no remainder) by itself and 1.

21. Using LOCATE and TAB, write a program that will draw a football made of asterisks. (Hint: use the equation for a circle.)

    RUN

Advanced Exercises

Each of the following exercises requires the development of a detailed algorithm. The program should not be written until all details of the algorithm have been worked out.

22. Write a program to simulate a simplified version of the game "21". A deck of cards numbered 1 to 10 is used and any number can be repeated since the deck contains many cards. The computer starts by asking you how many cards you want. It then deals you the cards, which are randomly picked, and totals their value. If the value exceeds 21, you automatically lose. If your value is under 21, the computer deals itself three randomly picked cards. The winner is the one with the highest score equal to or less than 21. Write your program so that the game can be played 10 consecutive times with the winner of each game winning one point. At the end of the 10 games print out the total winnings for you and the computer. The example below shows only the last four of the ten games:

    How many cards do you want? 3
    You : 8 5 1
    Me : 8 3 3
    I have 14 and you have 14 so we draw.

How many cards do you want? 2
You : 7 2
Me : 8 7 4
I have 19 and you have 9 so I WIN!

How many cards do you want? 3
You : 8 7 4
Me : 2 1 7
I have 10 and you have 19 so YOU WIN!

How many cards do you want? 3
You : 2 2 9
Me : 1 7 9
I have 17 and you have 13 so I WIN!
My winnings = 6
Your winnings = 3

23. (a) Write a program that displays the dart board shown below. Have the computer fire ten random shots at the board, using an asterisk to indicate the spot hit. The top of the outer square is on line 3 and its two vertical sides are at TAB(10) and TAB(30).

RUN

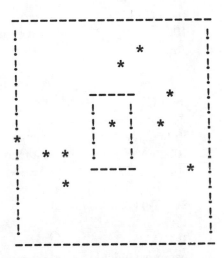

(b) Rewrite the program to give you the score at the end of a game. A hit in the center square is worth 10 points, the outer square 4 points, and the region outside both −1 points.

24. Design a program that will act as a computerized cash register for the school book store. The book store inventory is as follows:

Item	Code #	Price
Notebook	100	$1.59
Folder	101	$0.79
Blue Pen	200	$0.29
Red Pen	201	$0.29
Black Pen	202	$0.29
Textbook	300	variable
Ruler	400	$0.59
Calculator	500	$21.00
Misc.	600	variable

The program allows a salesperson to enter the product code and quantity of an item. If the item has a variable price, (code 300 or 600), the program asks for the price. The item code, item name, quantity, unit price and total prices are displayed in a "window" located at the center of the screen. When all the items have been entered, the salesperson enters 0 in response to the item code. The program calculates and displays a total, including tax, (rounded to the nearest cent), in the window. It also calculates and displays the amount of change the customer receives.

RUN

<school> BOOK STORE

Item Code? 100
Quantity? 3

Item Code	Item	Unit Price	Quantity	Total Price
100	Notebook	$1.59	3	$4.77

<school> BOOK STORE

Item Code? 300
Quantity? 1
Price? 15.00

Item Code	Item	Unit Price	Quantity	Total Price
100	Notebook	$1.59	3	$4.77
300	Textbooks	$15	1	$15

<school> BOOK STORE

Item Code? 0

Item Code	Item	Unit Price	Quantity	Total Price
100	Notebook	$1.59	3	$4.77
300	Textbooks	$15	1	$15

SUBTOTAL		$19.77
TAX		$1.19
TOTAL		$20.96
Amount tendered		$21.00
CHANGE		$.04

Press <ENTER> for another sale?

5

SUBSCRIPTED VARIABLES

DIM

ERASE

OPTION BASE

DIM

ERASE

OPTION BASE

DIM

ERASE

OPTION BASE

*T*he FOR...NEXT loop is an important tool since it instructs the computer to carry out a series of instructions a specific number of times. This chapter further explains how loops are used to carry out various programming tasks.

There are tasks that the simple variables we have used so far cannot do easily. In this chapter, therefore, we will look at a more complex type of variable, called a subscripted variable, that will increase a program's ability to store and use data.

Nested Loops

In Chapter 3, the FOR...NEXT and WHILE...WEND statements were explained as methods for producing loops. These loops are good for situations where only one condition determines how many times the loop is executed. Examples have been previously given where a FOR...NEXT loop produced a single multiplication table, and a WHILE...WEND loop was used to create a loop which continued until a variable equaled a certain value. To program multiple repetitive conditions nested loops should be used. A nested loop is a loop which is located entirely within another loop. For example,

```
    ┌──10 FOR I = 1 TO 10
    │  ┌──20    FOR K = 1 TO 5
    │  │  30       PRINT K, I;
    │  └──40    NEXT K
    └──50 NEXT I
```

shows a properly nested loop. The beginning and the end of different loops must never overlap. For example, the following arrangement of loops is not allowed:

```
    ┌──10 FOR J = 1 TO 10
    │  ┌──20    FOR K = 1 TO 5
    │  ├──30 NEXT J
    └──┴──40    NEXT K
```

These two loops overlap because the end of the first loop, NEXT J, comes before the end of the second loop, NEXT K. If this sample program were run, it would produce:

NEXT WITHOUT FOR ERROR IN 40

Indenting loops makes their structure more visible, thereby helping to prevent this error.

Program 5.1   This program uses two nested loops to print the multiplication table from 0 × 0 to 6 × 12. The outer loop uses X as a loop counter from 0 to 12. The value of X is then used as the first factor each time a new multiplication fact is calculated. The inner loop uses Y to produce the number by which X will be multiplied each time the inner loop is repeated.

```
10 CLS
20 LOCATE 3,5
30 PRINT "|  0    1    2    3    4    5    6"
40 LOCATE 4,5
50 PRINT "+--------------------------------"
60 FOR X = 0 TO 12
70    T = 7
80    LOCATE X+5,1: PRINT X; TAB(5); "|";
90    FOR Y = 0 TO 6
100       PRINT TAB(T); X*Y;
110       T = T + 5
120    NEXT Y
130 NEXT X
140 END
```

RUN

```
     |  0    1    2    3    4    5    6
     +--------------------------------
 0   |  0    0    0    0    0    0    0
 1   |  0    1    2    3    4    5    6
 2   |  0    2    4    6    8   10   12
 3   |  0    3    6    9   12   15   18
 4   |  0    4    8   12   16   20   24
 5   |  0    5   10   15   20   25   30
 6   |  0    6   12   18   24   30   36
 7   |  0    7   14   21   28   35   42
 8   |  0    8   16   24   32   40   48
 9   |  0    9   18   27   36   45   54
10   |  0   10   20   30   40   50   60
11   |  0   11   22   33   44   55   66
12   |  0   12   24   36   48   60   72
```

- **Lines 10-50:** Clear the screen and print the headings for the multiplication table.
- **Line 60:** Initiates the outer loop of the two nested loops. X is used as the first multiplicand in the calculation in line 100.
- **Line 70:** Sets T, which is used as the TAB position, to the starting value of 7.
- **Line 80:** Positions the cursor and prints the vertical scale.
- **Line 90:** Starts the inner loop of the pair of nested loops. Y is used as the second multiplicand in the calculation on line 100.
- **Line 100:** Prints the product of X and Y at position T on the current print line.
- **Line 120:** Ends the inner loop initiated by line 90. This loop will continue until the terminating value is reached. Then, the outer loop will be executed.
- **Line 130:** Ends the outer loop which was started in line 60.

Line 100 multiplies X and Y. The first time the outer loop is executed, X and Y have values of 0. After line 100 prints the first product, the inner loop is repeated and Y now has a value of 1, while X still has the value 0. Now, line 100 calculates a product of 0. The inner loop continues until Y reaches the terminating value of 6. The outer loop now increases the value of X to 1 and the inner loop is re-initialized. Each time the inner loop is re-initialized in this way, the value of Y is reset to 0 on line 90. Notice that the value of X is increased only when the Y loop is terminated and program control is passed to line 130.

Program 5.2   This program nests 3 loops to calculate and print all the possible combinations of quarters, dimes and nickels that add up to fifty cents:

```
10 PRINT "Quarters","Dimes","Nickels"
20 FOR Q = 0 TO 2
30    FOR D = 0 TO 5
40       FOR N = 0 TO 10
50          IF (Q * 25) + (D * 10) + (N * 5) = 50 THEN PRINT Q,D,N
60       NEXT N
70    NEXT D
80 NEXT Q
90 END

RUN
```

Quarters	Dimes	Nickels
0	0	10
0	1	8
0	2	6
0	3	4
0	4	2
0	5	0
1	0	5
1	1	3
1	2	1
2	0	0

In this program Q represents the number of quarters, D the number of dimes and N the number of nickels. The start and end values of the loops are determined by the maximum and minimum number of each coin that adds up to 50. For example, there can be as few as 0 quarters or as many as 2. Likewise, there may be as few as 0 dimes or as many as 5, and as few as 0 nickels or as many as 10. Because the loops are nested in this way, line 50 is able to check all the possible combinations that might add up to 50. However, only those combinations that equal 50 are printed. The output shows clearly how the outermost loop does not increase the value of Q until the value of D in the middle loop reaches 5, and the middle loop does not increase the value of D until the value of N in the innermost loop reaches 10. Each time the number of dimes and nickels is checked by repeating the middle and inner loops, the values of D and N are reset to 0 by lines 30 and 40.

Review

1. Write a program that uses nested loops to produce the following output:

OUTER LOOP = 1
INNER = 1   INNER = 2   INNER = 3   INNER = 4
OUTER LOOP = 2
INNER = 1   INNER = 2   INNER = 3   INNER = 4
OUTER LOOP = 3
INNER = 1   INNER = 2   INNER = 3   INNER = 4

2. Predict the output of the following program. Check your prediction by typing the program in and running it:

```
10 FOR A = 1 TO 10
20    PRINT "+";
30    FOR B = 1 TO 10
40      PRINT "*";
50    NEXT B
60    PRINT "+"
70 NEXT A
```

Subscripted Variables

An array uses a type of variable that allows the computer to employ more than one memory box to store the variable's value. An array is made up of numbered memory boxes, known as elements, that store either numeric or string data. To use an array instead of a simple variable, the programmer must tell the computer the name of the array and the subscript numbers of each of its elements. An array variable looks like this:

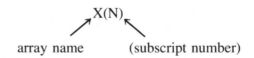

The array name is the name by which all the elements that are part of an array are known, and each individual box within an array is called a sub-scripted variable.

Continuing to use the idea of memory boxes, we see that an array with 3 subscripted variables storing numbers 7, 5 and 10 would look like this:

N(1)   N(2)   N(3)

| 7 | | 5 | | 10 |

It is important to realize that the subscript number is the number of the box and not the value stored within the box. For example, the array described here is a list of numbers named N( ) and the 3rd item on the list, subscripted variable N(3), has a value of 10.

The subscripted variables that make up an array are used much like simple variables. For instance, there can be both numeric or string sub-scripted variables. Also, subscripted variables are assigned values by using simple assignment, INPUT and READ statements, in the same way that simple variables are assigned values.

Program 5.3   This program uses an array with 4 subscripted variables to show how they are used in the same way as simple variables. Notice the difference between the subscript number and the value that a subscripted variable represents:

```
10 L(1) = 7
20 L(2) = 5
30 L(3) = 4
40 PRINT "L(1) ="; L(1), "L(2) ="; L(2), "L(3) ="; L(3),
   "L(4) ="; L(4)
50 PRINT "L(1 + 2) ="; L(1 + 2)
60 PRINT "L(1) + L(2) ="; L(1) + L(2)
70 L(4) = L(2) + L(3)
80 PRINT "L(4) ="; L(4)
90 L(1) = L(2) - L(3)
100 PRINT "NOW L(1) ="; L(1)
110 END

RUN
L(1) = 7         L(2) = 5        L(3) = 4         L(4) = 0
L(1 + 2) = 4
L(1) + L(2) = 12
L(4) = 9
NOW L(1) = 1
```

- **Lines 10-30:** Three of the subscripted variables that make up the array L( ) are assigned their values by separate assignment statements.
- **Line 40:** The contents of each of the four subscripted variables that make up the array are displayed. Since L(4) has not been assigned a value, its value is 0.
- **Line 50:** 1 is added to 2 to get 3. The computer then prints the contents of L(3), which is 4. Note that the computer did not add the values of L(1) and L(2).
- **Line 60:** L(1), which has a value of 7, and L(2), which has a value of 5, are added to get 12. The subscript is only the number of the box in which a value is stored and should not be confused with the value in the box. If the value of the subscript changes, the computer looks in a different box.
- **Line 70:** L(4) is assigned a new value by adding the contents of L(2) and L(3). The result of this operation assigns L(4) a value of 9.
- **Line 80:** The value of L(4) is displayed.
- **Line 90:** L(1) is given a new value. Its old value of 8 is replaced by 1 after the computer subtracts the value of L(3), which is 4, from the value of L(2), which is 5.
- **Line 100:** The new value of L(1) is displayed.

Review   3. Write a program that picks 10 random numbers from 1 to 100 and stores them in an array of subscripted variables. After the numbers are picked and stored, have the computer print each of the numbers and the name of the subscripted variable that stores it.

```
RUN
L( 1 ) = 8          L( 2 ) = 11
L( 3 ) = 2          L( 4 ) = 19
L( 5 ) = 11         L( 6 ) = 68
L( 7 ) = 5          L( 8 ) = 12
L( 9 ) = 76         L( 10 ) = 97
```

4. Using subscripted variables, write a program in which 3 numbers are entered. Then have the computer display them in reverse order.

```
RUN
ENTER A NUMBER ? 11
ENTER A NUMBER ? 19
ENTER A NUMBER ? 68

68
19
11
```

5. Write a program that allows 7 words to be entered from the keyboard. Then have the computer randomly select 4 of the words and write them as a sentence. The sentence need not make any sense and the words may be repeated:

```
RUN
ENTER A WORD? JACK
ENTER A WORD? AND
ENTER A WORD? JILL
ENTER A WORD? WENT
ENTER A WORD? UP
ENTER A WORD? THE
ENTER A WORD? HILL

UP WENT THE HILL
```

DIMensioning an Array

Without any special instructions the computer will allow a subscripted variable to have subscript values ranging from 0 to 10. This means a list of as many as 11 boxes can be set aside as part of an array:

A(0) A(1) A(2) A(3) A(4) A(5) A(6) A(7) A(8) A(9) A(10)

```
┌──┐ ┌──┐ ┌──┐ ┌──┐ ┌──┐ ┌──┐ ┌──┐ ┌──┐ ┌──┐ ┌──┐ ┌──┐
│  │ │  │ │  │ │  │ │  │ │  │ │  │ │  │ │  │ │  │ │  │
└──┘ └──┘ └──┘ └──┘ └──┘ └──┘ └──┘ └──┘ └──┘ └──┘ └──┘
```

If an array will need subscript values greater than 10, the computer must be told what the DIMensions of the array are, using a DIM statement. The format for a DIM statement is:

    10 DIM <variable name> (<dimension>)

In a program a DIM statement for a string array named N$( ) with subscript values up to 100 would be:

    20 DIM N$(100)

The DIMension value may be a number or a variable. For example,

    10 L = 100
    20 DIM N$(L)

will dimension an array that is equivalent to the variable in line 10.

If the array N$(L) were storing people's names and a programmer also wanted to store their ages, another array would have to be dimensioned. It could be dimensioned in a separate statement on a different line, or the above statement could be modified as follows:

```
10 L = 100
20 DIM N$(L), A(L)
```

If a programmer asks the computer to dimension an array and there is not sufficient space available for it in the computer's memory, this error message appears and the program halts:

?OUT OF MEMORY ERROR

A program must DIMension an array before the program tries to use any of the subscripted variables that make up the array. Also, the program must not use subscripted values that are higher than the number to which an array has been dimensioned. It is good programming style to place DIM statements at or near the beginning of a program, and to define all arrays in DIM statements, even those with less than 11 elements.

Program 5.4

In order to better organize its business, the Lawrenceville Lawn Service has computerized its customer list. They currently have 12 customers and want the computer to tell them which lawn to mow on which day of the week as well as the amount each customer is to be charged:

```
10 CLS
20 READ C
30 DIM N$(C), D$(C), P(C)
40 FOR J = 1 TO C
50    READ N$(J), D$(J), P(J)
60 NEXT J
70 PRINT "What day is today"
80 INPUT "(M, TU, W, TH, F, SA)"; A$
90 PRINT
100 IF A$ <> "M" AND A$ <> "TU" AND A$ <> "W" AND A$ <> "TH"
    AND A$ <> "F" AND A$ <> "SA" THEN 80
110 PRINT "Name","Charge"
120 FOR T = 1 TO C
130    IF D$(T) = A$ THEN PRINT N$(T),P(T)
140 NEXT T
150 PRINT "That's it for today"
200 REM  Number of customers
210 DATA 12
220 REM Name, Day to mow, Charge
230 DATA HACKER, M, 15, JONES, F, 12, JOHNSTON, TH, 18
240 DATA SMITH, SA, 25, BREWSTER, W, 20, WEBSTER, TH, 21
250 DATA CARNEY, TH, 10, MURPHY, W, 7, SMALL, TH, 12
260 DATA WEST, SA, 22, BURKE, M, 15, ZITHERMAN, TU, 12
999 END
```

- **Line 20:** C is the number of customers which is used to DIM the arrays that will store the name, day to mow and amount to charge each customer. Simply changing C and adding or deleting the appropriate data allows the lawn service to add or delete customers.

- **Line 30:** Since the lawn service has more than 10 customers, the arrays that store the customer information will have subscripted values greater than 10 so the arrays must be dimensioned. C is the number of N$( ), D$( ) and P( ) boxes created in the computer's memory. N$(C) stores the customer's name, D$(C) stores the day of the week that the customer's lawn is to be mowed, and P(C) stores the price that is to be charged.
- **Lines 40-60:** This loop reads the names, days of the week, and prices to charge from the data statements and assigns the data to the correct array. The loop counter, J, is used to change the subscript values each time the loop is repeated. For instance, when J = 1, N$(J) = "HACKER", D$(J) = "M" for Monday and P(J) = 15.
- **Lines 70-100:** These lines allow the user to input the day of the week for which information is needed. If the data entered is not correct, line 100 uses an IF...THEN with AND to send the computer back to line 80.
- **Line 110:** This line prints headings for the two columns of data that will be displayed.
- **Lines 120-140:** This loop searches through all the D$(T) subscripted variables for a match to the day entered as A$. When one of these subscripted variables has a value that is the same as A$, the customer's name, N$(T), and the price to charge them, P(T), are displayed.

```
RUN
What day is today?
(M, TU, W, TH, F or SA)? W

Name                    Charge
BREWSTER                $ 20
MURPHY                  $ 7
That's it for today.
```

In the run shown above, the value input as A$ was "W". The condition on line 130, IF A$ = D$(J), was not true until the loop had been repeated 5 times. When J had a value of 5, A$ did equal D$(5) because D$(5) is "W". This made the condition on line 130 true, so N$(5), which is BREWSTER, and P(5), which is 20 were displayed.

- **Line 150:** This message is printed when all the data for the day requested has been displayed.
- **Lines 200-210:** REM and DATA statements that allow the lawn service to change the number of its customers by changing only this number and adding or deleting the proper data.
- **Line 220:** A REM statement that shows the data is arranged by name, day of the week and price so that another programmer can easily add or delete customers.
- **Lines 230-260:** The data that will be used by the program.

Review	6. Write a program that picks 15 random numbers from 1 to 100, then prints them vertically and horizontally:

```
RUN
90
56
14
28
25
21
30
24
22
91
32
66
67
98
60
90 56 14 28 25 21 30 24 22 91 32 66 67 98 60
```

Double Subscripted Variables

The computer can also use double subscripts to name a variable. This is similar to single subscripting except that there are two numbers within parentheses instead of one. For example:

$A(1,5)$ $B3\$(7,3)$ $C\$(4,9)$

are all double subscripted variables. It is helpful to visualize them as placed in rows and columns, rather than in a single column (as is the case with a single subscripted variable). Double subscripted variables provide a convenient technique for dealing with problems where the data is two-dimensional in nature, such as the location of seats in a theater.

The box analogy is again helpful. The first integer in the subscript identifies the row and the second the column in which the variable is located. For example, A(2,3) is located at the second row, third column.

	COL 1	COL 2	COL 3	COL 4
ROW 1	A(1,1)	A(1,2)	A(1,3)	A(1,4)
	☐	☐	☐	☐
ROW 2	A(2,1)	A(2,2)	A(2,3)	A(2,4)
	☐	☐	☐	☐
ROW 3	A(3,1)	A(3,2)	A(3,3)	A(3,4)
	☐	☐	☐	☐

Program 5.5   A classroom has 5 rows of seats with 3 seats in each row. The following program randomly selects seats for a class of 14 students, leaving one seat empty:

```
10 RANDOMIZE TIMER
20 DIM N$(5,3)
30 FOR X = 1 TO 14
40    READ S$ : REM  Get a student
50    R = INT(RND * 5) + 1 : REM  Row #
60    C = INT(RND * 3) + 1 : REM  Column #
70    IF N$(R,C) <> "" THEN 50 : REM  Is seat occupied?
80    N$(R,C) = S$
90 NEXT X
100 REM  PRINTing the seating assignments
110 FOR R1 = 1 TO 5
120    FOR C1 = 1 TO 3
130       IF N$(R1,C1) = "" THEN PRINT "Empty",
                           ELSE PRINT N$(R1,C1),
140    NEXT C1
150    PRINT
160 NEXT R1
170 DATA ANNE, SON, SHERRY, CINDY, ERIC, LESTER, KIM
180 DATA JOHN, BONNIE, SANDRA, HELEN, DAVID, ROB, JOE
999 END

RUN
DAVID          HELEN          KIM
SON            Empty          ANNE
SANDRA         LESTER         JOHN
CINDY          ROB            BONNIE
JOE            ERIC           SHERRY
```

- **Line 10:** Ensures that a new set of random numbers is generated each time the program is run.
- **Line 20:** DIMensions a double subscripted array N$( ).
- **Line 30:** Starts a loop which will be executed 14 times to randomly assign students to seats.
- **Line 40:** Reads in a student's name (S$).
- **Lines 50-60:** Generates two random integers to be used as row and column subscripts.
- **Line 70:** If the seat at position R,C is not empty (equal to null " "), a new position is generated.
- **Line 80:** If the seat at position R,C is empty, assigns the student to that seat.
- **Line 90:** Completes the loop started in line 30.
- **Line 110:** Initializes the outer loop of a pair of nested loops which will determine the row subscript.
- **Line 120:** Initializes the inner loop of a pair of nested loops which will determine the column subscript.
- **Line 130:** If the seat at position R,C is equal to a null character (" ") then prints "Empty"; otherwise, prints the student's name at that position.
- **Line 140:** Completes the inner loop started in line 120.
- **Line 150:** Prints a blank line so that the next row begins printing at the correct place.
- **Line 160:** Completes the outer loop started in line 110.
- **Lines 170-180:** Data used by the READ in line 40.

The computer allows 3,4, etc., all the way up to 255 dimensions in a subscripted variable (e.g., DIM X(5,5,8,2,3,19)). However, the more dimensions that a subscripted variable has, the fewer the elements it may contain. This is because limited space is available in the computer's memory.

Review

7. Use a double subscripted variable X$(I,J) for which the row variable I runs from 1 to 5 and the column variable J from 1 to 3. Enter the letters, A,B,C, as the first row, D,E,F as the second, up to M,N,O as the fifth. Have the program print the following, making the rows become columns: (Hint: Use READ...DATA.)

```
A   D   G   J   M
B   E   H   K   N
C   F   I   L   O
```

Some Final Notes on Subscripted Variables

Subscripted strings and numeric variables greatly enhance the programmer's ability to store and deal with large quantities of data within a program. Remember, that if the program is run again, all of the stored data in the computer's memory is erased which means that all of the boxes become either null (" ") or zero at the start of the next run. A method for permanently storing data in disk files is presented in Chapters 10 and 11.

ERASE

Large arrays use up much of the computer's memory. If an array is no longer needed, it can be erased in order to free space. The statement,

100 ERASE B

will remove the array, B, and its contents from the computer's memory.

OPTION BASE

The lowest numbered element in a subscripted variable is numbered 0 (for example A(0), B$(0), A$(0,0)). If the 0 element is not wanted, it is possible to start numbering at 1 rather than 0. This can be done by using the statement

10 OPTION BASE 1

which must appear in a program before any reference is made to a subscripted variable or a DIM statement is executed.

End of Chapter Problem

A store that deals only in weekly magazines from the 1950's needs a program to keep track of its inventory. The magazines are dated from 1950 to 1959 and are stored in bins separated by year and title. The current titles are TIME, LIFE and THE NEW YORKER.

	TIME	LIFE	THE NEW YORKER
1950	23	34	43
1951	23	52	47
1952	35	.	.
.	.	.	.
.	.	.	.
1958	.	52	29
1959	9	11	23

Write a program to store the inventory information in a doubly subscripted array and provide for the updating of the information resulting from the buying or selling of magazines.

Algorithm:
1. Read data and load array
2. Ask for activity choice
    1 = buy
    2 = sell
    3 = exit
3. Update inventory quantities
4. Print out data
5. Repeat steps 2 through 4 until finished

Variables
Input:

User activity selection	: CHOICE
Number of magazines exchanged	: NUM
Title of magazine	: N$

Output:

Number of magazines	: MAG (R,C)

Other: (Constants, subscripts, etc.)

Row subscript (Year)	: R
Column subscript (Title)	: C
Addition/subtraction flag	: SWITCH

Program 5.6

```
10 DIM MAG(10,3)
20 M$ = "Not enough in stock... try again..."
30 FOR R = 1 TO 10
40     FOR C = 1 TO 3
50         READ MAG(R,C)
60     NEXT C
70 NEXT R
80 INPUT "ENTER (1)-BUY  (2)-SELL  (3)-QUIT"; CHOICE
90 IF CHOICE < 1 OR CHOICE > 3 THEN 80
100 IF CHOICE = 1 THEN SWITCH = 1
              ELSE IF CHOICE = 2 THEN SWITCH = -1
                                ELSE 999
110 INPUT "ENTER TITLE, YEAR AND NUMBER OF MAGAZINES "; N$, Y, NUM
```

```
120 IF N$ = "TIME" THEN C1 = 1
                    ELSE IF N$ = "LIFE" THEN C1 = 2
                              ELSE C1 = 3
130 R1 = (Y - 1950) + 1
140 IF MAG(R1,C1) < NUM AND SWITCH = -1 THEN PRINT M$ : GOTO 80
150 MAG(R1,C1) = MAG(R1,C1) + NUM * SWITCH
160 REM          DATA OUTPUT ROUTINE
170 PRINT "YEAR", "TIME", "LIFE", "NEW YORKER"
180 PRINT "==============================================="
190 FOR R = 1 TO 10
200     PRINT (R + 1949),
210     FOR C = 1 TO 3
220         PRINT MAG(R,C),
230     NEXT C
240     PRINT
250 NEXT R
260 PRINT
270 INPUT "Another transaction Y/N "; REPLY$
280 IF REPLY$ = "Y" THEN 80
290 DATA 23, 34, 43, 23, 52, 47, 35, 12, 22, 9
300 DATA 50, 32, 42, 12, 17, 23, 38, 51, 7, 12
310 DATA 26, 47, 16, 12, 7, 52, 29, 9, 11,23
999 END


RUN
ENTER (1)-BUY  (2)-SELL  (3)-QUIT? 1
ENTER TITLE, YEAR AND NUMBER OF MAGAZINES ? TIME, 1957, 12
```

YEAR	TIME	LIFE	NEW YORKER
==			
1950	23	34	43
1951	23	52	47
1952	35	12	22
1953	9	50	32
1954	42	12	17
1955	23	38	51
1956	7	12	26
1957	59	16	12
1958	7	52	29
1959	9	11	23

```
Another transaction Y/N ? N
```

- **Lines 30-70:** Form a pair of nested loops which will READ in the DATA for the array MAG( ). The inner loop determines the column of the array and the outer loop, the rows.
- **Lines 80-90:** Accept the user's choice of activity (Buy, Sell, or Exit).
- **Line 100:** The SWITCH variable is assigned a value depending upon whether an addition (buying) or subtraction (selling) is desired. If CHOICE = 3, however, the program ends.
- **Line 110:** Asks the user to input the transaction information.
- **Lines 120-130:** Test the input data to find the correct row and column for a specific magazine. The column is based upon the magazine title while the row is calculated by subtracting the year from 1950 and adding 1. This will give a row between 1 and 10.
- **Line 150:** Calculates a new total for that magazine by adding or subtracting the amount entered based upon the value of SWITCH.
- **Lines 190-250:** Form a pair of nested loops to print a table of the values stored in MAG( ).

EXERCISES

1. Using a nested loop, have the computer print a rectangle consisting of eight lines of thirty asterisks each:

```
RUN
******************************
******************************
******************************
******************************
******************************
******************************
******************************
******************************
```

2. Input values for X(L) with L = 1 to 6. Print the values of L and X(L) in two columns with L proceeding in the order 1, 3, 5, 2, 4, 6.

3. Enter 15 letters of the alphabet (not necessarily different) and print them in reverse order as a single block of letters.

4. Using a data statement, have the computer enter one letter of the alphabet for each element of A$ (L,J) where L runs from 1 to 8 and J from 1 to 3. The letters are first to be printed as an 8 word sentence, each word consisting of 3 letters. Then, the letters are to be printed again as a 3 word sentence, each word consisting of 8 letters. The words may or may not make sense.

5. What is the output of the following programs?

   (a)
   ```
   10 FOR L1 = 1 TO 3
   20    FOR L2 = 5 TO 6
   30        PRINT L1, L2
   40    NEXT L2
   50 NEXT L1
   ```

   (b)
   ```
   10 FOR X = 10 TO 15 STEP 2
   20    FOR Y = 15 TO 10 STEP –2
   30        IF Y = X THEN 99
   40        IF X < Y THEN PRINT X: GOTO 60
   50        PRINT Y
   60    NEXT Y
   70 NEXT X
   99 END
   ```

(c)   10 FOR S = 1 TO 10
      20   READ A(S)
      30 NEXT S
      40 PRINT A(3), A(7), A(10)
      50 DATA 23, 12, 45, 2, 87, 34, 89, 17, 2, 35, 70

6. The following program will not run properly. Correct it so the output will look like this:

```
RUN
3              4
4              3
4              4
5              3
5              4


10 FOR A = 3,5
20      FOR B = 1, 4
30            IF A * B < = 10 GOTO 50
40            PRINT AB
50      NEXT A
60 NEXT B
```

7. What is the exact output for the following program?

```
10 READ B1, B2, B3, B4, B5, B6
20 FOR X = 1 TO 6
30      READ B(X)
40 NEXT X
50 PRINT "B4 ="; B4;" But B(4) = "; B(4)
60 PRINT B1 + B2 + B3
70 PRINT B(1) + B(2) + B(3), B(1 + 2 + 3)
80 DATA 3, 7, 4, 1, 8, 12
90 DATA 14, 42, 69, 86, 12, 111
```

8. The following program is designed to generate random integers between 1 and 99, inclusive, until it encounters a duplicate. At that point it should print how many numbers it has found and then print all of them. However, there are a number of errors in the program. Correct them to produce output similar to:

```
RUN
Duplicate after 8 numbers
97   11   2   78   62   96   55


20 FOR X = 1 TO 100
30      N(X) = INT (99 * RND (1) + 1)
40      FOR Y = 1 TO 100
50            IF N(X) < > N(Y) THEN 70
60            PRINT "Duplicate after ";X;" numbers"
70            FOR I = 1 TO X: PRINT N(X); " ";: NEXT I
80            NEXT Y
90 NEXT X
```

9. A Pythagorean triple is a set of three integers which are lengths of the sides of a right triangle (C^2 = A^2 + B^2). Find all sets of three integers up to C = 50 which are Pythagorean triples. For example, A = 3, B = 4, C = 5 is a solution.

10. Stan's Grocery Store has 3 aisles and in each aisle there are five items. Write a program that will read 15 items into the subscripted variable L$(X,Y), dimensioned 3x5. Let his customers type in the item they want to buy and be informed by the computer of the aisle and the item's number. An input of ZZZ halts the program.

```
RUN
What are you looking for? apples
You will find apples in aisle #1, item #4
What are you looking for? milk
You will find milk in aisle #2, item #3
What are you looking for? broccoli
I'm sorry, we don't have broccoli
What are you looking for? ZZZ
```

11. Pick 20 random integers between 10 and 99, inclusive. Print the odd integers on one line and the even integers on the next line. The output should look like this:

```
RUN
Odd Integers: 49  25  21  13  63  77  29  77  27  43
Even Integers: 66  56  18  24  28  70  56  62  48  76
```

12. Find the average of four grades for each of five students. Print each student's name, four grades and average in columns with headings. The last student's average should be underlined and the class average printed below it in the same column:

```
RUN
Student #1? DON
Enter four grades? 42, 86, 99, 99
Student #2? LESTER
Enter four grades? 50, 55, 45, 34
Student #3? LIZ
Enter four grades? 100, 98, 99, 97
Student #4? ROB
Enter four grades? 67, 72, 71, 68
Student #5? SUE
Enter four grades? 89, 91, 93, 90
```

NAME	1	2	3	4	AVE.
DON	42	86	99	99	81.5
LESTER	50	55	45	34	46
LIZ	100	98	99	97	98.5
ROB	67	72	71	68	69.5
SUE	89	91	93	90	90.75
					77.25

13. Write an extended version of the game high-low. In this game, the computer picks a secret random number from 1 to 100 and gives the player an unlimited number of chances to guess it. For each wrong guess the computer tells whether to guess higher or lower and stores the guess in a subscripted variable. If the player guesses the same number twice, the computer produces the message "WAKE UP! You guessed that number before".

14. Mr. and Mrs. Charles Windsor have decided to start a bank account for their newborn son, Harry. They open the account with $500. At the beginning of each successive year they deposit $60 or more. When Harry is 21, how much money will be in the account? (Assume the interest rate to be 6% compounded quarterly.)

15. Write a program that rolls two dice 1000 times and prints the number of times each different point total (2, 3, 4, 5..., 12) appeared. The output should resemble the following:

```
RUN
    Point Total                    Times Appearing
        2                              23
        3                              50
        4                              87
        5                              106
        6                              147
        7                              157
        8                              150
        9                              104
       10                              86
       11                              65
       12                              25
```

16. Write a program which makes up 15 "words" (i.e. groups of letters, whether pronounceable or not) composed of from one to seven randomly chosen letters and prints them. (Hint: use addition of strings. For example, if A$(2) = "B" and A$(12) = "L", then A$(2) + A$(12) = "BL".)

17. Dr. Marcus Welby wants you to program the computer to keep track of his busy schedule.

    (a) Write a program to allow a patient to chose the day and time he or she wants to see the doctor. There are 5 days and 6 time slots for each day. If the desired slot is empty, the patient enters his or her name. If it is full, the program asks for another slot.

    (b) Add the steps needed to allow Dr. Welby to print his schedule for any particular day.

Advanced Exercises

The following exercises require the development of a detailed algorithm. The program should not be written until all details of the algorithm have been worked out.

18. The game Penny Pitch is common in amusement parks. Pennies are tossed onto a checkerboard on which numbers have been printed. By adding up the numbers in the squares on which the pennies fall, a score is accumulated. Write a program which simulates such a game in which ten pennies are to be randomly pitched onto the board shown below:

Have the computer print the board with an X indicating where each penny has landed and then the score. Below is a sample run. Note that more than one penny can land on one square:

```
RUN
1    1    1    1    X    1
1    2    2    2    2    1
X    2    3    3    2    X
1    X    3    X    2    1
1    2    2    2    X    1
X    1    1    X    1    X

Score = 14
```

19. Use the computer to play a modified game of Othello. Have it randomly fill an 8 × 8 subscripted variable with X's and O's and print the array by row (horizontal) and column (vertical). Examples are shown below. The X's are for player 1, the O's for player 2. Have the program ask the players alternately for the row and column of the opponent's piece that should be flipped (changed from an X to an O or vice versa). All of the opponent's pieces along the horizontal or vertical line passing through the flipped piece are also flipped. For example, if player 1 flipped the 0 at (8,1) board A would be changed to board B. After ten turns for each player, the player left with the most pieces wins.

		1	2	3	4	5	6	7	8
(a)	1	X	X	O	O	X	O	X	O
	2	O	O	O	X	X	O	X	X
	3	X	O	X	X	O	X	O	O
	4	O	O	X	O	X	O	X	O
	5	O	O	X	X	X	O	X	O
	6	O	O	X	O	O	X	X	O
	7	O	O	X	X	O	X	O	X
	8	X	X	O	X	X	O	X	X

(b)	1	2	3	4	5	6	7	8
1	X	X	X	X	X	X	X	X
2	O	O	O	X	X	O	X	X
3	X	O	X	X	O	X	O	X
4	O	O	X	O	X	O	X	X
5	O	O	X	X	X	O	X	X
6	O	O	X	O	O	X	X	X
7	O	O	X	X	O	X	O	X
8	X	X	O	X	X	O	X	X

20. Write a program that will produce a computerized mailing list. The program should be able to record up to twenty names, addresses and phone numbers. It prompts the user for one of four options: Insert data, Delete data, Print list or EXIT. The program should be written so that new data will be inserted into the first empty element, including an element that has been previously deleted.

MAILING LIST

Choose an option:
1—Insert a name
2—Delete a name
3—Display a list
4—EXIT

Choose an option? 1
Name? Rick Deckert
Address? L.A. Towers Apt. 9609
City & State? Los Angeles California
Telephone Number? 555-1752

Choose an option? 1
Name? Tony Montana
Address? 300 Orange Way
City & State? Ft. Lauderdale Florida
Telephone Number? 867-5309

Choose an option? 4

6

PROGRAMMING TECHNIQUES

Writing programs that work properly and are well written requires planning and organization. Because the computer must be given many specific instructions in order to carry out even simple tasks, a program can easily become long and complex. Therefore, writing a program is made much easier if time is first spent carefully planning it. This is usually done by first developing a detailed algorithm that will act as an outline for the computer program.

    This chapter will explain new techniques and statements that help simplify lengthy and complex programs. In addition, a series of techniques that can be employed to find and correct programming errors will be covered.

The Need for Subroutines

    To simplify longer, more complex programs, it is a good practice to to divide them into sections called subroutines. These subroutines can be activated or called from anywhere in the program. For instance, a long program can be divided into a main section followed by a series of subroutines. The main section describes the order in which the subroutines will be called, while each subroutines is written as if it were a short program that had only a simple task to perform. Another important use of subroutines is to reduce the size of a program by allowing a routine that is used several times to be written only once. Each time the programmer wants the computer to perform that task the program instructs the computer to call that subroutine.

GOSUB, RETURN

    GOSUB is the instruction that calls a subroutine. The computer is sent to the beginning of a subroutine by the statement:

    20 GOSUB <line number>

When the subroutine has completed its task, the computer is told by the statement:

    230 RETURN

to return to the line following the one which called the subroutine. For example:

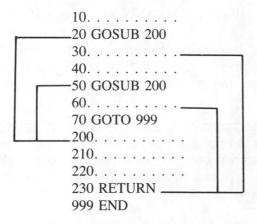

```
    10. . . . . . . . .
    20 GOSUB 200
    30. . . . . . . . .
    40. . . . . . . . .
    50 GOSUB 200
    60. . . . . . . . .
    70 GOTO 999
    200. . . . . . . . .
    210. . . . . . . . .
    220. . . . . . . . .
    230 RETURN
    999 END
```

When line 20 calls the subroutine at line 200, the RETURN on line 230 will send the computer back to line 30. Similarly, when line 50 calls the subroutine at line 200, the RETURN will send the computer back to line 60. Though GOTO and GOSUB are similar, by using GOSUB and RETURN the computer keeps track of where the program should go for its next instruction when the subroutine is finished.

Usually subroutines are placed toward the end of a program. Therefore, a GOTO, such as the one on line 70, is important in order to keep the computer from trying to execute a subroutine without being sent there by a GOSUB. When the computer executes a RETURN statement without having been sent by a GOSUB statement, an error will occur and the following message will appear:

?RETURN WITHOUT GOSUB IN <line number>

To make subroutines stand out as part of the structure of a program each subroutine should begin with a REM statement describing its function. A blank REM or two before and after each subroutine will make it stand out even more. For example:

```
10. . . . . . . . .
20 GOSUB 200 : REM ** Name of Routine **
30. . . . . . . . .
40. . . . . . . . .
50 GOSUB 200 : REM ** Name of Routine **
60. . . . . . . . .
70 GOTO 999
180 REM
190 REM
200 REM ** Name of Routine ***
210. . . . . . . . .
220. . . . . . . . .
230. . . . . . . . .
240 RETURN
250 REM
999 END
```

Throughout the remainder of this book, we will use REMs to identify subroutines and to make them a visible part of a program's structure.

The GOSUB and RETURN statements can be used in many situations. For instance, GOSUB can call a subroutine from an IF...THEN statement:

50 IF H = 1 THEN GOSUB 100

Although it is possible to use more than one RETURN statement in a subroutine, this is considered poor programming style. Each subroutine should have only one RETURN statement, which is located at its end.

Program 6.1

Given the numbers of pennies, nickels, dimes and quarters as input, this program will output the total amount of money represented. One subroutine will process and report the amount of money involved for each of the four types of coins:

```
10 A$ = "PENNIES" : V = 1
20 GOSUB 200 : REM  Accumulator
30 A$ = "NICKELS" : V = 5
40 GOSUB 200 : REM  Accumulator
50 A$ = "DIMES"   : V = 10
60 GOSUB 200 : REM  Accumulator
70 A$ = "QUARTERS" : V = 25
80 GOSUB 200 : REM  Accumulator
90 PRINT "The total value of the coins is $"; T / 100
100 GOTO 999
200 REM
210 REM  ****  Subroutine Accumulator  ****
220 REM
230 PRINT "Number of "; A$;
240 INPUT N
250 PRINT N; A$; " ="; N * V; "Cents"
260 T = T + (N * V)
270 RETURN
999 END

RUN
Number of PENNIES? 4
 4 PENNIES = 4 Cents
Number of NICKELS? 9
 9 NICKELS = 45 Cents
Number of DIMES? 3
 3 DIMES = 30 Cents
Number of QUARTERS? 6
 6 QUARTERS = 150 Cents
The total value of the coins is $ 2.29
```

- **Line 10:** Assigns the type, A$, and value, V, of the first coin.
- **Lines 20-80:** Send the program to the Accumulation Subroutine, which begins on line 200, 4 times. Each time, the subroutine is executed with a different value for the variables A$ and V.
- **Line 90:** Prints the total value of the coins after the fourth RETURN from the subroutine.
- **Line 100:** Skips the subroutine and sends the program to the END statement at line 999. Without this line the subroutine would be executed a fifth time resulting in a RETURN WITHOUT GOSUB error.
- **Lines 200-270:** ✳✳✳ Accumulation Subroutine ✳✳✳
  Asks the user to input the number of each of the coins and then print their value in cents and adds it to the total.

Review

1. Write a program in which names are input and then printed. If DONALD is input, use a subroutine to underline the name:

```
RUN
NAME? MARY
MARY

NAME? SUE
SUE

NAME? DONALD
DONALD
------
```

ON...GOSUB

The ON...GOSUB statement is like a special type of IF...THEN instruction. It allows a program to branch to a number of different subroutines:

    40 ON N GOSUB 100, 200, 300

When the value of N is 1, the program will branch to the first subroutine listed which begins at line 100. When the value of N is 2, it will branch to the second subroutine at line 200 and when N is 3, it will go to the third. If the value of N is less than 1 or greater than the number of subroutines listed, the program will drop down to the next line ignoring the ON...GOSUB statement. This statement allows a program to branch to a specific subroutine without having to write a long list of IF...THEN statements.

ON can also be used with an arithmetic expression in place of the variable:

    50 ON INT(6 * RND + 1) GOSUB 10, 20, 30, 40, 50, 60

This line will cause the computer to branch to one of six subroutines depending on the random number that is chosen.

Program 6.2

This program uses ON...GOSUB to deliver a movie review:

```
1 REM    N = Your choice of movie
2 REM   A$ = Your choice to see another review
10 CLS
20 PRINT "SELECT A MOVIE REVIEW:"
30 PRINT "1 - STAR WARS"
40 PRINT "2 - THE EMPIRE STRIKES BACK"
50 PRINT "3 - RETURN OF THE JEDI"
60 PRINT : PRINT "Choose the review by number."
70 INPUT "Type 1, 2, or 3:"; N
80 IF N < 1 OR N > 3 THEN 10
90 PRINT
100 ON N GOSUB 200, 300, 400
110 PRINT
120 INPUT "Another review (YES/NO)"; A$
130 IF A$ = "YES" THEN 10
140 GOTO 999
200 REM
210 REM   **** STAR WARS ****
220 REM
230 PRINT "Luke battles the Empire,"
240 PRINT "rescues the Princess,"
250 PRINT "destroys the Death Star and
260 PRINT "gets his picture on Burger King"
270 PRINT "glasses."
280 RETURN
300 REM
310 REM   **** THE EMPIRE STRIKES BACK ****
320 REM
330 PRINT "The Rebel Alliance is temporarily"
340 PRINT "set back and Han is captured"
350 PRINT "and frozen."
360 RETURN
```

```
400 REM
410 REM  **** RETURN OF THE JEDI ****
420 REM
430 PRINT "Luke learns his real"
440 PRINT "identity and the Empire is"
450 PRINT "defeated."
460 RETURN
470 REM
999 END
RUN
SELECT A MOVIE REVIEW:
1 - STAR WARS
2 - THE EMPIRE STRIKES BACK
3 - RETURN OF THE JEDI

Choose the review by number.
Type 1, 2, or 3:? 1

Luke battles the Empire,
rescues the Princess,
destroys the Death Star and
gets his picture on Burger King
glasses.

Another review (YES/NO)? NO
```

Lines 10 through 70 display a list of user options called a menu. Line 80 checks the value of variable N to make sure that it is one of the three numbers listed. Any number greater than 3 or less than 1 would cause the ON N GOSUB statement on line 100 to be ignored. Once the computer reaches line 100, it branches to the subroutine that contains the selected review.

ON...GOTO

The ON instruction may also be used with the GOTO instruction. This form of the ON statement is useful when a program has no need to return to the point where the ON statement called those lines:

```
60 ON N GOTO 100, 200, 300
```

Program 6.3

This program prints either a rectangle, a triangle, or a diamond based upon the choice of a random number:

```
10 CLS
20 RANDOMIZE TIMER
30 ON INT(3 * RND + 1) GOTO 100, 200, 300
100 REM
110 REM -- RECTANGLE --
120 REM
130 PRINT "**********"
140 FOR S = 1 TO 5
150 PRINT "*        *"
160 NEXT S
170 PRINT "**********"
180 GOTO 999
```

```
200 REM
210 REM -- TRIANGLE --
220 REM
230 PRINT TAB(7); "*"
240 FOR L = 6 TO 2 STEP -1
250 PRINT TAB(L); "*"; TAB(14 - L); "*"
260 NEXT L
270 PRINT "*************"
280 GOTO 999
300 REM
310 REM -- DIAMOND --
320 REM
330 PRINT TAB(7); "*"
340 FOR L = 6 TO 1 STEP -1
350 PRINT TAB(L); "*"; TAB(14 - L); "*"
360 NEXT L
370 FOR L = 2 TO 6
380 PRINT TAB(L); "*"; TAB(14 - L); "*"
390 NEXT L
400 PRINT TAB(7); "*"
410 REM
999 END

RUN
            *
          *   *
        *       *
      *           *
    *               *
  *                   *
*                       *
  *                   *
    *               *
      *           *
        *       *
          *   *
            *
```

The ON...GOTO on line 30 waits for the computer to pick randomly a 1, 2 or 3 and then sends the program to the lines required to draw the appropriate shape.

Review

2. Write a program to draw five cards from a deck. The computer picks two random numbers, the first between 1 and 4, inclusive, and the second between 1 and 13, inclusive. An ON...GOSUB statement should use the first number to pick each suit. The second represents the card's value within the suit.

```
RUN
CARD 1 IS THE 4 OF CLUBS
CARD 2 IS THE 10 OF DIAMONDS
CARD 3 IS THE 12 OF HEARTS
CARD 4 IS THE 1 OF CLUBS
CARD 5 IS THE 11 OF HEARTS
```

3. Write a program using an ON...GOTO statement that prints out one of four different possible vacation destinations depending on the number entered (A).

If A = 0	Print "ENGLAND"
A = 1	Print "FLORIDA"
A = 2	Print "NEW YORK"
A = 3	Print "CALIFORNIA"

PLANNING A PROGRAM

Now that you are familiar with most of the BASIC commands, it is important to refine your programming techniques. As problems become more sophisticated and the programs to solve them more complex, the development of a clear and detailed algorithm is increasingly important. A useful technique is to determine how a problem can be solved using only pencil and paper. The same step-by-step sequence used in producing this algorithm can usually be translated directly into a computer program.

A common mistake is to write a program before the problem and its solution are fully understood. Premature "coding" (program instructions) frequently results in a program which requires extensive modification, with the consequence that statements do not flow logically. For example, when excessive GOTO and IF...THEN statements have been added, the sequential flow is often destroyed and the program lacks clarity. You are urged to plan a program as thoroughly as possible before going to the computer. As the computer pioneer R.W. Hamming declared, "Typing is no subsitute for thinking."

"Top-Down" Planning

The correct method for planning the solution to a lengthy problem is called "top-down" planning, which involves working on the major portions of the solution first and leaving specifics until later. The problem is first broken down into large blocks with details of the blocks filled in later. We will use subroutines to code each of the large blocks. The true value of "top-down" planning becomes apparent in solving large problems which involve lengthy programs.

To demonstrate "top-down" planning we will solve a problem which involves computing the payroll for a small company with five employees. Each employee receives a weekly paycheck computed as follows:

1. The gross (total) pay is based on the employee's hourly wage times the hours worked per week; for every hour over 40 hours, the employee receives 1.5 times the hourly wage; over 50 hours, 2 times the hourly wage.

2. Taxes are deducted based on the following schedule:

GROSS PAY (in dollars)		PERCENTAGE
199 or less	—	0%
200-299	—	10%
300-399	—	15%
400-499	—	25%
over 500	—	50%

3. Social security (FICA) is deducted at 6.25% of the gross salary.

4. Participants in the company pension plan can have 10% of their gross wages subtracted and saved, but not all employees have elected to join the pension plan.

5. There is a vacation fund which allows employees to subtract from 1 to 15% of their gross wages and is only available to those who are members of the pension plan.

First, we must determine what information the computer must have for each employee:

1. name
2. hourly wage
3. hours worked (which vary from week to week)
4. pension plan signified by 1 (yes), or 0 (no).
5. vacation plan percentage

This information would be best stored in a disk file, but since files are not discussed until Chapters 10 and 11, we will store the information in DATA statements structured as follows:

900 DATA SMITH, 4.25, 1, 5

The statement contains the employee's name, the hourly wage, a 0 or 1 for the pension plan, and a percentage for the vacation plan. Since the hours worked vary, they will be input from the keyboard when the program is run.

Next, let's determine the large blocks by deciding what major tasks the program should perform.

1. Load information into arrays from the DATA statements and input the hourly wage from the keyboard.
2. Compute the employee's gross pay.
3. Compute all deductions.
   (a) taxes and social security
   (b) pension and vacation plans
4. Print out payroll.

We have four major tasks, with the third divided into two subdivisions. Using this information we can now outline our program without filling in the specific details.

```
100 GOSUB 1000 : REM LOAD ARRAY AND ACCEPT INPUT
200 GOSUB 2000 : REM GROSS PAY
300 GOSUB 3000 : REM DEDUCTIONS
400 GOSUB 4000 : REM PRINT PAYROLL
```

Each of these major tasks should now be planned and the appropriate variable names assigned.

1. Load Arrays:
   a. Read data for each employee:

Name	: EMPLOYEE$( )
Hourly Rate	: RATE( )
Deduction Code	: DEDUCTION( )
Vacation Fund%	: VACPERCT( )

   b. INPUT hours worked, HOURS( ).
   c. Read tax rate from DATA statement, TAXRATE( ).

2. Gross Pay
   a. Calculate gross pay, GROSS( ), based upon the following schedule:

Hours > 50	—	double time
40 < Hours <= 50	—	time and a half
Hours <= 40	—	straight time

   b. Round off GROSS( ) to nearest cent.

3. Deductions:
   a. Calculate tax, TAX( ), based upon the graduated scale.
   b. Calculate social security, SS( ), based upon a fixed rate (6.25%).
   c. Check if employee is participating in pension and vacation funds. If the employee is, then:

      1. Calculate pension plan, PENSION( ), based upon a fixed rate of 10%.
      2. Calculate vacation fund deduction, VACATION( ), based upon a variable rate chosen by each employee.

   d. Round all deductions to nearest cent.

4. Print Out:
   a. Print a detailed transaction record for each employee, stating hours worked, rate, gross pay and deductions.
   b. Calculate net pay, NET, by subtracting deductions from gross pay.
   c. Round net pay to nearest cent.
   d. Print net pay.

In the planning of the four major tasks, note that three of the four require that dollar and cents calculations be rounded. Therefore, rather than repeating the rounding routine three times, it is better to add a fifth subroutine, ROUNDING, which can be called by the other subroutines. This is a good example of what often occurs in using "top-down" design. As the plan is refined, it becomes necessary to alter the plan to futher simplify it. For this reason we add:

5. Rounding:
   a. Round number input to the nearest cent (.01).

The following diagram shows the relationships between the main routine and the subroutines.

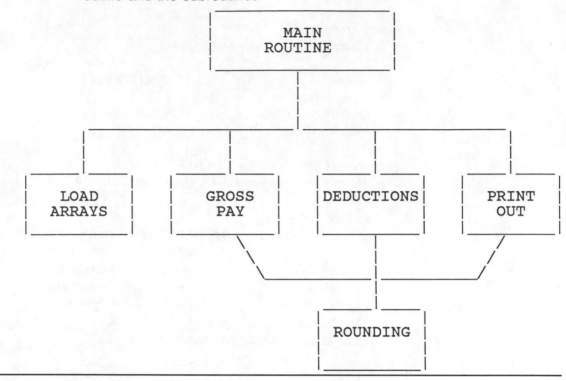

Program 6.4

```
10 REM    EMPLOYEE$()   ===>>   Name of employee
20 REM    WAGE()        ===>>   Hourly rate
30 REM    DEDUCTION()   ===>>   Deduction code
40 REM    VACPERCT()    ===>>   Percentage of gross salary put
50 REM                         into the employees vacation fund
60 REM    GROSS()       ===>>   Gross salary
70 REM    TAX()         ===>>   Taxes withheld from employee
80 REM    SS()          ===>>   Social security deduction
90 REM    PENSION()     ===>>   Deduction for the pension fund
100 REM   VACATION()    ===>>   Deduction for the vacation fund
110 REM   HOURS()       ===>>   Hours worked
120 REM   ROUND         ===>>   Temporary variable used in
130 REM                        the rounding routine
140 REM   TAXRATE()     ===>>   Schedule of available tax rates
150 REM
160 DIM EMPLOYEE$(5), WAGE(5), DEDUCTION(5), VACPERCT(5), GROSS(5)
170 DIM TAX(5), SS(5), PENSION(5), VACATION(5), HOURS(5)
180 REM
190 REM ******* Beginning of the Main Body ********
200 GOSUB 1000  : REM    ****    LOAD ARRAYS ROUTINE
210 FOR I = 1 TO 5
220      GOSUB 2000 : REM    ****    GROSS PAY ROUTINE
230      GOSUB 3000 : REM    ****    DEDUCTIONS ROUTINE
240 NEXT I
250 GOSUB 4000  : REM    ****    PRINT OUT ROUTINE
260 GOTO 9999
270 REM
280 REM ******* End of the Main Body ********
```

```
1000 REM
1010 REM        *****    LOAD ARRAYS ROUTINE    *****
1020 REM
1030 FOR I = 1 TO 5
1040    READ EMPLOYEE$(I), WAGE(I), DEDUCTION(I), VACPERCT(I)
1050    PRINT "Enter number of hours ";EMPLOYEE$(I);
              " worked this week";
1060    INPUT HOURS(I)
1070    IF HOURS(I) < 0 OR HOURS(I) > 168 THEN PRINT "REENTER..."
                                    : GOTO 1050

1080 NEXT I
1090 FOR I = 1 TO 5
1100    READ TAXRATE(I)
1110 NEXT I
1120 DATA  BIDWELL, 7.65, 1, 4
1130 DATA  WANG, 3.35, 0, 0
1140 DATA  ZAHARCHUK, 5.00, 0, 0
1150 DATA  DINGLE, 5.00, 1, 2
1160 DATA  NILSON, 6.45, 1, 3
1170 DATA 0, .1, .15, .35, .50
1180 RETURN
2000 REM
2010 REM        *****    GROSS PAY ROUTINE    *****
2020 REM
2030 GROSS(I) = 0 : H = HOURS(I)
2040 IF HOURS(I) > 50 THEN 2050
                     ELSE IF HOURS(I) > 40 THEN 2060
                                          ELSE 2070
2050 GROSS(I) = ((H - 50) * WAGE(I) * 2) : H = 50
2060 GROSS(I) = GROSS(I) + ((H - 40) * WAGE(I) * 1.5) : H = 40
2070 GROSS(I) = GROSS(I) + (WAGE(I) * H)
2080 ROUND = GROSS(I) : GOSUB 5000
2090 GROSS(I) = ROUND
2100 RETURN
3000 REM
3010 REM        *****    DEDUCTIONS ROUTINE    *****
3020 REM
3030 BASE = INT (GROSS(I) * .01)
3040 IF BASE > 5 THEN BASE = 5
3050 TAX(I) = GROSS(I) * TAXRATE(BASE)
3060 ROUND = TAX(I) : GOSUB 5000
3070 TAX(I) = ROUND
3080 SS(I) = GROSS(I) * .0625
3090 ROUND = SS(I) : GOSUB 5000
3100 SS(I) = ROUND
3110 IF DEDUCTION(I) = 0 THEN RETURN
3120 PENSION(I) = GROSS(I) * .1
3130 ROUND = PENSION(I) : GOSUB 5000
3140 PENSION(I) = ROUND
3150 VACATION(I) = GROSS(I) * (VACPERCT(I) / 100)
3160 ROUND = VACATION(I) : GOSUB 5000
3170 VACATION(I) = ROUND
3180 RETURN
```

```
4000 REM
4010 REM        *****    PRINT OUT ROUTINE    *****
4020 REM
4030 FOR I = 1 TO 5
4040    PRINT
4050    PRINT "NAME            ===>> "; EMPLOYEE$(I)
4060    PRINT "Pay Rate        ===>> $"; WAGE(I)
4070    PRINT "Hours Worked ===>>   "; HOURS(I)
4080    PRINT "Gross Pay       ===>> $"; GROSS(I)
4090    PRINT "Deductions"
4100    PRINT "    Taxes       ===>> $"; TAX(I)
4110    PRINT "    FICA        ===>> $"; SS(I)
4120    PRINT "    Pension     ===>> $"; PENSION(I)
4130    PRINT "    Vac. Fund ===>> $"; VACATION(I)
4140    PRINT
4150    NET = GROSS(I) - (TAX(I) + SS(I) + PENSION(I) + VACATION(I))
4160    ROUND = NET : GOSUB 5000
4170    NET = ROUND
4180    PRINT "NET PAY         ===>> $"; ROUND
4190    PRINT : INPUT "Hit the ENTER key to continue "; REPLY$
4200 NEXT I
4210 RETURN
5000 REM
5010 REM        *****    ROUNDING ROUTINE    *****
5020 REM
5030 ROUND = INT ( 100 * ROUND + .5) / 100
5040 RETURN
9999 END


RUN
Enter number of hours BIDWELL worked this week? 40
Enter number of hours WANG worked this week? 25
Enter number of hours ZAHARCHUK worked this week? 12
Enter number of hours DINGLE worked this week? 55
Enter number of hours NILSON worked this week? 32


NAME            ===>> BIDWELL
Pay Rate        ===>> $ 7.65
 Hours Worked ===>>    40
 Gross Pay      ===>> $ 306
 Deductions
    Taxes       ===>> $ 45.9
    FICA        ===>> $ 19.13
    Pension     ===>> $ 30.6
    Vac. Fund ===>> $ 12.24

NET PAY         ===>> $ 198.13

Hit the ENTER key to continue ?
```

```
NAME            ===>> WANG
Pay Rate        ===>> $ 3.35
Hours Worked ===>>    25
Gross Pay       ===>> $ 83.75
Deductions
    Taxes       ===>> $ 0
    FICA        ===>> $ 5.23
    Pension     ===>> $ 0
    Vac. Fund ===>> $ 0

NET PAY         ===>> $ 78.52

Hit the ENTER key to continue ?

NAME            ===>> ZAHARCHUK
Pay Rate        ===>> $ 5
Hours Worked ===>>    12
Gross Pay       ===>> $ 60
Deductions
    Taxes       ===>> $ 0
    FICA        ===>> $ 3.75
    Pension     ===>> $ 0
    Vac. Fund ===>> $ 0

NET PAY         ===>> $ 56.25

Hit the ENTER key to continue ?

NAME            ===>> DINGLE
Pay Rate        ===>> $ 5
Hours Worked ===>>    55
Gross Pay       ===>> $ 300
Deductions
    Taxes       ===>> $ 45
    FICA        ===>> $ 18.75
    Pension     ===>> $ 30
    Vac. Fund ===>> $ 6

NET PAY         ===>> $ 200.25

Hit the ENTER key to continue ?

NAME            ===>> NILSON
Pay Rate        ===>> $ 6.45
Hours Worked ===>>    32
Gross Pay       ===>> $ 206.4
Deductions
    Taxes       ===>> $ 20.64
    FICA        ===>> $ 12.9
    Pension     ===>> $ 20.64
    Vac. Fund ===>> $ 6.19

NET PAY         ===>> $ 146.03

Hit the ENTER key to continue ?
```

- **Lines 10-140:** This is the variable declaration section of the program. Each variable used is listed, along with a short description of its purpose. In long programs it is especially useful to include a variable declaration section.
- **Lines 160-170:** All of the array variables are DIMensioned to accommodate five employees.
- **Lines 180-280:** This is the main body of the program which calls the four main subroutines. The first is the subroutine LOAD ARRAYS, which fills the array variables with their values. The FOR...NEXT loop in lines 210-240 causes the second and third subroutines, GROSS PAY and DEDUCTIONS, to be executed for each employee separately. Finally, the payroll is printed by the subroutine PRINT OUT. When the main body has completed execution, line 260 sends the program to the END statement at line 9999.
- **Lines 1000-1180:** This is the subroutine LOAD ARRAY, where all the array variables are filled with their values. This is accomplished using the READ...DATA statements in lines 1040 and 1100 and the INPUT statement in line 1060. Line 1180 RETURNs the program to the main body when the loading process is complete.
- **Lines 2000-2100:** This subroutine, GROSS PAY, is called from line 220 of the MAIN ROUTINE. It figures each employee's gross pay for the week including any overtime. It also calls the ROUNDING subroutine to round the employee's gross pay to the nearest cent. Line 2100 RETURNs this subroutine to line 230 of the MAIN ROUTINE.
- **Lines 3000-3180:** This subroutine, DEDUCTIONS, is used to determine how much of each employee's weekly paycheck should be withheld. Every employee must pay taxes and social security, and these deductions are calculated and stored in lines 3030 to 3100. Line 3030 uses the variable BASE to determine the correct TAXRATE for each employee. Note that the subroutine ROUNDING, on line 5000, is called after each deduction to round the amount to the nearest cent. Only certain employees have decided to contribute to the pension and vacation funds. If the employee does not want to contribute to these funds, the program is sent back to the MAIN ROUTINE. Those who do contribute have their deductions calculated in lines 3120 to 3170. Finally, the subroutine RETURNs to the MAIN ROUTINE at line 3180.
- **Lines 4000-4210:** This is the subroutine PRINT OUT, where the payroll reports are displayed. In line 4150, the net pay is calculated by subtracting all the deductions from the gross pay.
- **Lines 5000-5040:** These lines comprise the subroutine ROUNDING, which is sent a number in the variable ROUND and rounds it to the nearest hundredth (i.e., the nearest cent).

The length of this program demonstrates the need for "top-down" planning. Review it carefully and use it as a model upon which you can base the design of longer programs.

Finding Errors —Debugging

No matter how carefully planned, the longer a program the more likely it is to contain errors. Debugging is the process of locating errors or "bugs" in a program and correcting them. Obviously, when a program has been broken down into well-defined subroutines, it is easier to locate and correct any problems. There are two basic types of errors which will cause a program to work improperly: run time and logic errors.

Run Time Errors   Run time errors, which cause the computer to halt execution, are usually of two types. The first is created when a statement is typed improperly:

> 10 REED X,Y

should be

> 10 READ X,Y

The second type is caused by an instruction that tells the computer to carry out a task that is not in agreement with the computer's rules of operation. For example,

> 10 READ A$, B
> 20 DATA 25, SMITH

will cause the computer to halt the program because the computer will try to assign the numeric variable B the string of characters "SMITH". Since the rules of BASIC do not allow this, a SYNTAX ERROR results.

Logic Errors   If a program does not break any of BASIC's rules, the computer will accept the program and run it. Remember, however, that computers always do what you tell them to do, which is not always what you want them to do. Errors that cause an output different than what is expected are called logic errors, and frequently result from an incorrect analysis of the program's task.

Program 6.5   The Skyhook International Company wrote this short program to keep track of the number of skyhooks it has in inventory. There are initially 145 hooks:

```
10 CLS
20 INPUT "Hooks in order "; ORDER
30 HOOK = 145
40 HOOK = HOOK - ORDER
50 PRINT "Hooks now on hand"; HOOK
60 PRINT
70 INPUT "Another order "; A$
80 IF A$ = "YES" OR A$ = "yes" THEN 20 ELSE 999
999 END

RUN
Hooks in order ? 45
Hooks now on hand 100

Another order ? YES
Hooks in order ? 30
Hooks now on hand 115

Another order ? NO
```

The program at first appears to work, but the output is obviously incorrect since the company cannot have more hooks left after filling the second order than it had after filling the first. The programmer has made a logic error by placing line 30, which set the initial value of variable HOOK, out of sequence. This causes the computer to keep resetting the value of HOOK to 145 each time the program is repeated rather than keep this variable equal to the result of HOOK minus the value of ORDER. Moving line 30 to the beginning of the program will correct this logic error. This simple, but common logic error was easy to locate. In longer programs locating such errors can be considerably more difficult.

Review

4. Find the logic error in the following program and correct it:

```
10 FOR J = 0 TO 10
20     A = J / 2
30     IF A = INT (J / 2) THEN 10
40     PRINT A
50 NEXT J
```

5. Find and correct the logic error in this program:

```
10 REM Program to PRINT the 5 times table
20 FOR I = 1 to 12
30     J = 1
40     I = J * 5
50     PRINT J; "* 5 ="; I
60 NEXT I
```

Hand Tracing

One way to create confidence in a program's output is to manually trace the results of a program using test data. This is called hand tracing. It is best to use test data that covers the range of anticipated program input. If the program produces the same results as those obtained by manual tracing this range, the program can usually be considered reliable.

Program 6.6

This program assigns variable N a value using READ and is then supposed to calculate and print the sum of the first N integers. For example, if N is 5 the sum should equal 1 + 2 + 3 + 4 + 5 or 15:

```
10 CLS
20 READ N
30 IF N = 99 THEN 999
40 FOR C = 1 TO N
50     S = S + C
60 NEXT C
70 PRINT
80 PRINT "The number of integers ="; N
90 PRINT "The sum of those integers ="; S
100 GOTO 20
110 DATA 3, 5, 10, 99
999 END
```

```
RUN

The number of integers = 3
The sum of those integers = 6

The number of integers = 5
The sum of those integers = 21

The number of integers = 10
The sum of those integers = 76
```

If the output for the program is checked by hand for N = 3, S = 6 (1 + 2 + 3) is a correct answer. However, if the programmer relies only on this test data, then a serious logic error will be overlooked. A problem with the test data technique is that data chosen for the test may bypass the bug. A test by hand using N = 5, has S = 15 (1 + 2 + 3 + 4 + 5) as the result, but does not agree with the output of the program.

The problem now is to find the place in the program where the error occurs. One way to do this is to "play computer". In fact, if this is done as part of the planning of the program, errors like this can most often be avoided in the first place.

To find this program's bug, the programmer makes a table that shows each variable in the program and then traces the value of each variable line-by-line, recording the value as each line is executed.

Line	N	C	S	
10	0	0	0	
20	3	0	0	
40	3	1	0	
50	3	1	1	
60	3	2	1	
50	3	2	3	
60	3	3	3	
50	3	3	6	
70-90				(Print 3,6)
20	5	3	6	
40	5	1	6	
50	5	1	7	(Error! S should be 1)

The program begins at line 10 with each of the variables having an initial value of 0. A value is not changed unless there is an assignment statement. The error begins to become apparent when the computer is told to go back to line 20. Variable N is assigned a new value so the program can calculate the sum of the first 5 integers. On line 40, variable C is reassigned a value of 1 by FOR C = 1 TO N. However, when the computer executes line 50 to begin calculating the new sum, variable S still has its old value of 6. The computer was not instructed to set the value of variable S back to 0 so the program began calculating the sum of the first 5 integers by adding 1 to 6. This is a common error which causes a program to produce incorrect output.

Use of Additional PRINT Statements

It is often useful to place additional PRINT statements at a number of program locations to check the value of variables. For example, the addition of the line

35 PRINT S

to Program 6.6 would prove S was not starting at an intital value of 0, as it should, after the loop had been executed once.

Another technique is to place a line in a program to indicate whether the program is following a proper sequence. Placing PRINT statements at the beginning of subroutines helps to outline if the routines are being called properly. For example,

200 PRINT "Subroutine Deductions"

will prove whether the program has reached this subroutine. These extra PRINT statements can later be removed when no longer needed.

STOP and CONTinue

Deliberately halting a program at certain points is a useful debugging technique. STOP is similar to the END statement, but unlike END, STOP displays the line number where the break in the program occurred. A program halted by a STOP instruction can be resumed at the point of the interruption by typing CONTinue. Breaking a program in this way becomes a useful debugging tool because the current value of any variable can be displayed using immediate mode.

Program 6.7

A STOP statement is added to Program 6.6 to test results of the hand tracing:

```
10  CLS
20  READ N
30  IF N = 99 THEN 999
40  FOR C = 1 TO N
45      IF S > 6 THEN STOP
50      S = S + C
60  NEXT C
70  PRINT
80  PRINT "The number of integers ="; N
90  PRINT "The sum of those integers ="; S
100 GOTO 20
110 DATA 3, 5, 10, 99
999 END

RUN
The number of integers = 3
The sum of those integers = 6
Break in 45
Ok
PRINT N, C, S
 5              2              7
Ok
CONT
```

```
Break in 45
Ok
PRINT N, C, S
 5               3               9
Ok
```

When the program tries to calculate the value of the first 5 integers, the IF...THEN on line 45 becomes true so the STOP command produces the BREAK IN 45 message and halts the program. The programmer then types PRINT and the names of the 3 variables in question (N, C and S) in immediate mode. Typing CONT tells the computer to continue the program from the next statement. This again produces the incorrect output and again forces a BREAK IN 45 message. Now the programmer should realize that the bug is caused by not setting the value of S back to 0.

This error can be corrected by adding an instruction to set S back to 0 and erasing line 45:

```
25 S = 0
45
```

Now a run of the program produces the correct results:

```
RUN

The number of integers = 3
The sum of those integers = 6

The number of integers = 5
The sum of those integers = 15

The number of integers = 10
The sum of those integers = 55
```

Review

6. This program should calculate the areas and perimeters of several rectangles. Hand trace the program to make sure that it produces the correct output:

```
10 FOR F = 1 TO 3
20     READ L, W
30     P = (2 * L) + (2 * W)
40     A = L * W
50     PRINT A, P
60 NEXT F
70 DATA 5, 3, 7, 9, 8, 8
```

TRON-TROFF

To follow the sequence in which the lines of a program are executed, type the command TRON before typing RUN. Each line number will then be printed as the line is processed by the computer, thus allowing the programmer to trace program flow easily. To stop the line tracing, the command TROFF is typed after the computer completes its run.

Program 6.8   This program prints all the combinations of quarters and dimes which add up to $1.00:

```
10 REM   Q = Quarters
20 REM   D = Dimes
30 REM
40 FOR Q = 0 TO 4
50     FOR D = 0 TO 10
60         IF (25 * Q) + (10 * D) = 100 THEN
               PRINT "Q =";Q,  "D ="; D
70         NEXT D
80 NEXT Q
999 END
RUN
Q = 0              D = 10
Q = 2              D = 5
Q = 4              D = 0
Ok
TRON
Ok
RUN
[10][20][30][40][50][60][70][60][70][60][70][60]
[70][60][70][60][70][60][70][60]
[70][60][70][60][70][60]Q = 0                    D = 10
[70][80][50][60][70][60][70][60][70][60][70][60]
[70][60][70][60][70][60][70][60]
[70][60][70][60][70][80][50][60][70][60][70][60]
[70][60][70][60][70][60]Q = 2                    D = 5
[70][60][70][60][70][60][70][60][70][60][70][80]
[50][60][70][60][70][60][70][60]
[70][60][70][60][70][60][70][60][70][60][70][60]
[70][60][70][80][50][60]Q = 4                    D = 0
[70][60][70][60][70][60][70][60][70][60][70][60]
[70][60][70][60][70][60][70][60]
[70][80][999]

Ok
TROFF
Ok
```

Follow the program flow carefully for both loops. Notice that each time a NEXT statement is executed, it returns the program to the statement following the corresponding FOR...TO statement. For programs that are long and complicated, involving a number of subroutines, TRON is especially useful.

ON ERROR GOTO and RESUME

If an error can be anticipated before a program is run, it may be "trapped" using the ON ERROR GOTO statement, which then allows the program to continue execution. When an error is encountered, this statement suppresses the printing of an error message and causes the program to jump to a specified line. For example,

30 ON ERROR GOTO 60

sends the program to line 60 if an error occurs.

An example of a frequently encountered error is that of taking the square root of a negative number. To trap this error the ON ERROR GOTO statement must be placed in the program before the error occurs. Then, if there is an error, the program will jump to the specified line.

The RESUME statement performs two functions after an error has been trapped. It returns the program to the point where the error occurred and resets the error trap so that new errors may be trapped. If the RESUME statement is not used, the program will continue from the point where it was sent by the ON ERROR GOTO statement and will thereafter be unable to trap any future errors. It is important to correct an error before executing the RESUME statement; otherwise, the error may occur again, putting the program into an infinite loop or cause it to produce undesired output.

Program 6.9   This program finds the square roots of a number supplied by the user. Note that the statement SQR(X) finds the positive square root of X and ABS(X), the absolute value of X. These statements will be explained in greater depth in Chapter 9:

```
10 REM    Find the square roots of X,
20 REM    where X is entered by the user.
30 REM
40 ON ERROR GOTO 200
50 INPUT "What is X "; X
60 R = SQR(X)
70 PRINT "The square roots of"; X; "are +"; R; "and -"; R
80 PRINT
90 INPUT "Do you want another square root "; A$
100 IF A$ = "YES" OR A$ = "yes" THEN 40 ELSE 999
200 PRINT "The square root of"; X; "is an Imaginary Root!"
210 X = ABS(X)
220 RESUME
999 END

RUN
What is X ? 4
The square roots of 4 are + 2 and - 2

Do you want another square root ? YES
What is X ? -25
The square root of-25 is an Imaginary Root!
The square roots of 25 are + 5 and - 5

Do you want another square root ? yes
What is X ? 2
The square roots of 2 are + 1.414214 and - 1.414214

Do you want another square root ? no
```

Note that if an error occurs, the program goes to line 200 and prints a message. Line 210 assigns X the absolute value of X, thereby eliminating the error by removing the minus sign. The RESUME at line 220 sends the program back to line 60, which is the line where the error occurred. Now the square root is calculated using the absolute value of X.

RESUME can also be used with a line number. For example,

120 RESUME 50

would send the program back to line 50 for a new INPUT rather than continue at line 70.

ERR and ERL

Program 6.9 has the drawback of handling all errors alike whether they are anticipated or not. The ERR and ERL functions allow the program to be more discriminating in handling errors.

ERR returns a number that identifies the specific error that has occurred. For example, the statement

20 PRINT ERR

will return a number corresponding to an error listed below.

Code	Explanation	Code	Explanation
1	NEXT without FOR	26	For without NEXT
2	Syntax error	27	Out of paper
3	RETURN without GOSUB	29	WHILE without WEND
4	Out of data	30	WEND without WHILE
5	Illegal function call	50	FIELD overflow
6	Overflow	51	Internal error
7	Out of memory	52	Bad file number
8	Undefined line number	53	File not found
9	Subscript out of range	54	Bad file mode
10	Duplicate Definition	55	File already open
11	Division by zero	57	Device I/O Error
12	Illegal direct	58	File already exists
13	Type mismatch	61	Disk full
14	Out of string space	62	Input past end
15	String too long	63	Bad record number
16	String formula too complex	64	Bad File name
17	Can't continue	66	Direct statement to file
18	Undefined user definition	67	Too many files
19	No RESUME	68	Device Unavailable
20	RESUME without error	69	Communication buffer overflow
21	Unprintable error	70	Disk Write Protect
22	Missing operand	71	Disk not Ready
23	Line buffer overflow	72	Disk media error
24	Device Timeout	73	Advanced Feature
25	Device Fault	—	Unprintable error

ERL returns a number equal to the line number where the most recent error occurred. For example,

30 PRINT ERL

prints the appropriate line number.

Program 6.10   This program allows the user to make up a team of up to eight members and then list the name of the person chosen when that player's number is input. The program will respond correctly to two different types of errors: Out of data and Subscript out of range:

```
10 REM    Pick the player's you want on your
20 REM    team out of the players available.
30 REM
40 ON ERROR GOTO 200
50 INPUT "Enter number of players"; X
60 FOR I = 1 TO X
70    READ N$(I)
80 NEXT I
90 INPUT "Enter player number"; Y
100 PRINT "Player number"; Y; "'s name is "; N$(Y)
110 INPUT "Do you want to pick another "; A$
120 IF A$ = "YES" OR A$ = "yes" THEN 90 ELSE 999
200 IF ERR = 4 THEN PRINT "Out of data...REENTER" :
                  RESTORE : RESUME 50
210 IF ERR = 9 THEN PRINT "Subscript out of range in line"; ERL :
                  RESUME NEXT
220 PRINT "Error number"; ERR; "occurred in line"; ERL :
          RESUME NEXT
230 DATA MIKE, GREG, BRUCE, HEIDI, PAUL
240 DATA CAROL, FRED, EILEEN
999 END
```

```
RUN
Enter number of players? 10
Out of data...REENTER
Enter number of players? 7
Enter player number? 5
Player number 5 's name is PAUL
Do you want to pick another ? YES
Enter player number? 12
Player number 12 's name is Subscript out of range in line 90
Do you want to pick another ? NO
```

- **Line 40:** When an error is detected, program control is passed to line 200.
- **Lines 50-80:** Read in as many names as specified by the user.
- **Lines 90-100:** Print out the name of the person chosen by the user.
- **Lines 110-120:** Ask the user if another player need be picked and if so, branch to line 90.
- **Line 200:** Checks to see if the user attempts to read beyond the end of the data. If so, the data is RESTORED and the program begins again.
- **Line 210:** Because no DIM statements was used, a "Subscript out of range" error could occur in either line 70 or 100.
- **Line 220:** Other errors are trapped by this statement. ERR tells which error it was and ERL tells where it occurred. This is a good programming practice since errors other than 4 and 9 may occur.

EXERCISES

1. What output is produced by the following program?

   ```
   10 FOR X = 1 TO 5 STEP 2
   20     READ K1, K2
   30     A = A + K1 − K2
   40     B = B − K1 + K2
   50 NEXT X
   60 PRINT A,B
   70 DATA 1, 3, 2, 4, 3, 5
   80 END
   ```

2. Trace the following program by hand and determine its output. Use the TRON command to check your results on the computer.

   ```
   10 READ N,A,B
   20 FOR I = 1 TO N
   30     FOR J = 2 TO N + 1
   40         A = 2 * A + B
   50         B = 2 * B + A
   60     NEXT J
   70     PRINT A ; B
   80 NEXT I
   90 DATA 3, −1, 2
   100 END
   ```

3. Input an integer from 1 to 4. The integer should cause one of the following four suggestions to be printed:

   NEVER LEAVE DISKS ON TOP OF A MONITOR
   UNPLUG YOUR COMPUTER DURING A LIGHTNING STORM
   OPEN THE DRIVE DOOR BEFORE POWERING OFF
   OPENING THE CASE WILL VOID YOUR WARRANTY

4. The following simple programs have errors in logic (i.e., the program runs, but the output is illogical). Find and correct the errors.

   (a)
   ```
   10 READ A,B,C
   20 PRINT A + B + C
   30 GOTO 20
   40 DATA 1, 2, 3, 4, 5, 6
   50 END
   ```

(b)

```
10 FOR X = 1 TO 10
20     IF X > 5 THEN 50
30     PRINT X; "IS GREATER THAN 5"
40     GOTO 60
50     PRINT X; "IS LESS THAN 5"
60 NEXT X
70 END
```

(c)

```
10 READ A,B,C
20 FOR X = 1 TO 10
30     Y = (A * B) / (C − X)
40     IF Y < 1 THEN 50
50     PRINT "Y < 1"; Y
60 NEXT X
70 DATA 20, 10, 5, 5, 10, 20
80 END
```

5. Write a program which reads the dimensions of a triangle from a DATA statement and prints its area and perimeter if it is a right triangle. The program should call a subroutine to check whether the triangle is a right triangle.

6. The following program is designed to arrange sets of numbers in descending order. If the second number is larger than the first, the computer interchanges the two values. (This occurs in lines 30 and 40.) Explain the output and correct the program to give the desired output.

```
10 READ A,B
20 IF A > B THEN 50
30 A = B
40 B = A
50 PRINT A, B
60 GOTO 10
70 DATA 10, 20, 20, 10
80 END

RUN
20                    20
20                    10
Out of DATA in 10
```

7. Isolated in his ski-lodge in the Swiss Alps, Bjorn Rich often gets his mail late. As a result, the statements from his Swiss bank account rarely arrive on time. To solve this problem, write a program to assist Bjorn in keeping his account up to date. Have three subroutines which take care of deposits, withdrawals, interest (5.75% annual rate compounded quarterly), or exit. Round all displayed values to the nearest cent.

```
RUN
Withdrawal (1), Deposit (2), Calculate Interest (3), or Exit (4)
Selection? 2
How much would you like to deposit? 500.00
Your balance now stands at 500 dollars.
Selection? 3
How many months since last calculation? 5
Your balance now stands at 507.19 dollars.
Selection? 1
How much would you like to withrawal? 175.50
Your balance now stands at 331.69 dollars.
Selection? 3
How many months since last calculation? 1
Too soon.
Your balance now stands at 331.69 dollars.
Selection? 4
```

8. Structure the following programs by adding spaces and REM statements and by indenting where appropriate:

(a)

```
1 REM THIS PROGRAM DECIDES WHICH MOVIE WE WILL SEE
2 RANDOMIZE TIMER
3 N = INT(20*RND + 6)
4 X = 1
5 FORK = 1TON
6 X = X*-1
7 IFK = NTHENPRINT"WEWILLSEE";ELSEPRINT
8 IFX>0THENPRINT"DUNE"ELSEPRINT"RETURN OF THE JEDI"
9 NEXTK
10 END
```

(b)

```
1 DIMJ(10,10)
2 FORX = 0TO9
3 PRINTTAB(X*4 + 6);X + 1;
4 NEXTX
5 PRINT
6 FORX = 0TO8
7 PRINTTAB(X*4 + 7);"– –";
8 NEXTK
9 PRINTTAB(43);"– –";
10 FORX = 1TO10
11 FORY = 1TO10
12 J(X,Y) = X + Y
13 IFF = 0 THENPRINTX;":";
14 PRINTTAB(F*4 + 6);J(X,Y);
15 F = F + 1
16 IFF = 0 THENPRINT:F = 0
17 NEXTY
18 NEXTX
19 END
```

9. The area of any triangle found from Hero's formula is:

$$AREA = \sqrt{S\,(S-A)\,(S-B)\,(S-C)}$$

where A, B, and C are the respective lengths of each leg of the triangle and S is the semiperimeter (S = (A + B + C) / 2). Write a program that uses Hero's formula in a subroutine to calculate the area of a triangle.

10. Let X and Y be the coordinates of a point in a plane. Write a program which randomly picks X and Y, each as an integer from −5 to 5, inclusive. The user of the program is to guess X and Y. A subroutine must be used to print the distance between the guessed point and the actual point after each guess. The user is to be given 3 guesses and, if unsuccessful, is then to be given the value of X as well as 2 more tries to guess Y.

11. Write a program that uses the Quadratic formula:

$$X = \frac{-b \pm \sqrt{b^2 - 4ac}}{2a}$$

to find the roots of an equation. Input a, b, and c and have the computer print the two roots. Your program should contain an error trap for the error that will occur if the computer attempts to take the square root of a negative number. When this situation arises have the computer print "ROOTS ARE IMAGINARY".

12. (a) Give the exact order in which the lines of the following program are executed.

(b) If line 80 is changed to

        80 DATA 3, 0, 4, −5, −1, −8, 1, 5, 999

what will be the output?

```
10 READ X
20 IF X = 999 THEN 90
30 ON SGN(X) + 2 GOSUB 50, 60, 70
40 GOTO 10
50 N = N + 1 : RETURN
60 Z = Z + 1 : RETURN
70 P = P + 1 : RETURN
80 DATA 6, −1, 0, 999
90 PRINT "N =";N, "Z =";Z, "P =";P
100 END
```

**Advanced
Exercises**

Each of the following exercises requires the development of a detailed algorithm. The program should not be written until all details of the algorithm have been worked out.

13. A FOR...NEXT loop can sometimes be used as a "delay". Notice the effect of the following program lines:

```
     . . .
     . . .
100 FOR X = 1 TO 500
110 NEXT X
     . . .
     . . .
```

When the program reaches line 100, it cycles between lines 100 and 110 five hundred times, causing a delay. The amount of time it takes to complete a FOR...NEXT loop depends on the computer's internal clock. Approximately 800 iterations, or cycles, equal one second of real time on most micro computers. Keep in mind, however, that this value may have to be adjusted depending on how much time other program lines outside the loop require to execute. Consider the following example:

```
100 FOR X = 1 TO 800
110 NEXT X
120 FOR I = 1 TO 5
130     C(I) = C(I) / 2
140 NEXT I
```

If the loop in lines 100-110 requires 1 second to execute and the loop in lines 120-140 requires .5 seconds to execute, then the total time required for this section of code to execute is 1.5 seconds.

Using the above information, develop an algorithm and then a program for a count-down timer. The program allows a timing interval to be entered, then begins counting down while displaying the time remaining at the center of the screen. When the interval has expired, the computer sounds an alarm by executing the BEEP statement, which has the format:

```
140 BEEP
```

Check your computer timer with a watch and make the appropriate changes in the program to make it accurate.

```
RUN
Enter the timer interval in the format MM,SS? 10,00



                10 :0 0
```

14. Modify the algorithm and program in problem 13 to act as a digital clock. The program allows the clock to be set to the current time and has it display the time in a user-selectable 12 or 24 hour format in the center of the display. (Note: In 24 hour mode, midnight is 00:00:00).

15. Write a program using a doubly subscripted array that keeps track of a car dealer's inventory at two different showrooms, DOWNTOWN and UPTOWN (up to twenty vehicles each). The initial inventory is as follows:

Downtown

Model	Price
Mustang	8975
Daytona	9950
Capri	10111
Sunbird	8900
Family Truckster	15195

Uptown

Model	Price
Cougar	13765
Mach 5	86050
Fox	7500
Corvette	15781
Kit	750987

The dealership's total sales should initially be assigned a value of 0.

The program asks the user whether a sale is made (delete from inventory) or a shipment is received (add to inventory), and at which showroom the transaction occurs. For a sale, the program checks to see if there is a trade-in vehicle involved. If so, it adjusts the purchase price of the vehicle being bought and adds the traded vehicle to the respective showroom's inventory. Finally, the program displays the dealership's total sales from both showrooms. Display the information in tabular form.

```
RUN
                              CAR INVENTORY

          DOWNTOWN                              UPTOWN
MODEL                PRICE          MODEL                PRICE
MUSTANG              8975           COUGAR               13765
DAYTONA              9950           MACH 5               86050
CAPRI                10111          FOX                  7500
SUNBIRD              8900           CORVETTE             15781
FAMILY TRUCKSTER     15195          KIT                  750987



The dealership's total sales are $ 0 .

Did we:
S - Sell a car
R - Receive an order
I - Display inventory
<E - EXIT>
Enter S, R, I or E? S
Model of car sold? MUSTANG
Enter a 1 for DOWNTOWN or 2 for UPTOWN showroom? 1
MUSTANG sells for $ 8975 .
Is there a trade (Y/N)? N
MUSTANG sold for $ 8975 .
```

```
Enter S, R, I or E? S
Model of car sold? FOX
Enter a 1 for DOWNTOWN or 2 for UPTOWN showroom? 2
FOX sells for $ 7500 .
Is there a trade (Y/N)? Y
Model of car to trade? NOVA
Trade allowance? 500
Our selling price? 700

FOX sold for $ 7000 .


Enter S, R, I or E? R
What model did we receive? ESCORT
How much did we pay for it? 4800
How much will we sell it for? 7200
Shipped to DOWNTOWN (1) or UPTOWN (2) showroom? 1


Enter S, R, I or E? I
                                 CAR INVENTORY

          DOWNTOWN                          UPTOWN
MODEL                 PRICE      MODEL                 PRICE
DAYTONA               9950       COUGAR                13765
CAPRI                 10111      MACH 5                86050
SUNBIRD               8900       NOVA                  700
FAMILY TRUCKSTER      15195      CORVETTE              15781
ESCORT                7200       KIT                   750987




The dealership's total sales are $ 11175 .
Enter S, R, I or E? E
```

7

STRING FUNCTIONS AND DATA TYPES

ASC

STRING$

LEN

INKEY$

VAL

MID$

LEFT$

RIGHT$

PRINT USING

*M*odern computers have resulted from the union of the binary number system with the principles of electricity. The binary number system uses only two digits, 0 and 1, and can be represented by the two states of an electric circuit, off or on. Digital computers are possible because they operate by reducing all data to binary code. This chapter explains how different types of data are stored using the binary system. Also explained are techniques to improve the computer's ability to format output.

Binary Code

The most familiar number system, the decimal system, uses ten digits, 0, 1, 2, 3, 4, 5, 6, 7, 8, 9 and is therefore called base ten. In contrast, the binary system, which uses only the digits 0 and 1, is base two.

In the base ten system, columns are used to represent powers of ten with the first column left of the decimal point representing 10^0, the second 10^1, the third 10^2, and so on. For example, in the number 458, 8 represents 8×10^0, 5 represents 5×10^1, and 4 represents 4×10^2. The number itself represents the sum: $4 \times 10^2 + 5 \times 10^1 + 8 \times 10^0$.

The base two system works identically except the columns represent the powers of two instead of ten. For example, in the number 101, the 1 on the right represents 1×2^0, the 0 represents 0×2^1, and the 1 on the left represents 1×2^2. The number itself represents the sum of $1 \times 2^2 + 0 \times 2^1 + 1 \times 2^0$, which is equal to five in the base ten system.

Base Two   **Base Ten**

$$11 = 1 \times 2^1 + 1 \times 2^0 \qquad\qquad\qquad\qquad = 3$$
$$1011 = 1 \times 2^3 + 0 \times 2^2 + 1 \times 2^1 + 1 \times 2^0 \qquad = 11$$
$$11001 = 1 \times 2^4 + 1 \times 2^3 + 0 \times 2^2 + 0 \times 2^1 + 1 \times 2^0 \quad = 25$$

To convert a number from base ten to base two, we must find which powers of two add up to the number. Since $13 = 8 + 4 + 1$, the base two representation for 13 is 1101 ($1 \times 8 + 1 \times 4 + 0 \times 2 + 1 \times 1$).

6 =	4	+	2	+	0							= 110
=	$1*2^2$	+	$1*2^1$	+	$0*2^0$							
29 =	16	+	8	+	4	+	0	+	1	+		= 11101
=	$1*2^4$	+	$1*2^3$	+	$1*2^2$	+	$0*2^1$	+	$1*2^0$			
52 =	32	+	16	+	0	+	4	+	0	+	0	= 110100
=	$1*2^5$	+	$1*2^4$	+	$0*2^3$	+	$1*2^2$	+	$1*2^1$	+	$0*2^0$	

Computer Memory and Processing

The computer is composed of a solid-state electronic memory which stores information and a central processing unit (CPU) which performs calculations, makes decisions, and moves information.

Because electricity has two basic states, ON and OFF, it is ideal for expressing binary numbers. When a circuit (called a "flip-flop") is ON it stands for a "1", and when OFF stands for a "0". By designing computers to contain millions of simple flip-flop circuits, huge quantities of information can be stored.

A single binary digit (0 or 1) is called a "bit", and eight of these bits constitute a "byte". Single characters require one byte and integers two bytes of memory for storage. The memory stores both instructions for the CPU and data as binary digits.

The power of a computer is vastly increased when it is capable of storing letters and special characters as well as numbers. In order to do this, a code has been established to translate letters and special characters into numbers which can then be stored in binary form. This code has been standardized by the computer industry as the American Standard Code for Information Interchange (ASCII). In this code, each letter of the alphabet, both upper and lower case, each symbol, and each function used by the computer is represented by a number. For example, the name JIM is translated by the computer into ASCII numbers 74, 73, 77. In turn these numbers are then stored by the computer in binary form.

$$J = 74 = 0100\ 1010$$
$$I = 73 = 0100\ 1001$$
$$M = 77 = 0100\ 1101$$

In order for the computer to store a name such as JIM, or any piece of non-numeric information, it must be entered in the form of a string, converted character by character into ASCII numbers, and then stored in memory as binary numbers. The following is a table of the ASCII character codes available on the computer:

ASCII value	Character	ASCII value	Character	ASCII value	Character	ASCII value	Character	ASCII value	Character
0	(null)	52	4	104	h	156	£	208	╨
1	☺	53	5	105	i	157	¥	209	╤
2	☻	54	6	106	j	158	Pt	210	╥
3	♥	55	7	107	k	159	ƒ	211	╙
4	♦	56	8	108	l	160	á	212	╘
5	♣	57	9	109	m	161	í	213	╒
6	♠	58	:	110	n	162	ó	214	╓
7	(beep)	59	;	111	o	163	ú	215	╫
8	◘	60	<	112	p	164	ñ	216	╪
9	(tab)	61	=	113	q	165	Ñ	217	┘
10	(line feed)	62	>	114	r	166	ª	218	┌
11	(home)	63	?	115	s	167	º	219	█
12	(form feed)	64	@	116	t	168	¿	220	▄
13	(carriage return)	65	A	117	u	169	⌐	221	▌
14	♫	66	B	118	v	170	¬	222	▐
15	☼	67	C	119	w	171	½	223	▀
16	►	68	D	120	x	172	¼	224	α
17	◄	69	E	121	y	173	¡	225	β
18	↕	70	F	122	z	174	«	226	Γ
19	‼	71	G	123	{	175	»	227	π
20	¶	72	H	124			176	░	228	Σ
21	§	73	I	125	}	177	▒	229	σ
22	▬	74	J	126	~	178	▓	230	μ
23	↨	75	K	127	⌂	179	│	231	τ
24	↑	76	L	128	Ç	180	┤	232	Φ
25	↓	77	M	129	ü	181	╡	233	Θ
26	→	78	N	130	é	182	╢	234	Ω
27	←	79	O	131	â	183	╖	235	δ
28	(cursor right)	80	P	132	ä	184	╕	236	∞
29	(cursor left)	81	Q	133	à	185	╣	237	Ø
30	(cursor up)	82	R	134	å	186	║	238	ϵ
31	(cursor down)	83	S	135	ç	187	╗	239	∩
32	(space)	84	T	136	ê	188	╝	240	≡
33	!	85	U	137	ë	189	╜	241	±
34	"	86	V	138	è	190	╛	242	≥
35	#	87	W	139	ï	191	┐	243	≤
36	$	88	X	140	î	192	└	244	⌠
37	%	89	Y	141	ì	193	┴	245	⌡
38	&	90	Z	142	Ä	194	┬	246	÷
39	'	91	[	143	Å	195	├	247	≈
40	(	92	\	144	É	196	─	248	°
41	)	93	]	145	æ	197	┼	249	•
42	*	94	∧	146	Æ	198	╞	250	·
43	+	95	—	147	ô	199	╟	251	√
44	,	96	`	148	ö	200	╚	252	ⁿ
45	-	97	a	149	ò	201	╔	253	²
46	.	98	b	150	û	202	╩	254	■
47	/	99	c	151	ù	203	╦	255	(blank 'FF')
48	0	100	d	152	ÿ	204	╠		
49	1	101	e	153	Ö	205	═		
50	2	102	f	154	Ü	206	╬		
51	3	103	g	155	¢	207	╧		

Review

1. Convert the following decimal numbers to their binary equivalent:

   a. 92   d. 127
   b. 13   e. 35
   c. 7   f. 63

2. Convert the following binary numbers to their decimal equivalent:

   a. 100111   d. 111001
   b. 010011   e. 101010
   c. 001010   f. 010101

Data Types

When information is entered into the computer, it can take one of three forms: characters, integers, or floating point numbers. An integer is a number without decimal places, while a floating point number has either a decimal point and decimal places or an implied decimal point. For example, the number 29 could be either integer or floating point, but 29.73 is definitely floating point.

Floating point numbers can be specified to be either single precision or double precision. A single precision floating point number is stored in the computer with seven significant figures, and up to seven are printed, but only six are accurate. A double precision floating point number is accurate to seventeen significant figures but rounded to sixteen when printed.

Storage of an integer requires 16 bits (2 bytes), a floating point number either 32 or 64 bits (4 or 8 bytes), depending on whether it is single or double precision, and an ASCII character 8 bits (1 byte). Because of storage requirements it is important to distinguish among the several forms. When files are presented in Chapters 10 and 11, the significance of this will become apparent.

The four data types employ different symbols to inform the computer which is being used. Strings of ASCII characters use the familiar symbol ($) for string variable names (e.g., G$, B3$). Integers, which have the disadvantage of being restricted to the range –32768 to 32767, are denoted by a percent sign (%). For example, B% and Z% are variable names for integers. While integers have a severe range limitation, they are processed fastest by the computer. Single precision floating point variables are denoted by an exclamation mark (!), (e.g., C!, HI!). Double precision floating point variables are denoted by a number sign (#), (e.g., G7#, E#). While they are more accurate, calculations involving double precision numbers are the slowest. Variable names without any declaration symbols (#, !, $, %) are considered single precision, floating point variables.

The precision of constants as well as variables can be declared and will then determine the precision of the calculations in which they are used. For example, a single precision division,

PRINT 2/3

produces

.6666667

while a double precision division,

PRINT 2# / 3#

produces

.6666666666666667

ASCII Code—
ASCII Character
Conversions

Earlier in this chapter, ASCII code was described as a method by which the computer converts information in the form of strings into numbers. Commands exist to convert strings into ASCII values and vice versa:

Function Format	**Operation**
X = ASC (P$)	Converts only the first character of the string P$ to its ASCII code number.
P$ = CHR$(X)	Assigns the character with the ASCII code number X to P$, which now contains only one character.
P$ = STRING$ (X,Y)	Generates a string, P$, of length X composed of characters all having the ASCII code number Y.

Program 7.1

This program demonstrates the use of ASCII character conversions:

```
10 REM    C$ = Character input
20 REM    A  = ASCII value of C$
30 REM    K$ = New string
40 REM    Y$ = Indicator
50 REM
60 INPUT "Enter any character"; C$
70 A = ASC(C$)
80 PRINT "The ASCII value of "; C$; " is "; A
90 K$ = STRING$(17,A)
100 PRINT "'"; CHR$(A); "' repeated 17 times looks like this ";
110 PRINT K$
120 INPUT "Would you like to run this again"; Y$
130 IF ASC(Y$) = 89 OR ASC(Y$) = 121 THEN 10
140 END

RUN
Enter any character? R
The ASCII value of R is   82
'R' repeated 17 times looks like this RRRRRRRRRRRRRRRRR
Would you like to run this again? N
```

- **Line 60:** A single character (letter or digit) is entered by the user.
- **Line 70:** Uses the ASC( ) function to assign A the numeric value of the ASCII code for the first character in C$.
- **Line 90:** Assigns a string 17 characters long with the ASCII value A to K$.
- **Line 130:** Uses the ASC( ) function to check if the user had entered a "Y" or a "y" in response to line 120.

Review

3. Write a program that allows the user to input a letter. Have the computer print that letter's ASCII code and then print the letter that comes two letters after it in the alphabet. If Y or Z is the letter input, then A or B should be returned respectively. Have the program stop if a non-alphabetic character is input:

```
RUN
A LETTER FROM THE ALPHABET PLEASE? R
THE ASCII OF 'R' IS 82
TWO LETTERS AFTER R IS 'T'
A LETTER FROM THE ALPHABET PLEASE? Y
THE ASCII OF 'Y' IS 89
TWO LETTERS AFTER 'Y' IS 'A'
A LETTER FROM THE ALPHABET PLEASE? *
```

String Manipulation Functions

The computer offers the programmer a variety of statements and functions to manipulate string information.

LEN

When dealing with string data, it is often important to determine the length, which is the number of characters contained in a certain data item. One use for this operation is to center headings on a report. The LEN function is used to accomplish this and takes the form:

$$L = LEN(A\$)$$

where L is a numeric variable assigned a value equal to the number of characters in the string variable A$.

Program 7.2

The following program demonstrates how the LEN function could be used to center report headings:

```
10 REM CENTER REPORT HEADINGS
20 FOR I = 1 TO 3
30    READ H$
40    L = LEN(H$) : T = INT((80 - L) / 2)
50    PRINT TAB(T); H$
60 NEXT I
70 DATA Acme Widget Co, Sales Report, 1st Quarter 1984

RUN

                    Acme Widget Co
                     Sales Report
                  1st Quarter 1984
```

Notice how the variables L and T are used in this example. The variable L is assigned the length of the report heading H$ read in line 30. In order to center the heading on the sales report, the length of the string is subtracted from the total width of the screen, 80. This value is divided by 2 to get the number of spaces to be TABbed in line 50.

**String Modification
MID$, LEFT$,
RIGHT$,**

It is possible to isolate one part of a string using the MID$, LEFT$, or RIGHT$ functions. The LEFT$ and RIGHT$ functions are similar and take the form:

$$L\$ = LEFT\$(B\$,N)$$

and

$$R\$ = RIGHT\$(B\$,N)$$

In the first example, L$ is assigned a substring of B$ starting from the left-most character up to and including the Nth character, while the second example assigns R$ a substring of B$ consisting of the rightmost N characters. For example, if

$$B\$ = \text{``COMPUTER''} \text{ and } N = 3$$

then

$$L\$ = \text{``COM''}$$
$$R\$ = \text{``TER''}$$

More powerful than either LEFT$ or RIGHT$ is the MID$ function. It takes the form

$$M\$ = MID\$(B\$,N,L)$$

where M$ is assigned a substring of B$ beginning with the Nth character and running for a length of L characters. For example,

```
10 B$ = "COMPUTER"
20 M$ = MID$ (B$, 4, 3)
30 PRINT M$

RUN
PUT
```

Besides isolating parts of strings, the programmer can "build" strings, using the addition (+) symbol. Unlike arithmetic addition, string addition joins two strings together. For example,

```
10 A = 20 : B = 40
20 A$ = "20" : B$ = "40"
30 PRINT A + B
40 PRINT A$ + B$
50 END

RUN
60
2040
```

Notice how the arithmetic addition of the numbers 20 and 40 yields 60 while the string addition of the strings "20" and "40" yields "2040".

Program 7.3   This program reads a sentence from a DATA statement and then prints it repeatedly, subtracting a word each time. It will then take a second sentence and add a word each time it is printed.

```
10 READ S$
20 FOR I = LEN(S$) TO 1 STEP -1
30    IF MID$(S$,I,1) = " " THEN PRINT LEFT$(S$,I-1)
40 NEXT I
50 READ S$
60 FOR I = LEN(S$) TO 1 STEP -1
70    IF MID$(S$,I,1) = " " THEN PRINT RIGHT$(S$,LEN(S$)-I)
80 NEXT I
90 DATA "I seem to keep forgetting one word "
100 DATA " But I think its coming back to me now"
110 END

RUN
I seem to keep forgetting one word
I seem to keep forgetting one
I seem to keep forgetting
I seem to keep
I seem to
I seem
I
now
me now
to me now
back to me now
coming back to me now
its coming back to me now
think its coming back to me now
I think its coming back to me now
But I think its coming back to me now
```

- **Line 10:** Assigns S$ the sentence contained in the first DATA statement.
- **Line 20:** Initiates a loop which will check for blank spaces in the sentence S$. The loop checks the sentence from the last character of the sentence (LEN(S$)) to the first.
- **Line 30:** When the MID$ function finds a blank space at position I in S$, the sentence is printed from the beginning to the position prior to where the blank was found (I-1) using LEFT$.
- **Line 40:** Ends the loop started in line 20.
- **Line 50:** Assigns S$ the second sentence from the DATA statements.
- **Line 60:** (Same as Line 20).
- **Line 70:** When the MID$ function finds a blank space at position I in S$, the sentence is printed from the place where the blank was found to the end of the sentence using RIGHT$.
- **Line 80:** Ends the loop started in line 60.

Review   4. What is the exact output of the following programs?

```
a. 10 A$ = "RESPECT"
   20 B$ = "COINCIDE"
   30 C$ = "STIFLE"
   40 PRINT MID$ (A$, 4, 2) + LEFT$ (C$, 3) + RIGHT$ (B$, 4)
   50 END
```

b. 10 W$ = "HOTDOG"
   20 FOR X = 1 TO 5
   30   IF LEFT $ (W$, X) > RIGHT$ (W$, X) THEN PRINT "LEFT "
   40   IF LEFT $ (W$, X) < RIGHT$ (W$, X) THEN PRINT "RIGHT "
   50 NEXT X
   60 END

Using Menus: INKEY$

The INKEY$ statement is used to enter data a character at a time and takes the form:

   A$ = INKEY$

When INKEY$ is executed, the computer scans the keyboard to determine if a key has been pressed and if one has, assigns the character or digit to the variable A$. If no key has been pressed during its scan a null character ("") is assigned. To allow time for a user to respond, it is necessary to place the INKEY$ statement within a delay loop which employs an IF...THEN statement. For example,

   20 A$ = INKEY$: IF A$ = "" THEN 20

will cause INKEY$ to continue scanning the keyboard until a key has been pressed. There are substantial differences between the INKEY$ and INPUT statements. First, INKEY$ does not require hitting the ENTER key. Second, INKEY$ does not supply a question mark (?) as a prompt to the user and third, INKEY$ does not display the character entered.

It is good programming style to make a program as simple and easy to use as possible. INKEY$ can be used to do this by giving the user a "menu" of choices. For example:

   CHOOSE THE TYPE OF PROBLEM TO REVIEW:

   1. ADDITION
   2. SUBTRACTION
   3. MULTIPLICATION
   4. DIVISION

   TYPE THE NUMBER OF YOUR SELECTION:

If INKEY$ is used to enter the selection, the computer will respond as soon as a number is typed.

Another method is to give the program user yes or no options:

   TYPE Y FOR YES OR N FOR NO.

Using INKEY$ simplifies these inputs by allowing a single keystroke to instruct the computer.

Although INKEY$ appears to have limited applications since only one character may be entered, this may be overcome by incorporating INKEY$ with a WHILE...WEND loop which employs MID$ and string addition.

Program 7.4   This program allows the user to enter a string of characters one character at a time until an asterisk (∗) is input:

```
10   WHILE  T$<> "*"
20      T$ = INKEY$ : IF T$ = "" THEN 20
30      A$ = A$+T$
40   WEND
50   A$ = MID$(A$,1,LEN(A$)-1)
60   PRINT A$
70 END

RUN
HELLO, CAN YOU SEE ME?
```

The MID$ function in line 50 truncates the asterisk from A$ by assigning A$ to a substring of itself, which is one character less than its total length. Since INKEY$ does not print what is entered, if line 60 were removed, this program could be used as the input routine for a word-guessing game or for entering security passwords.

**Input
Protection: VAL( )**   It is often useful to change the string character or characters of a number into its numeric value. This is done by assigning a numeric variable the VAL( ) of the string characters:

A = VAL(<string>)

The string that is within the parentheses can be either a string variable or a string of characters within quotation marks:

A = VAL(A$)
B = VAL("23")

VAL( ) will convert all combinations of the characters 0-9 into numeric values. The first non-numeric character that the computer encounters will halt the conversion of characters to numbers. A string that begins with a non-numeric character will be assigned a value of 0:

PRINT VAL("1234")
1234

PRINT VAL("2") + VAL("3")
5

PRINT VAL("007 JAMES BOND")
7

PRINT VAL("TWO")
0

An important use for VAL( ) is in preventing the accidental input of incorrect data that will halt a program with an error message. Errors caused by typing a non-numeric character when the computer is expecting numbers can be eliminated by using a string variable to input all data. After the data is entered as a string, it can then be changed into its numeric value using VAL( ). The following examples show how this technique can be used with INPUT or INKEY$:

```
50 INPUT "TYPE A NUMBER"; N$
60 N = VAL(N$)
```

or

```
80 A$ = INKEY$ : IF A$ = "" THEN 80
90 A = VAL(A$)
```

It is good programming style to prevent errors by using "preventive programming" techniques like this whenever possible.

Review

5. Write a program that will analyze a user's input and state whether it is numeric or alphanumeric.

```
RUN
? 14254
THE INPUT WAS NUMERIC

RUN
? 1K42P054
THE INPUT WAS ALPHANUMERIC
```

PRINT USING

The PRINT USING statement allows the programmer to format an entire line of output into zones of variable length. These zones may contain a series of numbers, strings, or a combination of both. The general form of PRINT USING is:

PRINT USING "<format>"; <variables or expressions>

The format may be either a string variable or a string enclosed within quotation marks. Its purpose is to inform the computer of the format which will be used in printing the variables or expressions. The format is made up of special symbols and characters which all have unique meanings. For example, the number sign (#) reserves a position for a single digit of numerical data.

Program 7.5

This program demonstrates some simple applications of the number sign symbol in a PRINT USING statement:

```
10 A = 25.68 : B = 3.21 : C = 2.4
20 PRINT USING "##.#   #.#   #"; A, B, C
30 PRINT
40 PRINT USING "##.##   #.#   #.#"; 3.798, 2.78, 3.55
50 END

RUN
25.7   3.2   2

 3.80   2.8   3.6
```

Notice how the format portion of the PRINT USING statement determines exactly where each digit will be printed and where the separate numbers will be spaced relative to one another. One of the most useful features of the PRINT USING statement is its ability to round numbers as demonstrated in line 20 where the value of variable A, 25.68 is printed as 25.7 because only the tenths digit is asked for in the format.

Formatting Numbers—#

Program 7.6

This program demonstrates a common problem with non-formatted computer output, the lack of uniformity of printed numbers:

```
10 FOR X = 1 TO 5
20    READ NUM
30      PRINT NUM
40 NEXT X
50 DATA 12398, 421, 54, 456789, 453
60 END

RUN
 12398
 421
 54
 456789
 453
```

The # symbol in the PRINT USING statement reserves one space for each # used in the output format. If line 30 is rewritten employing PRINT USING, it provides the user with a more logically structured list of numbers:

```
30 PRINT USING "######"; NUM

RUN
 12398
   421
    54
456789
   453
```

Notice how blank spaces were added to the left of the numbers so that they are right justified. If not enough spaces have been allotted in a numeric zone for a number to be properly printed, it will still be printed but preceded by a percent sign (%).

```
30 PRINT USING "#####"; NUM

RUN
12398
  421
   54
%456789
  453
```

More Numerical Formatting—.,$ $$ **$

Often the numbers printed by the computer will be decimal numbers and numbers with dollar signs. To provide for a decimal number, the period "." is used. It is placed at the position in a numeric format where the decimal point will be located. Similarly, the comma "," is used to indicate its location in a numeric format. This way, the number 438926.78 could be printed 438,926.78. In Program 7.6 line 30 could be edited so that the output would contain commas and decimal points:

```
30 PRINT USING "###,###.##"; NUM

RUN
 12,398.00
    421.00
     54.00
456,789.00
    453.00
```

When performing operations dealing with money, the $, $$ and **$ symbols may be used. The single dollar sign prints the "$" in the column where it is placed. It will be left justified in respect to the number it is associated with. The dual "$$" symbol will insert a "floating" dollar sign in the numeric field. In other words, the dollar sign will be placed directly in front of the first digit in the field. This technique is used when writing invoices or checks so that additional numbers cannot be inserted "accidentally" between the dollar sign and the first number. To further enhance the effect of the floating dollar sign, asterisks may be used to fill any leading blanks in a numeric field. The "**$" symbol fills all leading blanks with asterisks and also prints a floating dollar sign.

Program 7.7

This program illustrates the numeric format features of PRINT USING.

```
10 READ N
20 PRINT USING "######";N
30 PRINT USING "$######.##"; N
40 PRINT USING "$$###,###.##";N
50 PRINT USING  "**###,###.##";N
60 PRINT USING "**$###,###.##";N
70 DATA 12345.678

RUN
  12346
$ 12345.68
   $12,345.68
***12,345.68
***$12,345.68
```

**Formatting String Output—& ! **

When designing output, the format may have to take into account string variables. Often, it is necessary to output the entire string. If this is the case, the ampersand "&" character is used. It will represent a variable length string, which is to be located at that position in the ouput. If, however, only part of a string is needed, i.e., a person's initial or the first 5 letters of a last name, then the exclamation mark "!" or backslash "\\" character is used. The exclamation mark "!" is used to display only the first character of a string. This is especially useful for outputting initials. When only a partial string is needed, the backslash characters should be used. When there is no space between the backslash characters, the first 2 characters of a string are displayed. If there is one space between slashes, then 3 characters are printed. Therefore, if there are N number of spaces between slashes, N+2 characters are printed.

Program 7.8

This program demonstrates the use of the different formatting characters:

```
10 READ F$, M$, L$
20 PRINT USING "& & &"; F$, M$, L$
30 PRINT USING "!\\ \ \"; F$, M$, L$
40 PRINT USING "! ! !"; F$, M$, L$
50 DATA COMPUTERS, ARE, FUN
60 END

RUN
COMPUTERS ARE FUN
CAR FUN
C A F
```

Another possible technique is to place the format portion of the PRINT USING statement into a string. For example,

```
10 F$ = "##.#        ##      \      \ "
```

can be used later in a PRINT USING statement:

```
70 PRINT USING F$; A, B, N$
```

This technique is especially useful in formatting columns in a table so that they line up with their appropriate headings. The headings are typed in the line directly above the line containing the format string. By lining up the quotation marks in each of the lines, it is easy to produce the correct format:

```
10 PRINT "            Bank of America"
20 PRINT "          Quarterly Dividend Report"
30 PRINT
40 PRINT "Name                                    Amount "
50 PRINT "---------------------------------------------"
60 F$ = "\          \ will receive  **$###,###.##"
70 READ N$, D
80 WHILE N$ <> "ZZZZ"
90      PRINT USING F$; N$, D
100     READ N$, D
110 WEND
120 PRINT
130 DATA B Presley, 34564.22, M Porter, 22176.78
140 DATA M Bidwell, 66543.99, C Tibbetts, 12388.45
150 DATA H Crane, 23176.88, G Schwinn, 9176.33
160 DATA ZZZZ, 999
999 END
```

```
RUN
                  Bank of America
            Quarterly Dividend Report

    Name                              Amount
    -------------------------------------------
    B Presley       will receive    ***$34,564.22
    M Porter        will receive    ***$22,176.78
    M Bidwell       will receive    ***$66,544.00
    C Tibbetts      will receive    ***$12,388.45
    H Crane         will receive    ***$23,176.88
    G Schwinn       will receive    ****$9,176.33
```

- **Lines 10-50:** Produce headings for the Quarterly Dividend Report.
- **Line 60:** Stores the format employed by the PRINT USING statement in F$.
- **Line 70:** Reads in a shareholder's name N$, and dividend D.
- **Line 80:** Initiates a WHILE...WEND loop which will print the table for the report until the name "ZZZZ" has been read.
- **Line 90:** A PRINT USING statement is used to format the report.
- **Line 100:** This READ statement is used to continue reading the data while still in the loop. It is placed at this position so that the check for the terminating condition (N$ = "ZZZZ") will occur before the loop can be executed again.
- **Line 110:** Completes the loop initiated in line 80 and checks for the terminating condition.

The following table shows the valid characters which may be used in designing a PRINT USING format:

Symbol	Use	Examples
#	Reserve space for one digit.	### ##
.	Indicate location of decimal point within number sign (#) field.	#.### ###.##
,	Specify location of one or more commas within a # field.	##,###.## #,###
+	Display the sign of the number being printed. The + may be placed before or after the # field.	+###.# ####.##+
−	Display a leading or trailing minus sign regardless of the sign of the number.	−###.## ###−
$$	Display a single dollar sign just prior to the leftmost digit of a # field.	$$###.## $$#,###
**	Replace any leading blanks in a # field with asterisks.	**####.## **##.##
**$	This combines ** and $$ such that a single dollar sign will be displayed just prior to the leftmost digit in a # field. Any leading spaces remaining will be filled with asterisks.	**$###.## **$#.##

^ ^ ^ ^	Output a number in scientific notation.	#.### ^ ^ ^ ^
!	Output only the first character of a string.	!
\ \	Output only the first two characters of a string.	\ \
\ <n-2 spaces> \	Output the first n characters of a string.	\ \ \ \
_	Any single character preceded by an underscore will be printed.	_#
&	Allows a string of any length to be inserted in the output where specified.	&
<any other char>	Output any characters not in this table as though they were in a normal print statement.	ABCD Q12R

Review

6. Write a program to read in the data for the 5 employees of Wright Mfg. Corp. Calculate the gross pay (hours × rate) and deduct 25% (for taxes) to get the net pay. Display a formatted table of the employees, their hours, rate, gross pay and net pay using the following data:

NAME	HOURS	RATE
Mike	25	$10.00
Carol	37	$ 9.00
John	26	$ 6.00
Heidi	35	$ 7.00
Maggie	15	$ 5.00

End of Chapter Problem

The following is a program for a word guessing game which can be played by either one or two players. In the one-player game, the computer will choose a word at random from a list stored in DATA statements. In the two-player game, one player must "secretly" enter a word for the other player to guess. When the word has been chosen, the computer prompts the user to enter a letter. If the letter is in the word, the computer assigns it to its appropriate position in a blank string and prints the string. When the initially blank string is equal to the word, the game is over. The player continues to guess letters until either the word is guessed or 10 guesses have been made.

Algorithm:
1. Choose either one or two player game or exit.
2. If one player game, computer chooses a random word.
3. If a two player game, one player enters a word "secretly" using INKEY$.
4. Player picks a letter.
5. Computer checks to see if the letter is in the word.
6. If the letter is in the word then place the letter in the correct spot in an initially blank string.
7. If the string is equal to the word then the player wins.
8. Repeat steps 4 through 7 up to 10 times or until the word is guessed.
9. If the string is not equal to the word, then the player loses.
10. Go to step 1.

Variables:

Activity chosen by the player(s)	: PICK$
Word which the player has to guess	: WORD$
A one character string used in the construction of a word in a 2 player game	: T$
The letter guessed by the player	: G$
A string built from correct guesses.	: GUESS$

Program 7.10

```
10   CLS : LOCATE 9,10
20   PRINT "1) USER TO GUESS COMPUTER'S WORD"
30   PRINT TAB(10);"2) ONE PLAYER TO GUESS ANOTHER PLAYER'S WORD"
40   PRINT TAB(10);"3) EXIT PROGRAM"
50   PRINT TAB(10);"   ENTER SELECTION "
60   PICK$ = INKEY$ : IF PICK$ = "" THEN 60
70   P = VAL(PICK$) : IF P < 1 OR P > 3 THEN 10
80   ON P GOSUB 100, 200, 999
90   GOTO 10
100  REM
110  REM   **** WORD INPUT BY COMPUTER ****
120  REM
130  RANDOMIZE TIMER : RESTORE
140  FOR I = 1 TO INT(RND * 15 + 1)
150     READ WORD$
160  NEXT I
170  GOSUB 400
180  RETURN
200  REM
210  REM   **** WORD ENTERED BY PLAYER ONE ****
220  REM
230  PRINT "TYPE IN A WORD, FOLLOWED IMMEDIATELY BY AN ASTERISK (*)"
240  WORD$ = "" : T$ = ""
250  WHILE T$ <> "*"
260     T$ = INKEY$ : IF T$ = "" THEN 260
270     WORD$ = WORD$ + T$
280     PRINT "*";
290  WEND
300  WORD$ = LEFT$(WORD$, LEN(WORD$)-1)
310  GOSUB 400
320  RETURN
400  REM
410  REM   **** GUESS ROUTINE ****
420  REM
430  CLS : LOCATE 6,10
440  L = LEN(WORD$) : G = 1
450  PRINT "THE WORD HAS"; L; "LETTERS"
460  LOCATE 10,10
470  GUESS$ = STRING$(L,221)
480  PRINT GUESS$
490  WHILE G < 11
500      LOCATE 18,10 : PRINT "THIS IS GUESS #"; G; "OF 10"
510      LOCATE 19,10 : INPUT "GUESS A LETTER"; G$
520      FOR J = 1 TO L
530         IF MID$(WORD$,J,1) <> G$ THEN 550
                            ELSE MID$(GUESS$,J,1) = G$
540         LOCATE 10,10 : PRINT GUESS$
550      NEXT J
```

```
560        G = G + 1
570        IF GUESS$ = WORD$ THEN G = 11
580 WEND
590 LOCATE 14,10
600 IF GUESS$ = WORD$ THEN PRINT " Y O U   W I N "
                        ELSE PRINT "YOU LOSE...THE WORD WAS ";WORD$
610 FOR I = 1 TO 2000 : NEXT I : REM  DELAY
620 RETURN
700 REM
710 REM   **** PROGRAM DATA ****
720 REM
730 DATA COMPUTER, DISKETTE, BYTE, BINARY, STRING
740 DATA VARIABLE, SUBROUTINE, FUNCTION, NUMERIC, LETTER
750 DATA PROGRAM, LOOPS, SYNTAX, ERRORS, TESTING
999 REM
1000 REM   **** PROGRAM EXIT ROUTINE ****
1010 REM
1020 CLS
1030 END
RUN
```

```
        1) USER TO GUESS COMPUTER'S WORD
        2) ONE PLAYER TO GUESS ANOTHER PLAYER'S WORD
        3) EXIT PROGRAM
        ENTER SELECTION 1


        THE WORD HAS 6 LETTERS



        ------




        THIS IS GUESS # 1 OF 10
        GUESS A LETTER? N

              .
              .
              .

        THE WORD HAS 6 LETTERS


        BINARY


         Y O U   W I N



        THIS IS GUESS # 9 OF 10
        GUESS A LETTER? Y

        ENTER SELECTION 3
```

- **Lines 10-50:** Clear the screen and display a menu of activities.
- **Line 60:** Uses INKEY$ to assign a value to PICK$. This program line will continue to exectue until a key has been pressed.
- **Line 70:** The numeric value of PICK$ is assigned to P. If the value of P is not within the acceptable range, then the program begins again.
- **Line 80:** The program now branches to a subroutine based upon the value of P.
- **Lines 100-180:** ✶✶✶✶ WORD INPUT BY COMPUTER ✶✶✶✶
- **Line 130:** Ensure a different series of random numbers each time the program is run and also that the data is read from the beginning.
- **Lines 140-160:** Read in a random number of words from the DATA statements. The final word read in the loop will be the word that the user has to guess.
- **Line 170:** Branches to the GUESSING ROUTINE.
- **Lines 200-320:** ✶✶✶✶ WORD ENTERED BY PLAYER ONE ✶✶✶✶
- **Lines 250-290:** Build a word using INKEY$ and a WHILE...WEND loop.
- **Line 300:** Truncates the asterisk off WORD$ using LEFT$.
- **Line 310:** Branches to the GUESSING ROUTINE
- **Lines 400-610:** ✶✶✶✶ GUESSING ROUTINE ✶✶✶✶
- **Line 440:** Assigns L the length of the string in WORD$ and initializes the guess counter, G.
- **Line 470:** Initializes GUESS$ by assigning it a string of block characters (ASCII 221) which is L characters long.
- **Line 490:** Initiates a WHILE...WEND loop for guessing the word.
- **Line 520:** Initializes a loop which will control the checking of the word.
- **Line 530:** Incorporates the MID$ function to see if the guessed letter G$ is in WORD$. If it is, the MID$ statement is used to place the guessed letter in the correct position in GUESS$.
- **Line 540:** Shows the user how much of WORD$ has been guessed.
- **Line 550:** Completes the loop started in line 620.
- **Line 560:** Increments guess counter, G.
- **Line 580:** Completes the loop initiated in line 590.
- **Line 590:** Places the cursor at the tenth position of the 14th line on the screen.
- **Line 600:** If GUESS$ equals WORD$ then the player wins, otherwise the player has lost.

EXERCISES

1. Enter a string A$ and use a loop to print the ASCII number of each of its characters.

2. Input three letters, add their ASCII numbers, find the INT of one third of their sum and print the character corresponding to the result. Is there any meaning to this process?

3. Using properly selected ASCII numbers in a DATA statement, print the sentence "ASCII DID THIS!".

4. Using ASCII numbers 45 and 46 and the PRINT TAB statement, print the following figure:

   RUN

5. Enter the string THREE!@ $%STRING!@#$%FUNCTIONS. Use LEFT$, MID$, and RIGHT$ to print the phase "THREE STRING FUNCTIONS".

6. Enter a string A$ of any length. Print the length of A$ and the ASCII number of its first and last characters.

7. Write a program where you input a name and then have the computer print the ASCII number of the letter which appears most often in the name.

```
RUN
Name? FREDDY
D is the most common letter in FREDDY, which is ASC( 68 )
```

8. Find the binary equivalents of the decimal values given below:

   89, 74, 80, 107, 255, 129, 28, 39, 29, 24, 43

9. Find the decimal equivalents for the binary values given below:

$$1011, \ 10100, \ 1111, \ 1110, \ 1010011, \ 110011, \ 1011100$$
$$1101111, \ 11000000, \ 10000111$$

10. INPUT a string A$ which consists of the digits 0 to 9, inclusive, each to be used only once (e.g. 1956472038). Use string functions to obtain from A$ two numbers N1 and N2, N1 being the number represented by the first three digits in A$ and N2 the number represented by the last three digits. Print the sum of N1 and N2.

11. Let A$ consist of the first twelve letters of the alphabet. Using A$, construct the right triangle shown at the right:

```
RUN
A
AB
ABC
ABCD
ABCDE
ABCDEF
ABCDEFG
ABCDEFGH
ABCDEFGHI
ABCDEFGHIJ
ABCDEFGHIJK
ABCDEFGHIJKL
```

12. As a young boy Franklin Roosevelt signed his letters to his mother backwards: TLEVESOOR NILKNARF. Write a program that accepts a person's name and prints it backwards.

13. Using the ASCII chart given in the text, determine the output for the following program. Check by running the program:

```
10 FOR A = 1 TO 4
20     READ A$
30     PRINT ASC (A$)
40 NEXT A
50 DATA "W", "H", "7", "625"
60 END
```

14. The output of the following program is Jill's message to Jack. What is the message? Check by running the program:

```
10 FOR W = 1 TO 6
20      READ A$, B$, C$
30      PRINT LEFT$ (A$,1); MID$ (B$,2,2); RIGHT$ (C$,1)
40 NEXT W
50 END
60 REM data section
70 DATA JDO,ILXP,LUL
80 DATA SSS,HAYE,RRS
90 DATA HYF,OELR,EVP
100 DATA WER,LILO,VEL
110 DATA CIS,TOMH,EIE
120 DATA SRS,WOOI,SHN
```

15. Choose fifteen random integers from 65 to 90, inclusive, to serve as ASCII code numbers. Convert these fifteen integers to the fifteen characters for which they stand and print the results.

16. Write a program which produces a sentence containing twenty nonsense words. Each word can contain from two to five letters. Use random numbers and the ASCII code to produce the words.

```
RUN
SIJWX UDMP OJV EXUQN MAQ XU EX PGDSX
ZCTY RLZNH RXO YRZIH TALYS TWXO OZU
EV EXVPD RHQ NTRGG DA
```

17. Using random numbers and the ASCII code numbers from 32 to 126, inclusive, have the computer generate a string of 100 characters, allowing repetitions. Tabulate how many characters are letters, numbers or miscellaneous characters. Print the results including a list of the characters:

```
RUN
There are: 47 letters.
           16 numbers, and
           37 special characters
c'M ˜ ],CW,x4 = 6uWK n"CPT∗BmrGc Ymh)Ssn1RO2>Cw2Vqb + n
#>_'S( |Hfela4Ud^Qu{O4#h$r>O&$$8& = Q'p3$b5>}2!3XY#G4
```

18. You are a spy who will use the computer to produce a secret code.

    (a) INPUT a short message and have the computer type back what appear to be nonsense words. To produce the coded words, convert each letter of the original message into its corresponding ASCII code number, add two to each number and convert to characters to produce the message. Keep all spaces between the words in their original places and realize that the letters Y and Z are to be converted to A and B.

    (b) Write a program that will decode the following message:

    ```
    NCYTGPEGXKNNG
    UEJQQN
    ```

19. Write a program which prints a triangle made up of parts of the word "triangle". The triangle should be obtuse, and the program should ask for its height (A), how far to indent the bottom edge (B), and where the bottom edge ends (C).

```
RUN
A, B, and C? 10, 10, 20
T
 RI
  IAN
   ANGL
    NGLET
     GLETRI
      LETRIAN
       ETRIANGL
        TRIANGLET
         RIANGLETRI
```

20. Last night you were informed that your aunt had left you several million dollars. You decide to start your own corporation. In the tradition of DEC, GTE, RCA, IBM, and other great corporate conglomerates, you want your corporate name to be composed of initials, each standing for a word (e.g., Radio Corporation of American becomes RCA). Write a program which accepts up to ten words tand then prints a block of letters composed of the first letters of each word. For example, given "WE AWAIT SILENT TRYSTERO'S EMPIRE", the program should return "WASTE".

Advanced Exercises

Each of the following exercises requires the development of a detailed algorithm. The program should not be written until all details of the algorithm have been worked out.

21. Using string functions, write a program to play a word guessing game. Ask the player to guess a secret word. Search through each guess to see if the guess contains any correct letters. If any letters are correct, have the computer print them. If the entire word is guessed, type "YOU GUESSED IT!!".

```
RUN
Guess a word? HANGMAN
'A' is in the word.
'A' is in the word.
Guess a word? DATAPHONE
'A' is in the word.
'A' is in the word.
'E' is in the word.
Guess a word? TERMINAL
'E'is in the word.
'R' is in the word.
'A' is in the word.
'L' is in the word.
Guess a word? SCRABBLE
YOU GUESSED IT!!
```

22. Often, literary critics argue over the identity of the author of some ancient manuscript. To resolve such disputes, it is helpful to show similarities between the anonymous text and a text by a known author. Write a program which checks a text and tabulates the occurrences of each article ("a", "an", and "the"), each adverb (check for "ly"), and of each mark of punctuation (".", ",", "!", "?", ";", ":").

```
       RUN
       There are: 2 periods,
                  7 commas,
                  2 exclamation marks,
                  1 question marks,
                  0 semicolons,
                  1 colons,
                  4 'a's,
                  0 'an's,
                  3 'the's, and
                  5 adverbs
       in the passage.
```

Use the following DATA:

```
       DATA "    Dear Mr. Fields,"
       DATA "          We happily announce that you have won"
       DATA "    the grand prize in our Publisher's Warehouse"
       DATA "    Sweepstakes! What have I won, you may"
       DATA "    ask? You've won the following:"
       DATA "          1) a 1958 Edsel,"
       DATA "          2) a year's supply of puppy chow,"
       DATA "          3) a cuddly pair of siamese cats,"
       DATA "             and finally,"
       DATA "          4) a trip for 2 to the South Pole!"
       DATA "                    Sincerely,"
       DATA "                    M. West"
```

8

COLOR GRAPHICS
AND SOUND

*O*ften, a picture or graphic display is the best way to get a message across. Using a pie chart to represent sales percentages or a bar diagram to show a company's revenues are two examples. This chapter will deal with the BASIC statements needed to create graphic displays on the IBM PC and PCjr.

In order to create graphics on the PC, a Color/Graphics Monitor Adapter must be installed in your machine. The PCjr, on the other hand, has color graphics capabilities already built-in. It must be noted that there are differences in the graphics capabilities of these two machines. However, any graphics routine which runs on the PC also runs on PCjr. Basically, these differences stem from the fact that the PCjr has more screen modes which allow for greater color variation and flexibility. This chapter only covers material applicable to both machines.

MODE

On the PC with both the Color/Graphics and Monochrome Display Cards installed, the output is normally directed to the monochrome display. In order to activate the color display, first exit BASIC by typing the command SYSTEM. You will now see the 'A>' prompt. The MODE command is then used to switch the displays. The command

MODE CO80

will activate the color screen in 80-column mode. The command

MODE CO40

will accomplish the same except the screen will be in 40-column mode. In order to switch back to the monochrome display, the command

MODE MONO

is used. Since the graphics capabilities of the PCjr are built in, the MODE command is not needed.

There are three different screen modes: text, medium-resolution graphics and high-resolution graphics. A mode is merely the way the computer displays information on the screen. The first mode is called text mode because it allows character data (letters, numbers, special characters, etc.) to be displayed on the screen in a variety of text and background colors. The second, medium-resolution graphics mode, provides an area for graphing which is 320 horizontal positions by 200 vertical positions. Finally, the high-resolution graphics mode provides for pictures of even finer detail by further dividing the screen into an area of 640 horizontal positions by 200 vertical positions.

SCREEN

In order to create graphic displays, the computer must first be put into the correct mode. This is accomplished through the SCREEN statement

SCREEN <mode>,<burst>

where mode represents one of the three graphics modes and burst indicates whether to display output in black and white or color. Burst operates differently in different modes. The following chart shows the relationship between mode and burst in the three different graphics modes:

Mode	Meaning	Burst
0	text	0 = black & white 1 = color
1	medium-resolution	0 = color 1 = black & white
2	high-resolution	no effect

For example, the statement

10 SCREEN 0,0

puts the computer into text mode with a black and white display, while

10 SCREEN 1,0

puts the computer into medium-resolution graphics mode with the color turned on. The statement

10 SCREEN 2

puts the computer into high-resolution mode. Notice that burst was not used in this example because high-resolution mode produces pictures in only black and white. Since color is not available in high-resolution mode, the burst value has been omitted.

COLOR

The COLOR statement is needed to set the color characteristics of the display after a screen command has been issued. There are a total of 16 colors available; however, the number of colors is limited by which mode the computer is in. The available colors are:

Color Table

0 — BLACK	8 — GRAY
1 — BLUE	9 — LIGHT BLUE
2 — GREEN	10 — LIGHT GREEN
3 — CYAN	11 — LIGHT CYAN
4 — RED	12 — LIGHT RED
5 — MAGENTA	13 — LIGHT MAGENTA
6 — BROWN	14 — YELLOW
7 — WHITE	15 — BRIGHT WHITE

COLOR in Text Mode

When using the text mode (SCREEN 0,1), the COLOR statement takes the form

COLOR <foreground>,<background>,<border>

The foreground, or color of the text, may have a value of 0-15, inclusive. For example, having the foreground color equal to 5 will produce magenta characters. The characters can be made to blink on and off by adding 16 to the foreground value (producing a number between 16 and 31). Using the previous example, we could produce flashing magenta characters by inserting the foreground value of 21 (5 + 16 = 21). The background can only be a color with a value of 0-7, inclusive. Finally the border, or edge of the screen, can be any color, so it can take the value of 0-15. The statements

```
10 SCREEN 0,1
20 COLOR 0,4,8
```

produce black characters on a red background with a gray border.

It is possible to change one of the COLOR values without changing the other values. For example,

```
30 COLOR ,8
```

leaves the character and border colors at their current values and changes only the background to white. In other words, any value which is omitted in the COLOR statement will retain its current value. It is important to remember to insert the appropriate commas when only changing one or two of the values.

The CLS statement should be used following the COLOR statement. This not only clears the screen of unwanted text but also changes the screen color entirely to the background color.

Program 8.1

This program illustrates the different colors available in the text mode:

```
10 REM  Using SCREEN and COLOR in text mode
20 SCREEN 0,1
30 COLOR 0, 5, 1
40 CLS
50 LOCATE 4,11
60 PRINT "You can write in: BLACK"
70 FOR I = 1 TO 15
80    READ HUE$
90    COLOR I
100    PRINT TAB(29); HUE$
110 NEXT I
120 DATA BLUE, GREEN, CYAN, RED, MAGENTA, BROWN
130 DATA WHITE, GRAY, LIGHT BLUE, LIGHT GREEN
140 DATA LIGHT CYAN, LIGHT RED, LIGHT MAGENTA
150 DATA YELLOW, BRIGHT WHITE
```

```
                        RUN

                        You can write in: BLACK
                                          BLUE
                                          GREEN
                                          CYAN
                                          RED

                                          BROWN
                                          WHITE
                                          GRAY
                                          LIGHT BLUE
                                          LIGHT GREEN
                                          LIGHT CYAN
                                          LIGHT RED
                                          LIGHT MAGENTA
                                          YELLOW
                                          BRIGHT WHITE
```

- **Line 20:** Puts the computer into text mode with the color on.
- **Line 30:** Sets the background color to magenta, with black characters and a blue border.
- **Line 40:** It is important to notice what this program line does. When this statement is executed, the entire background becomes magenta. This does not automatically occur when the COLOR statement is executed. If this line were omitted, the background would only be magenta around the printed characters.
- **Line 50:** Moves the cursor to the beginning of the fourth line where the printing starts.
- **Line 60:** Displays the first line of output in black characters.
- **Line 70:** Initiates the loop which displays the names of the available foreground colors in their respective hues.
- **Line 80:** Reads the names of each color to be displayed.
- **Line 90:** Sets the foreground (text) color to the value of variable I.
- **Line 100:** Displays the value of HUE$ in its appropriate color. Notice how color #5 (magenta) is "invisible".
- **Line 110:** Completes the loop begun in line 70.
- **Lines 120-150:** Supply the data for HUE$.

Review

1. Write a program which will print the following output:

```
        RUN

        OLD GLORY IS MADE UP OF
                RED
                WHITE
        AND BLUE STRIPES.
```

using gray characters with a green background. Have the word for each color (red, white and blue) print in that color.

COLOR in
Graphics Mode

Of the two graphics modes, the COLOR statement can be used only in medium-resolution mode. This is because the high-resolution mode creates pictures only in black and white. The format for the COLOR statement in medium-resolution graphics mode is

COLOR <background>,<palette>

The background can have the value of 0-15, thus taking on any color available to the computer. Only the medium-resolution graphics mode contains the palette option, the value of which can be either 0 or 1. Each of the two palettes allows the programmer to select one of three foreground colors. In addition to these, it is possible to choose the background color (0), in which case the foreground and background will be the same.

Palette 0		**Palette 1**	
Color #	**Color Name**	**Color #**	**Color Name**
0	<background>	0	<background>
1	Green	1	Cyan
2	Red	2	Magenta
3	Brown	3	White

In both cases, color 0 is assigned to the background color which has been chosen by the COLOR statement. The statements

10 SCREEN 1,0
20 COLOR 12,1

puts the computer into medium-resolution graphics mode and selects a background color of light red (pink). The use of palette 1 means that the available plotting colors are cyan (1), magenta (2) and white (3), as well as the background color of light red (0). However, the statements

10 SCREEN 1,0
20 COLOR 14,0

would still put the computer into medium-resolution graphics mode and select a background color of yellow. Using palette 0 means that the colors green (1), red (2) and brown (3), as well as the background color of yellow (0), are available.

Review

2. What do each of the following sets of statements accomplish?

a. 10 SCREEN 0,1
   20 COLOR 12,6,8
   30 COLOR 5,,6
   40 COLOR 25,7
   50 COLOR ,3,3
   60 COLOR ,,1

b. 10 SCREEN 1,0
   20 COLOR 12,1
   30 COLOR 5
   40 COLOR ,0
   50 COLOR 5,1

PSET and PRESET   Graphics statements are needed to actually produce a picture. The simplest graphing statement to use is PSET, which will plot a single point on the screen at the position indicated. Of course, the computer must be in one of the two graphics modes (SCREEN 1 or SCREEN 2). The general form of the PSET statement is:

PSET (X,Y),<color>

The (X,Y) values refer to the horizontal (X) and the vertical (Y) coordinates which are to be used to plot the point. If the medium-resolution screen is used, X can have a value from 0 to 319 and in high-resolution mode, X can vary from 0 to 639. In either mode, however, the Y value can range from 0 to 199.

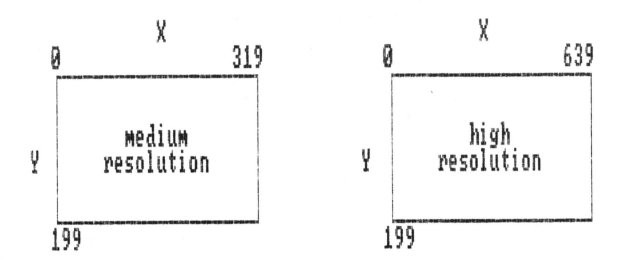

In medium-resolution graphics mode, the <color> value refers to the color of the point to be plotted, which is based upon the palette chosen in the most recent COLOR statement. For example,

```
10 SCREEN 1,0
20 COLOR 9,0
30 PSET (250,125), 2
```

will plot a red point at coordinates (250,125) on the medium-resolution screen. Remember that only four colors are available for plotting as determined by the preselected palette.

The PSET statement does not need the <color> value in high-resolution mode, since it automatically takes on the color white with a background color of black. If the <color> value is omitted in medium-resolution mode, a value of 3 is automatically assumed.

To "black-out" a plotted point, use the PRESET statement, which selects the background color to do its plotting. The PRESET statement takes the form:

PRESET (X,Y)

Program 8.2

This program will flash a point at (89,89) on and off 100 times. This is accomplished by setting the point on in line 30 and turning it off in line 50:

```
10 SCREEN 1, 0 : COLOR 12, 1
20 FOR K = 1 TO 100
30    PSET (89, 89), 3
40    FOR I = 1 TO 300 : NEXT I : REM Delay
50    PRESET(89, 89)
60    FOR I = 1 TO 300 : NEXT I : REM Delay
70 NEXT K
80 END
```

- **Line 10:** Puts the computer into medium-resolution graphics mode with a background color of light red using palette 1.
- **Line 20:** Starts a loop which turns a point on and off 100 times.
- **Line 30:** Uses PSET to plot a white point at location (89,89).
- **Line 40:** A delay loop to keep the point on the screen long enough to be seen.
- **Line 50:** Uses PRESET to turn off the point at location (89,89).
- **Line 60:** A second delay loop.
- **Line 70:** Completes the loop started in line 20.
- **Line 80:** Exits the program.

Program 8.3

This program draws a vertical line from (30,10) to (30,120) and then erases it by setting each point to the background color:

```
10 REM Green background, Palette 0
20 SCREEN 1,0 : COLOR 2,0
30 REM Plot the line
40 FOR Y = 10 TO 120
50    PSET (30,Y), 2 : REM Plot a point
60 NEXT Y
70 REM   Now erase the line
80 FOR Y = 10 TO 120
90    PRESET (30,Y) : REM Erase a point
100 NEXT Y
110 SCREEN 0,0 : WIDTH 80
120 END
```

- **Line 20:** Sets the computer to medium-resolution graphics mode and chooses a green background with palette 0.
- **Line 40:** Initiates the loop used to draw the line.
- **Line 50:** Plots a point used to form a line in color 2 (red).
- **Line 60:** Ends the loop started in line 40.
- **Line 80:** Initiates the loop which will "black-out" the line.
- **Line 90:** Uses PRESET to "black-out" the line point-by-point by plotting in the background color.
- **Line 100:** Completes the loop started by line 80.
- **Line 110:** Sets the screen back into text mode with the color off and the width set to 80-characters. This is a good programming practice.

Review

3. Write a program using PSET to draw 500 randomly placed "stars" on a black background. Print "STARRY STARRY NIGHT" on the 24th line.

LINE

In Program 8.3, the PSET statement was used to draw a line by plotting contiguous points with a FOR...NEXT loop. A more efficient way of getting the same output is to use the LINE statement. In its simplest form, the LINE statement is:

LINE (X1,Y1) – (X2,Y2), <color>

The LINE statement uses the same coordinate system as the PSET statement and plots a single line from (X1,Y1) to (X2,Y2). The <color> value will correspond to that color in the current palette. The statements

100 SCREEN 1,0 : COLOR 9,1
110 LINE (0,0) – (319,199), 2

draw a diagonal magenta line from the upper-left corner of the screen (0,0) to the lower-right corner (319,199).

Another way to use the LINE statement is to omit the first pair of coordinates

LINE – (X2,Y2), <color>

which draws a line from the last point referenced (i.e., by the last LINE, PSET, etc) to the point (X2,Y2). The <color> value works the same way as in the first example. The program lines

130 SCREEN 1,0 : COLOR 7,0
140 PSET (319,0), 3
150 LINE – (0,199), 3

draw a brown diagonal line from the upper-right corner of the screen (319,0), as referenced by the PSET in line 140, to the lower-left corner of the screen (0,199), as referenced in the LINE statement in line 150.

Besides drawing lines, the LINE statement can be adapted to draw boxes through use of the B (block) option. To construct a box, the LINE statement takes the form:

LINE (X1,Y1) – (X2,Y2), <color>,B

The statement above draws a box where points (X1,Y1) and (X2,Y2) represent opposite corners of the box:

Rather than just draw the outline of a box, the LINE statement can be further adapted to color in the box, using the BF (block-fill) option. It takes the form:

LINE (X1,Y1) – (X2,Y2), <color>, BF

Program 8.4

This program will draw a house employing the various features of the LINE statement:

```
10 REM Draw a house using the LINE statement
20 SCREEN 1,0: COLOR 0,0
30 REM Draw the roof
40 LINE (10,60) - (155,0), 2
50 LINE - (300,60), 2
60 REM Draw the body of the house
70 LINE (10,60) - (300,190), 2, B
80 REM Draw the doors and windows
90 LINE (140,120) - (170,190), 3, BF
100 LINE (60,80) - (90,100), 3, BF
110 LINE (220,80) - (250,100), 3, BF
120 END
```

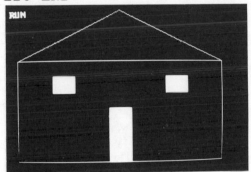

- **Line 20:** Puts the computer into medium-resolution graphics mode, sets the background to black and chooses palette 0.
- **Line 40:** Draws a red line from (10,60) to (155,0) which will be used as the left side of the roof.
- **Line 50:** Continues the red line drawn in line 40 to form the right side of the roof.
- **Line 70:** The block (B) option is used to form the body of the house in red.
- **Line 90:** The block-fill (BF) option is used to draw the door in brown.
- **Line 100-110:** The BF option is once again utilized to draw the windows of the house in brown.

Review

4. Write a program to draw 6 filled rectangles, each 60 × 30.

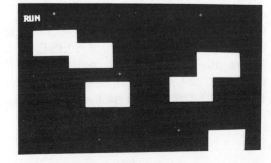

POINT

The POINT function returns the value of the color currently displayed at a specified point on the screen. The statement

70 N = POINT (X,Y)

will assign N a value between 0 and 3 when using medium-resolution mode. A value of 0 indicates that the color of the selected point is the same as the background color. A value of 1, 2 or 3 corresponds to a color from the current palette, as selected by the most recent COLOR statement. If −1 is returned by the POINT function, then the coordinates given are not on the screen. Remember that in medium-resolution mode, the X value must be between 0 and 319, while the Y value must lie between 0 and 199.

In high-resolution mode, the POINT function will return either 0 for a black point or 1 for a white point. A value of −1 is returned if the specified point is not on the screen. Remember that in high-resolution mode the X value must be between 0 and 639, while the Y value must lie between 0 and 199.

Program 8.5

This program illustrates the POINT function.

```
10  SCREEN 1,0 : COLOR 8,0
20  LOCATE 9,1
30  PSET (18,12), 1
40  LINE (10,20) - (85,20), 2
50  LINE (10,25) - (85,45), 3, BF
60  FOR T = 1 TO 4
70     READ X,Y : REM Coordinates
80     R = POINT (X,Y)
90     PRINT "Point at ("; X; ","; Y; ") is "; R
100 NEXT T
110 DATA 20,30,  18,12,  45,11,  47,20
120 END
RUN
```

```
Point at ( 20 , 30 ) is  3
Point at ( 18 , 12 ) is  1
Point at ( 45 , 11 ) is  0
Point at ( 47 , 20 ) is  2
Ok
```

- **Line 10:** Sets the computer to medium-resolution graphics mode with a gray background and palette 0.
- **Line 20:** Positions the text cursor at the beginning of the ninth line.
- **Lines 30-50:** Use PSET and LINE to draw figures of different colors.
- **Lines 60-100:** This loop reads in X and Y coordinates to determine the color of those positions using the POINT function.
- **Line 110:** Data used as the coordinates for the POINT function.

CIRCLE

The CIRCLE statement is used to draw a circle or ellipse on the screen while in one of the two graphics modes. The general form of the CIRCLE statement is:

CIRCLE (X,Y), <radius>, <color>

The coordinates (X,Y) specify the center of the circle and the <radius> specifies the distance from the center of the circle to its perimeter. In medium-resolution mode only, the <color> value is used to select a color from the current palette defined by the COLOR statement. It is not needed in high-resolution mode.

Program 8.6

Using the CIRCLE statement, this program produces the five-ring Olympic logo:

```
5 REM Draw the Olympic rings with the CIRCLE statement
10 SCREEN 1,0 : COLOR 8,0
20 FOR R = 20 TO 22
30     CIRCLE (50,50), R, 2
40     CIRCLE (99,50), R, 2
50     CIRCLE (148,50), R, 2
60     CIRCLE (74,70), R, 2
70     CIRCLE (124,70),R, 2
80 NEXT R
90 END
RUN
```

- **Line 10:** Sets the computer to medium-resolution graphics mode with a background color of gray using palette 0.
- **Line 20:** Initializes the loop which draws each of the circles three times with radii of 20, 21 and 22, respectively. This allows the program to draw thicker circles by drawing concentric circles with increasingly larger radii.
- **Lines 30-70:** These lines actually draw the circles which form the Olympic rings. Notice how the radius of each circle is represented by the variable R.
- **Line 80:** Ends the loop started in line 20.

The CIRCLE statement can be expanded to print just an arc of a circle by specifying the starting and ending angles in radians.

CIRCLE (X,Y), <radius>, <color>, <start>, <end>

To convert from degrees to radians, multiply the number of degrees by PI/180. For example:

$45° = 45 * (PI/180) = PI/4$ radians

The start and end angles specify where the drawing is to begin and end as follows:

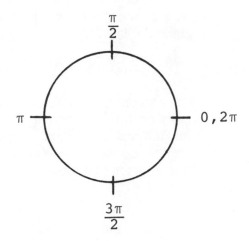

Any value between 0 and 2PI may be used. If either the <start> or <end> angle is negative, the arc will be connected to the center (X,Y) with a line. The angles are then treated as if they were positive.

Program 8.7
This program uses the arc features of the CIRCLE statement to draw a variety of arcs:

```
10 PI = 3.14159
20 SCREEN 1,0 : COLOR 0,1 : LOCATE 1,1
30 PRINT "Some Simple Arcs:"
40 CIRCLE (24,40), 20, 2, PI/2, PI
50 CIRCLE (175,40), 25, 1, 0, PI
60 CIRCLE (225,40), 25, 1, PI, 2*PI
70 LOCATE 11,1
80 PRINT "Arcs with negative angles:"
90 CIRCLE (122,120), 22, 3, -5*PI/4, -3*PI/4
100 CIRCLE (175,135), 38, 2, -3*PI/8, -5*PI/8
110 END
RUN
```

- **Line 10:** Sets PI equal to 3.14159.
- **Line 20:** Puts the computer into medium-resolution graphics mode with a black background using palette 1. The text cursor is placed in the upper-left corner.
- **Lines 40-60:** Draw arcs utilizing positive angles.
- **Lines 90-100:** Draw arcs with negative angles. Notice how the arcs with negative angles have lines connecting the perimeter to the center of the circle.

The CIRCLE statement can be further expanded to draw ellipses by including a ratio of the X-radius to the Y-radius:

CIRCLE (X,Y), <radius>, <color>, <start>, <end>, <ratio>

If the <ratio> is less than 1, then the <radius> is the X-radius. That is, the value input for the <radius> represents the horizontal distance from the center of the ellipse (X,Y) to its perimeter. The Y-radius will then be equal to <ratio> * <radius>.

If the <ratio> is greater than one, then the <radius> refers to the Y-radius, the vertical distance from the ellipse's center to its perimeter. The X-radius then equals <radius> / <ratio>. For example, the statement

70 CIRCLE (100,85), 60, 1,,,0.5

produces:

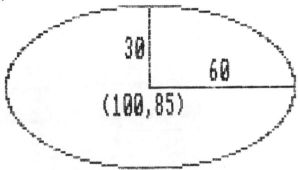

Program 8.8 This program draws a face using the CIRCLE statement and its ellipse function:

```
10 PI = 3.14159
20 REM Put computer into graphics mode
30 SCREEN 1,0 : COLOR 0,1
40 REM Draw the outline of the face
50 CIRCLE (150,90),140,3,,,,.5
60 REM Draw the nose
70 CIRCLE (150,80),35,3,,,7
80 REM Draw the eyes
90 CIRCLE (99,60),15,3
100 CIRCLE (199,60),15,3
110 CIRCLE (99,60),2,3
120 CIRCLE (199,60),2,3
130 REM Draw the mouth
140 CIRCLE (150,130),50,3,-PI,-2*PI,.4
150 END
```

- **Line 30:** Puts the computer into medium-resolution graphics mode with a background color of black using palette 1.
- **Line 50:** Uses the ellipse option of the CIRCLE statement to draw an oval face.
- **Line 70:** Uses the ellipse option of the CIRCLE statement to draw an oval nose.
- **Lines 90-120:** Use concentric circles to form the eyes.
- **Line 140:** Uses the arc and ellipse functions of the CIRCLE statement to form the mouth.

Review

5. Write a program to draw the pattern of concentric ellipses shown below. There is a total of 30 ellipses, with 10 of each color.

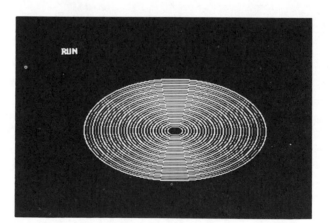

PAINT

The PAINT statement is used to color in a figure on the screen. The general form of the PAINT statement is:

PAINT (X,Y), <color>, <edge>

X and Y must be the coordinates of any point located within the figure to be painted. The figure will be shaded in the selected <color> from the current pallete. The color of the figure's outline must be specified in <edge>. For example, if a circle centered at (60,150) has a red perimeter and is to be filled in with the color green, use the statement:

PAINT (60,150), 1, 2

Program 8.9   This program employs the PAINT statement to draw a painter's palette with four paint blotches on it:

```
10 PI = 3.1415
20 SCREEN 1,0 : COLOR 0,0
30 LOCATE 1,15
40 PRINT "palette #1"
50 REM  Draw the outline of the palette
60 CIRCLE (150,90),140,2,5*PI/4,3*PI/4,.5
70 LINE (50,40) - (50,140), 2
80 REM  Draw the outlines for the paint blotches
90 CIRCLE (80,120), 25, 2,,,,.5
100 CIRCLE (120,50), 20, 2,,,1.5
110 CIRCLE (170,55), 20, 2,,,1.5
120 CIRCLE (260,80), 20, 2,,,1.5
130 REM  Fill in the palette and paint blotches with color
140 PAINT (150,90), 2, 2
150 CIRCLE (215,65), 20, 3,,,1.5
160 PAINT (170,55), 1, 2
170 PAINT (260,80), 3, 2
180 REM Label th paint blotches
190 FOR I = 0 TO 3
200     READ R,C
210     LOCATE R,C : PRINT I
220 NEXT I
230 DATA 7,15,8,21,9,27,10,32
240 END
```

RUN

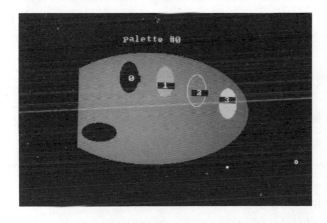

- **Line 20:** Puts the screen into medium-resolution graphics mode with a black background using palette 0.
- **Lines 30-40:** Display a title centered above the picture.
- **Lines 60-70:** Draw the outline of the palette using the CIRCLE and LINE statements.
- **Line 90:** Uses the CIRCLE statement to draw the thumb-hole in the palette.
- **Lines 100-120:** Use the CIRCLE statement to draw the paint blotches.
- **Line 140:** Uses the PAINT statement to fill in the palette with color 2.
- **Line 150:** Uses a CIRCLE statement to draw an oval in color 3 to represent the blotch for color 2. If this oval were drawn before line 140 is executed, the PAINT statement would have colored over it.
- **Lines 160-170:** Use the PAINT statement to color in the blotches for colors 1 and 3.

- **Lines 190-220:** Form a loop which will read in the cursor positions for the color labels and print at the appropriate positions.
- **Line 230:** Contains the data for the coordinates read in line 200.

Review

6. Using the Paint statement, rewrite Program 8.8 to fill in the face with color.

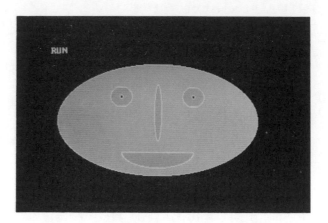

ADDING SOUND TO PROGRAMS

BEEP

The BEEP statement causes the computer to produce a short beep (a tone of 800 Hz for 1/4 second) to attract the user's attention. For example,

```
10 INPUT "ENTER NAME"; N$
20 IF N$ < "A" OR N$ > "Z" THEN BEEP : GOTO 10
```

will cause the computer to beep if a non-alphabetic name is entered.

SOUND

Some programs can be made more interesting if sound is used as part of the output. The BEEP statement works well, but it is limited to only one note of fixed duration. If a variety of sounds are desired, the SOUND statement is more applicable. The general form of the SOUND statement is

SOUND <frequency>, <duration>

where the frequency is in Hertz (cycles per second). The allowable frequency range is 37 to 32767 Hz. It should be noted that the human ear can only hear sounds up to approximately 20,000 Hz. Duration refers to how long the sound will be emitted and is measured in "clock ticks". There are 18.2 clock ticks per second. For example, the statement

SOUND 523,18.2

will play middle C for 1 second.

Substituting 0 for the duration will terminate the note created by any previous SOUND statement. The following chart shows the notes and their corresponding frequencies:

Note	Frequency (Hz)	Note	Frequency (Hz)
C	130.81	C	523.25
D	146.83	D	587.33
E	164.81	E	659.26
F	174.61	F	698.46
G	196.00	G	783.99
A	220.00	A	880.00
B	246.94	B	987.77
C	261.63	C	1046.50
D	293.66	D	1174.70
E	329.63	E	1318.50
F	349.23	F	1396.90
G	392.00	G	1568.00
A	440.00	A	1760.00
B	493.88	B	1975.50

Program 8.10

This program utilizes the SOUND statement to produce the sound of a fire engine siren whose pitch will first rise then fall.

```
10 REM Fire engine siren
20 LOW = 660
30 HIGH = 880
40 FOR J = 1 TO 10
50    FOR I = LOW TO HIGH STEP 15
60       SOUND I,.5
70    NEXT I
80    FOR I= HIGH TO LOW STEP -7
90       SOUND I,.5
100   NEXT I
110 NEXT J
120 END
```

- **Line 20:** Sets variable LOW to a frequency of 660 Hz (E).
- **Line 30:** Sets variable HIGH to a frequency of 880 Hz (A).
- **Line 40:** Initializes the loop which sounds the siren 10 times.
- **Line 50:** Initializes the loop which forms the rising half of the siren's pitch.
- **Line 60:** Notice how a variable is substituted for <frequency>.
- **Line 70:** Ends the loop started in line 50.
- **Line 80:** Initiates the loop which forms the falling half of the siren's pitch.
- **Line 90:** Produces the sound which decreases in pitch.

End of Chapter Problem

A bookstore needs a program that will keep track of when books are sold or returned and update the inventory. It carries only four books: one on computers, one on cats, one on exercise and one on cooking. The store would like the inventory displayed as a bar chart.

Algorithm:
1. Read in information on the books (name, stock amount).
2. Choose which option to perform (sold books, returned books, inventory chart, or exit).
3. Perform the selected activity(s):
    a. Sold books: decrease inventory
    b. Returned books: increase inventory
    c. Bar Chart: draw a graph dependent upon the quantity of books in stock
    d. Exit: Leave the program
4. A calculation routine will be needed since the Sold and Returned books routines differ only in that one adds books while the other subtracts books from inventory. Variable SWITCH is used to indicate which function is taking place.

Input:

Book Name	: BOOK$( )
Quantity	: STOCK( )
Name of Book	: LOOK$
Quantity Sold or Returned	: ADD

Output:
Vertical Bar Chart

Program 8.11

```
5 OPTION BASE 1
10 DIM BOOK$(4), STOCK(4)
20 FOR I = 1 TO 4
30     READ BOOK$(I), STOCK(I)
40 NEXT I
50 SCREEN 0,1 : COLOR 13,5,3 : CLS : LOCATE 6,1
60 PRINT TAB(9);"1: Selling Books"
70 PRINT TAB(9);"2: Returned Books"
80 PRINT TAB(9);"3: Inventory Bar Chart"
90 PRINT TAB(9);"4: Exit"
100 INPUT "Enter Selection : "; CHOICE
110 IF CHOICE < 1 OR CHOICE > 4 THEN BEEP: GOTO 100
120 ON CHOICE GOSUB 200, 300, 600, 999
130 GOTO 50
200 REM
210 REM   *******    Selling Books    *******
220 REM
230 SWITCH = -1
240 GOSUB 400
250 RETURN
300 REM
310 REM   *******    Returned Books    *******
320 REM
330 SWITCH = 1
340 GOSUB 400
350 RETURN
```

```
400 REM
410 REM   *******        Calculations      *******
420 REM
430 INPUT "Enter Book Name, How Many :"; LOOK$, ADD
440 I = 1
450 WHILE I < 5
460     IF BOOK$(I) <> LOOK$ THEN 500
470     IF (STOCK(I)+(ADD * SWITCH)) < 0 OR
            (STOCK(I)+(ADD * SWITCH)) > 180
            THEN PRINT "Amount exceeds inventory limits" : GOTO 430
480     STOCK(I) = STOCK(I) + (ADD * SWITCH)
490     I = 4 : CHECK = 1
500     I = I + 1
510 WEND
520 IF CHECK <> 1 THEN PRINT "BOOK NOT FOUND"
530 FOR D = I TO 1000 : NEXT D
540 RETURN
600 REM
610 REM   *******        Inventory Chart    *******
620 REM
630 SCREEN 1,0 : COLOR 1,1
640 WIDE = 12 : START = 104 : HUE = 1 : LOCATE 25,1
650 LINE (0,183) - (319,188), 3, BF
660 FOR I = 1 TO 4
670     LINE (START,180) - (START + WIDE,180 - STOCK(I)), HUE, BF
680     PRINT TAB(INT(START / 8)); I;
690     START = START + (WIDE * 2) : HUE = HUE + 1
700     IF HUE > 3 THEN HUE = 1
710 NEXT I
720 FOR D = 1 TO 2500 : NEXT D : REM  ***   delay
730 RETURN
740 REM
750 DATA COMPUTER, 100, CAT, 116
760 DATA EXERCISE, 165, COOKING, 76
999 REM
1000 REM  ******     EXIT PROGRAM  ******
1010 REM
1020 SCREEN 0,0 : WIDTH 80
1030 END
RUN
          1: Selling Books
          2: Returned Books
          3: Inventory Bar Chart
          4: Exit
Enter Selection : ? 3
```

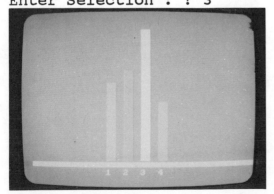

```
Enter Selection : ? 4
```

- **Lines 5-40:** Load the arrays for book title and initial stock quantity. OPTION BASE 1 allows the arrays to begin numbering array elements at 1. It is good programming practice to dimension arrays even though the computer may not require it.
- **Lines 50-90:** Display a menu on the colored text screen.
- **Line 100:** Inputs the user's selection.
- **Line 110:** Uses BEEP to warn the user of incorrect input.
- **Line 120:** ON...GOSUB branches to the selected routines.
- **Lines 200-250:** ∗∗∗ Selling Books ∗∗∗
Using the SWITCH variable allows the calculations in lines 470-490 to switch from addition to subtraction based upon the value of the variable (either 1 or −1). Control is then passed to the Calculation subroutine.
- **Lines 300-350:** ∗∗∗ Returned Books ∗∗∗
Once again, the SWITCH variable is used so that the same calculation routine used above may also be accessed. Control is then passed to the Calculation subroutine.
- **Lines 400-540:** ∗∗∗ Calculations ∗∗∗
Input the name and amount of the book in question. A WHILE...WEND loop checks the list of books against the name of the book input. If there is no match, then an appropriate message is printed. However, if the book is found, STOCK( ) is re-calculated based upon SWITCH.
- **Lines 600-730:** ∗∗∗ Inventory Chart ∗∗∗
- **Line 640:** Sets the width of the bars to 12, the starting (X) position of the bars to 104, the HUE (color of the bars) to 1 and also sets the position of the text cursor to the first position of the 25th line.
- **Line 650:** Draws the X-axis.
- **Line 660:** Starts the loop which will draw the four bars of the chart.
- **Line 670:** Draws a vertical bar which is 12 positions wide and STOCK(I) positions high. Note the variable HUE determines the color of the bar.
- **Line 680:** Prints the book's index number by TABbing (START / 8) positions. There are 8 horizontal positions and 8 vertical positions per text character.
- **Line 690:** Increases the START and HUE variables.
- **Line 700:** Resets HUE to 1 if it is greater than 3.
- **Line 710:** Completes the loop started in line 660.
- **Lines 999-1030:** Upon exiting the program, the computer is switched to black and white text mode and 80 column width.

EXERCISES

1. Have the computer draw a solid red rectangle with its upper left corner at (38,18), a length of 70 columns, and a height of 30 rows.

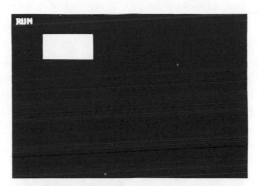

2. Have the computer draw a green letter L about two inches high in the upper left corner of the screen.

3. Using medium resolution graphics, draw a cyan vertical line and a white horizontal line which intersect at (140,80).

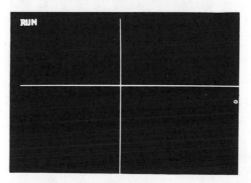

4. Have the computer construct a brown right triangle with the coordinates at (250,20), (250,110), (130,110).

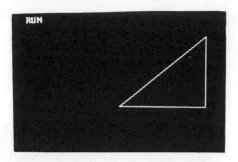

5. Place a flashing red notice on the text screen which advertises Uncle Bill's Whamburgers for $.79.

Today only!
   Uncle Bill's
WHAMBURGERS!
   Only $0.79

6. In high resolution mode draw the letter A with the top at (350,30) and the lowest point on the left side at (200,160).

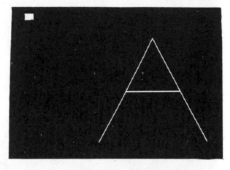

7. Have the computer generate 200 random integers between 1 and 10, inclusive. Using medium resolution graphics, plot a properly labeled bar graph showing the number of occurrences of each random number.

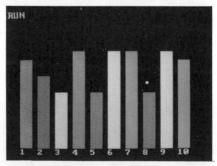

8. Produce the following Hatman in yellow with a green hat. The Hatman should be surrounded by the color red.

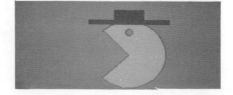

9. The following table shows production output per day for each employee of Papa's Pizza Parlor. Plot a bar graph showing the average output per week for each of Papa's employees.

Employee	Pizza Production
Smith	18, 12, 9, 10, 16, 22, 14
Munyan	12, 21, 19, 16, 28, 20, 22
Ricardo	18, 20, 14, 19, 11, 16, 23
Fazioli	23, 27, 18, 16, 21, 14, 24

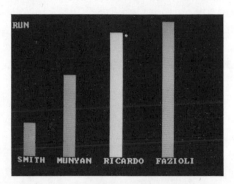

10. Using only a single CIRCLE statement and a single FOR...NEXT loop, have the computer produce the following sphere:

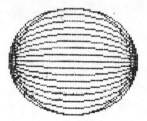

11. Using medium resolution graphics, have the computer produce the following figure:

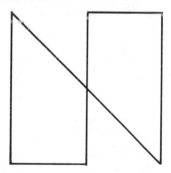

12. Using a single loop and one CIRCLE statement, produce the following wagon wheel in red:

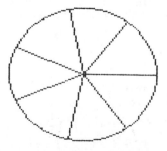

Advanced Exercises

Each of the following exercises requires the development of a detailed algorithm. The program should not be written until all details of the algorithm have been worked out.

13. Using medium resolution graphics, have the computer generate a 90 × 90 circular dart board using the colors 1 through 3, where brown (color 3, palette 0) occupies the center, red the middle band and green the outer band. Have the computer take ten random shots at points on the board. Use the POINT function to tabulate the computer's score. If the point of impact is within the brown area, the computer scores 3 points; if within the red, 2 points and green, 1 point. Show where each dart hits by plotting a small black circle at the point of impact.

14. Bilton Madley has converted all its board games into computer format. The only one they have not done is "Name That Tune". Using the SOUND statement, write a program that allows for 5 songs of 8 notes each to be stored, along with their respective durations, in DATA statements. The game should randomly choose a song and allow two players to each pick the number of notes in which they could guess the song. The player who inputs the least number of notes (greater than zero) will be told to guess the song after he or she has heard the clue. If the first player guesses wrong, the second player is given a chance to hear the number of notes he or she chose. If both guess wrong, the game continues by playing the song in its entirety for the first player and then the second. Points are awarded to each based on the following:

First player correct on chance 1—10 points
Second player correct on chance 1—5 points
Either player correct on chance 2—2 points
Data Statements

The game continues until all five songs have been played. Make sure not to play the same song more than once.

Use the following DATA when writing your program:

```
100 REM    Mary Had a Little Lamb
110 DATA 659,3, 587,3, 523,3, 587,3
120 DATA 659,3  659,3, 659,3, 587,3
130 REM    Three Blind Mice
140 DATA 659,6, 587,6, 523,12, 659,6
150 DATA 587,6, 523,12, 784,6, 698,6
160 REM    Happy Birthday
170 DATA 523,3, 523,3, 587,3, 523,3
180 DATA 698,3, 659,3, 523,3, 523,3
190 REM    Do Re Mi
200 DATA 523,5, 587,3, 659,3, 523,5
210 DATA 659,3, 523,3, 659,3, 587,5
220 REM  Beat It
230 DATA 784,7, 988,4, 1047,3, 1176,2
240 DATA 988,5, 1176,4, 1320,7, 1176,2
```

9

MATHEMATICAL FUNCTIONS

SQR

SGN

ABS

SIN

COS

TAN

ATN

LOG

EXP

DEF

*T*he ability to interpret and work with mathematical expressions has made the computer an indispensable tool for the mathematician. Since this chapter introduces the various mathematical functions that the computer can perform, it should be read by those who possess a sufficient mathematical background. It is not within the scope of this book to teach mathematics but instead to illustrate how the computer can be used to solve mathematical problems.

SQR, SGN and ABS

Since the following functions perform specific operations, they will be presented individually and then demonstrated together in one program.

The SQR function calculates the positive square root of a number. For example,

$$X = SQR(N)$$

assigns X the square root of N. The square root of a number is defined as that value which, when multiplied by itself, gives N.

In the expression SQR(X), SQR is the function name and X the argument. With the SQR function, the argument may be any mathematical expression with a non-negative value. For example, SQR(3 ∗ X + 5) is perfectly acceptable provided that the expression 3 ∗ X + 5 produces a non-negative value.

Note that the argument of a function must be enclosed within parentheses. In its evaluation of a mathematical function, the computer first evaluates the argument and then the function. Some functions have a limitation on the value of the argument. These limitations will be indicated as the functions are introduced.

In some situations it may be necessary to know if a variable is positive or negative. The SGN function has only three possible values: 1, 0, and –1. For example,

$$X = SGN(N)$$

assigns X the value 1 if N > 0, 0 if N = 0 and –1 if N < 0.

The ABS function can be used to find the absolute value of a number. If

$$X = ABS(N)$$

then X = N if N > = 0 and X = – N if N < 0.

Program 9.1

This program asks the user to input a number of which the square root is desired. The SGN function is used to avoid asking for the square root of a negative number, while the ABS function is used to print the square root of the absolute value of a negative number.

```
10 PRINT "To end this program, type 999"
20 INPUT "Enter a number"; N
30 IF N = 999 THEN 999
40 IF SGN(N) = -1 THEN PRINT "Negative number"; SQR(ABS(N))
                ELSE PRINT SQR(N)
50 GOTO 20
999 END

RUN
To end this program, type 999
Enter a number? -15
Negative number 3.872984
Enter a number? 14
 3.741657
Enter a number? 999
```

Review

1. What is X when X = ABS(–12 + 6 ∗ SGN(–9 + 9/3) + 1.8) – 18.2?

2. Write a program which will produce the following results:

```
RUN
Enter a number? 37.84
The sign of 37.84 is positive
Enter a number? –36
The sign of –36 is negative.
Enter a number? 999
```

Trigonometric Functions: SIN, COS, TAN

The computer can find the values of several trigonometric functions. The functions SIN(X), COS(X) and TAN(X) will produce the value of the sine, cosine, and tangent, respectively, of an angle X, where X is measured in radians. To convert an angle from degrees to radians, multiply it by 3.14159 and then divide the result by 180, since 180 degrees equals PI radians.

Program 9.2

The following program illustrates how the values of the sine, cosine and tangent can be found for an angle input in degrees:

```
10 PRINT "INPUT THE VALUE OF AN ANGLE IN DEGREES."
20 PRINT "TO STOP THE PROGRAM TYPE 999."
30 PI = 3.14159
40 INPUT "VALUE"; A
50 IF A = 999 THEN 999
60 X = A*PI/180
70 PRINT A;"DEGREES EQUALS";X;"RADIANS."
80 PRINT "SIN("; A; ") ="; SIN(X)
90 PRINT "COS("; A; ") ="; COS(X)
100 PRINT "TAN("; A; ") ="; TAN(X)
110 PRINT
120 GOTO 40
999 END
```

```
RUN
INPUT THE VALUE OF AN ANGLE IN DEGREES.
TO STOP THE PROGRAM TYPE 999.
VALUE? 30
 30 DEGREES EQUALS .5235984 RADIANS.
SIN( 30 ) = .4999997
COS( 30 ) = .8660256
TAN( 30 ) = .5773498

VALUE? 45
 45 DEGREES EQUALS .7853975 RADIANS.
SIN( 45 ) = .7071064
COS( 45 ) = .7071073
TAN( 45 ) = .9999986

VALUE? 999
```

Note that due to computer rounding error some of the values do not come out exactly as they should.

ATN

The only inverse trigonometric function supplied by the computer is the principle arctangent function ATN. The function ATN(X) is used to find the angle whose tangent is X. The value produced by the ATN function is in radians. Thus, the arctangent of 1 is PI/4 radians = .7853982. To convert an angle from radians to degrees, multiply it by 180 and then divide the result by 3.14159. The ATN function, just like the principal arctangent function in mathematics, gives values only between –PI/2 and PI/2 radians. There is no limitation on the value that the argument may assume.

Program 9.3

This program finds the angle whose tangent is entered and prints the result in degrees:

```
10 PRINT "TO STOP THE PROGRAM TYPE 999."
20 PI = 3.14159
30 INPUT "ENTER A TANGENT VALUE"; T
35 IF T = 999 THEN 999
40 R = ATN(T)
50 D = R* 180/PI
60 PRINT "The angle whose tangent is"; T; "is"; D; "degrees"
70 PRINT
80 GOTO 30
999 END

RUN
TO STOP THE PROGRAM TYPE 999.
ENTER A TANGENT VALUE? 1
The angle whose tangent is 1 is 45.00004 degrees

ENTER A TANGENT VALUE? 0
The angle whose tangent is 0 is 0 degrees

ENTER A TANGENT VALUE? 0.57735
The angle whose tangent is .57735 is 30.00001 degrees

ENTER A TANGENT VALUE? 999
```

Again, computer rounding error causes some of the results to be slightly inaccurate.

To find the principal arcsine of a number, it is necessary to use the trigonometric identity:

$$\text{ARCSINE}(X) = \text{ARCTAN} \frac{X}{\sqrt{1 - X^2}}$$

Therefore, to find the principal angle whose sine is X, the expression ATN (X / SQR(1 − X^ 2)) is used. This angle will be measured in radians and will be between −PI/2 and PI/2. The value of X, however, must be between −1 and 1, not inclusive.

To find the arccosine of X, use the expression ATN((SQR(1 − X ^ 2)) / X). This gives the angle which is between −PI/2 and PI/2 (whose cosine is X). In this expression, X must be between −1 and 1, inclusive, but not equal to 0.

Program 9.4   This program finds the arcsine and arcosine of X in both radians and degrees:

```
10 PRINT "TO STOP THIS PROGRAM TYPE 999."
15 PI = 3.14159
20 INPUT "VALUE";X
30 IF X = 999 THEN 999
40 S = ATN(X/SQR(1-X^2))
50 S1 = S * 180/PI
60 C = ATN(SQR(1-X^2)/X)
70 C1 = C * 180/PI
80 PRINT "THE ANGLE WHOSE SINE IS";X; "IS"; S; "RADIANS"
90 PRINT "THE ANGLE WHOSE COSINE IS"; X; "IS"; C; "RADIANS"
100 PRINT "THE ANGLE WHOSE SINE IS"; X; "IS"; S1; "DEGREES"
110 PRINT "THE ANGLE WHOSE COSINE IS"; X; "IS"; C1; "DEGREES"
120 PRINT
130 GOTO 20
999 END

RUN
TO STOP THIS PROGRAM TYPE 999.
VALUE? .5
THE ANGLE WHOSE SINE IS .5 IS .5235988 RADIANS
THE ANGLE WHOSE COSINE IS .5 IS 1.047198 RADIANS
THE ANGLE WHOSE SINE IS .5 IS 30.00003 DEGREES
THE ANGLE WHOSE COSINE IS .5 IS 60.00005 DEGREES

VALUE? .8777
THE ANGLE WHOSE SINE IS .8777 IS 1.071041 RADIANS
THE ANGLE WHOSE COSINE IS .8777 IS .499755 RADIANS
THE ANGLE WHOSE SINE IS .8777 IS 61.3662 DEGREES
THE ANGLE WHOSE COSINE IS .8777 IS 28.63388 DEGREES

VALUE? 999
```

Logarithms and the Exponential Function: LOG, EXP

The LOG function can be used to find natural logarithms, that is, logarithms to the base e. To find the natural logarithm of X, LOG(X) is used. Do not confuse the natural logarithm with the common logarithm. The common logarithm, that is logarithm base 10, can be found from the natural logarithm by using the formula

$$\log_{10}(X) = \frac{\ln(X)}{\ln(10)}$$

where ln(X) designates the natural logarithm of X. Therefore, to find $\log_{10}(X)$ simply use LOG(X)/LOG(10). The argument in the LOG function must always be positive.

The function EXP(X) is used to find values of the exponential function, $e \wedge x$, where e = 2.71828. This number is the same as the base of the natural logarithm function. The value of the argument cannot be greater than 88, because this will cause an ?OVERFLOW error.

Program 9.5

This program finds the natural (base e) and common (base 10) logarithms of X as well as the value of e^x:

```
10 PRINT "TO STOP THIS PROGRAM TYPE 999."
20 INPUT "ENTER X"; X
30 IF X = 999 THEN 999
40 PRINT "LN(X)="; LOG(X)
50 IF X < 88 THEN PRINT "E RAISED TO X ="; EXP(X)
60 T = LOG(X)/LOG(10)
70 PRINT "THE COMMON LOGARITHM OF"; X; "IS"; T
80 PRINT
90 GOTO 20
999 END


RUN
TO STOP THIS PROGRAM TYPE 999.
ENTER X? 1
LN(X)= 0
E RAISED TO X = 2.718282
The common logarithm of 1 is 0

ENTER X? 0.01
LN(X)=-4.60517
E RAISED TO X = 1.01005
The common logarithm of .01 is-2

ENTER X? 10000
LN(X)= 9.210341
The common logarithm of 10000 is 4

ENTER X? 999
```

DEF

A number of the standard mathematical functions have already been introduced in this chapter. In addition to these, the programmer can define other functions by using the DEF statement. The major advantage of DEF lies in the fact that the expression for the function need only be written once, even though the function can be evaluated at more than one location within the program. The form of the DEF statement is:

$$DEF\ FN\text{<function name>}\ (\text{<variable name>}) = \text{<expression>}$$

The function name may be any acceptable numeric variable name (e.g., FNA, FNF, FNG3). The variable name (i.e. the argument) following the function name must always appear within parentheses and may be any appropriate numeric variable. In the following example,

$$10\ DEF\ FNP(X) = X \wedge 2 - 2 * X - 1$$

P is the function name, X is the variable name, and $X^2 - 2X - 1$ is the expression used to compute the function's value. For instance, when X = 5, FNP(X) = 14 because $5 \wedge 2 - 2 * 5 - 1 = 14$.

Within a program future reference to a function is made using the function name, not the variable name. The variable name is called a "dummy"—it could be any variable name—and later on in a program when the function is evaluated the original variable name need not be used. For example, in evaluating the function P, it is possible to use the variable A.

```
20 A = 3
30 PRINT FNP(A)

RUN
 2
```

The value of variable A, which is 3, is now substituted into the function P and 2 is printed.

Program 9.6

The following program evaluates the polynomial function FNP(X) several times:

```
10 DEF FNP(X) = X^2 - 2*X - 1
20 PRINT "X",  "FNP(X)"
30 FOR A = 1 TO 5
40    PRINT A, FNP(A)
50 NEXT A
60 INPUT X
70 PRINT "The result of FNP("; X; ") is"; FNP(X)
80 END

RUN
X                    FNP(X)
 1                    -2
 2                    -1
 3                     2
 4                     7
 5                    14
? -10
The result of FNP(-10 ) is 119
```

When the function is evaluated at line 40, the variable in parentheses is A. When it is evaluated on line 70, the variable is X. The name of the variable in parentheses may be the same as or different from the variable name used in the DEF statement. Note also that if the DEF statement were not used, the formula on line 10 would have to appear twice (lines 40 and 70). Economy results because even though the function is defined once, it can be evaluated at any place within the program.

Another advantage of using the DEF statement is that it can be easily retyped to define a different function. This is illustrated by re-running Program 9.6 with line 10 changed to:

```
10 DEF FNP(X) = X^3 - 5*X^2 +1

RUN
X                 FNP(X)
 1                 -3
 2                 -11
 3                 -17
 4                 -15
 5                  1
? -10
The result of FNP(-10 ) is-1499
```

String functions may also be defined using DEF. This technique is handy for simplifying certain string operations such as their addition.

Program 9.7   This program illustrates how a user-defined string function can be implemented:

```
10 DEF FNG$(A$) = A$ + " is yellow"
20 B$ = "The SUN"
30 PRINT FNG$(B$); " and "; FNG$("Big Mellow"); "."
40 END

RUN
The SUN is yellow and Big Mellow is yellow.
```

Note the output produced by line 30. FNG$(A$) is evaluated twice, first with "The Sun" and then with "BIG Mellow".

User-defined functions may have more than one variable within the parentheses. For example, the statement

$$10 \text{ DEF FNR(A,B)} = \text{INT(RND} * (B - A + 1) + A)$$

defines the function FNR(A,B) which returns a random integer between A and B, inclusive. The statement

$$20 \text{ DEF FNC\$(X\$,Y\$,Z\$)} = X\$ + \text{", "} + Y\$ + \text{", "} + Z\$$$

defines a function which combines three string variables, and inserts commas between them.

Review

3. Write a program that will produce the following output. Two user-defined functions should be employed, one to convert degrees to radians, the other to convert radians to degrees.

> RUN
> DEGREES? 30
> That is .5235903 radians.
>
> RADIANS? .785375
> That is 44.99871 degrees.

End of Chapter Problem

One of the most valuable mathematical problems a computer is capable of solving is finding the area under a curve, a process which is usually difficult to do and requires integral calculus if done mathematically.

For most curves a trapezoid represents a good approximation of the area under the curve. Consider the graph of the function y = 1/t:

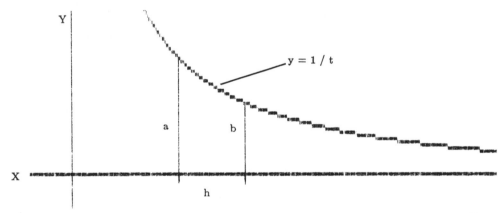

Note how closely a trapezoid fits the area between the limits 1 and X. The area of a trapezoid can be found from the formula

$$A = .5(a + b) h$$

where a and b are the altitudes of the trapezoid and h the base.

A single trapezoid is a good approximation for a function as simple as Y = 1 / T but for more complicated functions, such as Y = 1 / (T ^ 3), it is a poor approximation. Breaking the area into a large number of trapezoids and then summing the areas of the separate trapezoids usually increases the accuracy of the calculated area.

Algorithm:
1. Input the function.
2. Input the limits between which the area is desired.
3. Determine how many trapezoids the area is broken into.
4. Break the area down into small trapezoids.
5. Calculate the area of each trapezoid.
6. Sum the areas of all trapezoids.

Input:

Function to evaluate	: FNY(T)
Upper limit	: T1
Lower limit	: T2

Output:
> Area under graph   : Z

Program 9.8

```
10 DEF FNY(T) = 1/T
20 INPUT "Enter start point, end point"; Tl, T2
30 INPUT "Enter # of trapezoids"; X
40 H = (T2 - Tl) / X
50 FOR I = Tl TO (T2 - H) STEP H
60    A = .5 * (FNY(I) + FNY(I+H)) * H
70    Z = Z + A
80 NEXT I
90 PRINT "Area ="; Z
100 END

RUN
Enter start point, end point? 1,2
Enter # of trapezoids? 100
Area = .6931537
```

- **Line 10:** Defines the function to be used. Simply changing this line is all that is required to find the area under another curve.
- **Line 20:** Inputs the limits between which the area is to be calculated.
- **Line 30:** Inputs the number of trapezoids into which the area will be divided.
- **Line 40:** Calculates the base of each trapezoid by finding the total length along the horizontal axis (T2 − T1) and dividing it by the number of trapezoids.
- **Line 50:** Initiates a loop that will be executed once for each trapezoid. Notice that I is used to represent the value of the variable to be evaluated by the function. H is subtracted from T2 to avoid adding one too many trapezoids.
- **Line 60:** Calculates the area of a single trapezoid by evaluating the value of the function at the two altitudes (a and b) of the trapezoid and then by using the formula (A = .5 $*$ h $*$ (a + b)).
- **Line 70:** Sums the area of the separate trapezoids, which will be printed when complete at line 90.

Change line 10 to read

> 10 DEF FNY(T) = 1 / (T $\wedge$ 2)

Run the program twice, using the same endpoints, first using five trapezoids and then 1000 trapezoids. This shows that a large number of trapezoids must often be used to produce a good approximation. The correct answer is very close to 0.5.

```
RUN
Enter start point, end point? 1,2
Enter # of trapezoids? 5
Area = .4499189
Ok
RUN
Enter start point, end point? 1,2
Enter # of trapezoids? 1000
Area = .4997382
```

EXERCISES

1. When a number is input, have the computer generate its square roots. Be sure to account for a negative input. An input of 999 terminates the program.

   ```
   RUN
   ? -1
   No negative numbers allowed.
   ? 4
   N = 4          Square roots = +2 or -2
   ?999
   ```

2. Write a program which prints the integers from 121 to 144, inclusive, and their respective square roots. Label each column of output.

3. Write a program that will print a table of the COS(X) and SIN(X + 90°) where X varies from 0 to 360 degrees in increments of 10°.

4. Input a number N. If N is zero, print 0. Otherwise, print ABS(N)/N. What does the program do?

5. Input a number N and print the product of SGN(N) and N. What does this program do?

6. Input a number N, square it and print the square root of the result. What should the program produce?

7. Print a table consisting of 2 columns with headings showing each angle in radians and degrees. The angles in radians are to be 0, .25, .5, .75, ..., 3.0. Remember that 180° = pi radians.

8. Input an angle in degrees and convert it to a fraction of a revolution (1 rev. = 360°) and to radians.

9. Input an angle in degrees. Of the three functions sine, cosine and tangent, print the value of the one which has the greatest value.

   ```
   RUN
   Enter angle? 0
   COSINE = 1
   ```

10. For angles from 0° to 180° (at intervals of 10°) print the angle in degrees, the sine, the cosine, and the sum of their squares in columns with headings. What patterns emerge?

11. Input two numbers (A,B). Print the quantity FNP(B) − FNP(A), given that FNP(X) = $9X^3 - 7X^2 + 4X - 1$.

12. Input a number N. Print the values of FNJ(N) and FNJ(FNJ(N)), where FNJ(X) = 20 ∗ SQR (ABS(X)) − 10 ∗ SGN(X) + 5 ∗ INT(X).

13. Print a table (with headings) of X, the natural logarithm of X and the exponential function of X for X = 1 to 15.

14. Print a table (with headings) of X, the logarithm of X to the base 10, and 10 raised to the power X for X = 1 to 15.

15. What is the exact output of the following program? Check by running the program:

```
10 READ A,B,C,D
20 PRINT SQR (A), INT(B), SQR(INT(C)), INT(SQR(D))
30 DATA 25, –3.4, 9.7, 24
40 END
```

16. What is the exact output for the following program? Check by running the program:

```
10 DEF FN F(N) = 3 ∗ N − 6
20 FOR X = -4 TO 6 STEP 2
30      IF FN F(X) > 0 THEN PRINT "FNF(";X;") is positive"
40      IF FN F(X) = 0 THEN PRINT "FNF(";X;") is zero"
50      IF FN F(X) < 0 THEN PRINT "FNF(";X;") is negative"
60 NEXT X
70 END
```

17. Using three user-defined functions, have the computer evaluate the following for integers from -10 to 10:

$$X^2 + 3X + 2$$
$$LOG(X^2 + 1) - X$$
$$ATN(SIN(X))$$

18. Write a program to convert from polar to rectangular coordinates (i.e., from (r,θ) to (X,Y)).

19. If two functions, f and g, are inverse to each other, the following relations hold: f(g(x)) = x and g(f(x)) = x.

    (a) Tabulate the values of X, EXP(X) and LOG(EXP(X)) for X = −5 to 10.

    (b) Print a table for X = 1 to 151 of X, LOG(X), EXP(LOG(X)), using STEP 10.

    (c) Do EXP and LOG appear to be inverse to each other?

20. Produce your own sequence of random numbers without using the RND function. To do this, let X vary from 1 to 100 in steps of 1. Obtain SIN(X) and multipy this by 1000, calling the absolute value of the product Y. Divide INT(Y) by 16, and let the remainder R serve as your random number. (Hint: the remainder of A/B is A/B − INT(A/B).)

21. Six year old Dennis the Menace has decided to invest $.50 in the Last Chew Bubble Gum Company. Starting with the 11th year, he withdraws 5 cents at the beginning of each year. His money earns 8% interest compounded annually. The formula for interest compounded annually is $P = P_0 e^{it}$), where t is the elapsed time in years, P_0 is the initial deposit, P is the balance at time t, and i is the interest rate. In this case the formula would be $P = P_0 e^{.08t}$. How much is Dennis's deposit worth after 50 years?

22. Use the SIN function to generate the following:

RUN

```
                                        SHAZAM!
                                         SHAZAM!
                                          SHAZAM!
                                           SHAZAM!
                                          SHAZAM!
                                           SHAZAM!
                                           SHAZAM!
                                          SHAZAM!
                                         SHAZAM!
                                        SHAZAM!
                                       SHAZAM!
                                      SHAZAM!
                                     SHAZAM!
                                    SHAZAM!
                                   SHAZAM!
                                  SHAZAM!
                                 SHAZAM!
                                SHAZAM!
                               SHAZAM!
                              SHAZAM!
                             SHAZAM!
                            SHAZAM!
                            SHAZAM!
                            SHAZAM!
                             SHAZAM!
                              SHAZAM!
                               SHAZAM!
```

Advanced Exercise

The following exercise requires the development of a detailed algorithm. The program should not be written until all details of the algorithm have been worked out.

23. Write a program that will solve a triangle (compute the unknown sides and angles) for the following situations:

(a) given two sides and the included angle,

Sides 1 and 2? 3,3
Included angle? 60

Side	Angle
3	60.00001
3	60.00001
3	60

(b) given two angles and any side,

Angles 1 and 2? 60,60
Side? 3
Is that the included side <Y/N>? Y

Side	Angle
3	60
3	60
3	60

(c) given three sides,

Three sides? 3,4,5

Side	Angle
3	36.8699
4	53.1301
5	90

10

SEQUENTIAL FILES

OPEN

CLOSE

WRITE#

INPUT#

EOF

LINE INPUT

PRINT#

LINE INPUT#

So far we have discussed only two methods for saving data in the computer. Variables could be assigned a value (e.g., A = 5), or the data could be placed in DATA statements. There are two drawbacks to these methods. First, if it becomes necessary to update the data, program lines have to be retyped, thus altering the program and increasing the chance of error. Second, since the data is an integral part of a program, it cannot be accessed by other programs. The solution is to store the data in a file, which is a collection of related data items usually stored on a diskette. Since files are separate from programs, they can be updated without changing any part of a program. Also, a single data file can be accessed by many programs, allowing more flexible use of the data. Files and programs should not be confused. A program is a set of instructions that tells the computer what to do; a file is a separate set of data used by a program.

A computer file is analogous to a filing cabinet, which stores information that can be recalled and cross referenced. The computer file provides the means for storing large quantities of data indefinitely.

The computer utilizes two different file types: sequential and random-access. The sequential file is best adapted to situations requiring data to be recalled in the same order in which it was stored. Proceeding line-by-line from the beginning of the file, the computer reads the file sequentially until either all the desired information has been retrieved or the end of the file has been reached. If information is to be retrieved from a random location in the file (for example, a single entry in a mailing list), random-access files are better suited. Since they are more complex, random-access files will be discussed separately in the next chapter.

It is suggested that before proceeding with this chapter you first read Appendix B to become familiar with the Disk Operating System (DOS).

OPEN

The OPEN statement establishes a line of communication between a program and a file and prepares the file for use. The general format of the OPEN statement is:

OPEN "<mode>", <channel>, "<file name>"

The mode tells the computer how to access the data. The four modes of access are:

O: Sequential Output. The computer will output from a program to a file, starting at the beginning of the file. If the file does not already exist, it will automatically be created; otherwise, the new data will be written over any previously existing data stored in the file.

I: Sequential Input. The computer will input data from the file to a program starting at the beginning of the file. If the file does not already exist, it will print FILE NOT FOUND.

A: Sequential Output at End of File. The data will be output from a program and appended to the end of a previously created file. Previously stored data will be added to, not lost. If the file does not already exist, a new one will be created.

R: Random Input and Output. This option is discussed in Chapter 11.

When the computer opens a file, an electronic channel is needed to transfer information to a file from a program or to a program from a file. It is possible to have open from 1 to 3 files, on separate channels.

A file name is a unique label used by the computer to identify each file and program stored on a diskette. It is important to remember that files and programs must not have the same name and that the mode and the file name must be enclosed in quotation marks. For example,

> 10 OPEN "I", 2, "PAYROLL.DAT"

will open a file named PAYROLL.DAT for sequential input (I) on channel 2. It is a good convention to use the extension .DAT as part of each file name so that when the contents of a diskette are listed it will be obvious which names are those of data files.

CLOSE

Any file previously OPENed must be CLOSEd. This procedure is necessary in order to break the line of communication between a program and a file that was originally established by the OPEN statement. A file is closed by using the statement CLOSE followed by the channel that was specified when the file was opened. For example,

> 100 CLOSE 2

will close the file previously opened on channel 2. If the channel is omitted in the CLOSE statement, all previously opened files are closed. Closing a file ensures that all its information is properly stored. Do not remove a diskette from a drive on which files are open, since there is no way to guarantee whether all of the data has been written to the file until it is closed. Removing a disk prematurely may result in loss of data.

WRITE#

While the OPEN statement establishes a line of communication between a program and a file, the WRITE# command is used to place data from a program into a file.

> WRITE#<channel>, <variable>, <variable>...

Information assigned to the variable names mentioned in the WRITE# statement will be placed in the file associated with the specified channel. The WRITE# statement automatically places quotation marks around the string data and commas between numeric and string data in the file. The commas and quotation marks act as markers so that the computer can tell the different items of data apart when later reading them from the file.

Program 10.1   This program opens a sequential file named WORK.DAT on the diskette in drive B. In it are stored the names of four employees, their hourly wages and the number of hours they have worked. Note the structure of line 90:

```
10 REM   *** EMPLOYEE$ = Employee name
20 REM   *** WAGE = Rate per hour
30 REM   *** HOURS = Total hours worked
40 OPEN "O", 1, "B:WORK.DAT"
50 FOR EMPLOYEE = 1 TO 4
60       INPUT "NAME"; EMPLOYEE$
70       INPUT "WAGE"; WAGE
80       INPUT "TIME"; HOURS
90       WRITE#1, EMPLOYEE$, WAGE, HOURS
100      PRINT
110 NEXT EMPLOYEE
120 CLOSE 1
130 END


RUN
NAME? BOB BRACALENTE
WAGE? 6.00
TIME? 40

NAME? JOHN WANG
WAGE? 4.45
TIME? 10

NAME? MIKE BIDWELL
WAGE? 9.99
TIME? 42

NAME? HEIDI CRANE
WAGE? 7.65
TIME? 38
```

- **Line 40:** Opens an "O"utput file named WORK.DAT using channel 1.
- **Line 50:** Initiates a loop which will read in 4 sets of data and WRITE them to WORK.DAT.
- **Lines 60-80:** Input from the keyboard the information which will be written to the file.
- **Line 90:** Writes the data from the program to the file open on channel 1.
- **Line 110:** Completes the loop started in line 50.
- **Line 120:** Closes the line of communication between the file and the program.

Review   1. Write a program named CALENDAR.BAS that will create a sequential file MONTHS.DAT containing the names of the months of the year.

2. Write a program named SNOWHITE.BAS that will create a sequential file DWARF.DAT containing the name and number for each of the seven dwarves.

NUMBER	NAME
1	Dopey
2	Sleepy
3	Sneezy
4	Grumpy
5	Happy
6	Bashful
7	Doc

INPUT#

The INPUT# statement is used to transfer information from a sequential file to a program. Its format is similar to the WRITE# statement.

$$INPUT\#<channel>, <variable>, <variable>...$$

It is necessary that the order in which the variable names are listed in the INPUT# statement is the same as the order of the WRITE# statement that created the file. For example, a program that reads data from WORK.DAT created by Program 10.1 would have to input the data from the file to the program in the order EMPLOYEE$, WAGE, HOURS. After the file has been closed, the same channel number need not be used to access it at a later time. For example, a program accessing the file created by Program 10.1 might use channel 2 instead of channel 1.

Program 10.2

This program opens the file WORK.DAT created by Program 10.1, inputs data from the file to the program, and then prints the name and hours worked of each of the four employees.

```
10 REM   *** EMPLOYEE$ = Employee name
20 REM   *** WAGE = Rate per hour
30 REM   *** HOURS = Total hours worked
40 OPEN "I", 2, "B:WORK.DAT"
50 PRINT "NAME"; TAB(25); "HOURS WORKED"
60 FOR EMPLOYEE = 1 TO 4
70       INPUT #2, EMPLOYEE$, WAGE, HOURS
80       PRINT EMPLOYEE$; TAB(25); HOURS
90 NEXT EMPLOYEE
100 CLOSE 2
110 END

RUN
NAME                         HOURS WORKED
BOB BRACALENTE                  40
JOHN WANG                       10
MIKE BIDWELL                    42
HEIDI CRANE                     38
```

- **Line 40:** Opens the file WORK.DAT as an "I"nput file using channel 2.
- **Line 60:** Initiates the loop to print out the file.
- **Line 70:** Inputs data from the file to the program using channel 2.

- **Line 80:** Displays the information. Notice that even though WAGE is not printed, it must be read in line 70. This is necessary to keep the data being read from the file in proper sequence.
- **Line 90:** Completes the loop.
- **Line 100:** Closes the channel between the file and the program.

Review

3. Write a program named RETRIEVE.BAS that will retrieve the names of the first six months of the year from the file MONTHS.DAT.

4. Write a program named PRINTING.BAS that will read the names and numbers of the seven dwarves and print them out like this:

NUMBER	NAME
1	Dopey
2	Sleepy
3	Sneezy
4	Grumpy
5	Happy
6	Bashful
7	Doc

Updating Sequential Files

Specifying the "A"ppend mode in the OPEN statement tells the computer to append new information to the end of an existing file. When an OPEN command is executed instead with either the "O"utput or the "I"nput mode, the computer opens the file and prepares either to write to it or to read from it starting at the beginning of the file. If a programmer uses the "O"utput mode, the new information is written over that which was at the beginning of the file, thus destroying the old information. To avoid this loss of data, the "A"ppend mode instructs the computer to write new information starting at the current end of the file rather than the beginning.

Program 10.3

This program will update the old WORK.DAT file created by Program 10.1 so that it includes information on two new employees just hired:

```
10 REM   *** EMPLOYEE$ = Employee name
20 REM   *** WAGE = Rate per hour
30 REM   *** HOURS = Total hours worked
40 OPEN "A", 1, "B:WORK.DAT"
50 FOR EMPLOYEE = 1 TO 2
60       INPUT "NAME"; EMPLOYEE$
70       INPUT "WAGE"; WAGE
80       INPUT "TIME"; HOURS
90       WRITE#1, EMPLOYEE$, WAGE, HOURS
100      PRINT
110 NEXT EMPLOYEE
120 CLOSE 1
130 END

RUN
NAME? GREG ZAHARCHUK
WAGE? 5.55
TIME? 13

NAME? RICK MACDONWALD
WAGE? 6.54
TIME? 14
```

- **Line 40:** Opens the file WORK.DAT in "A"ppend mode on channel 1. This tells the computer to write any additional information starting at the current end of the file.
- **Lines 50-110:** As in Program 10.1, this loop inputs employee data and writes it to the file using channel 1.
- **Line 120:** Closes the channel between the file and the program.

There is no single command that will remove or alter outdated information in a sequential file. To change such a file, the corrected information must be transferred to a new file, after which the old file can be deleted.

Program 10.4   When an employee retires, this program removes the employee's name from the file WORK.DAT. All of the data is read sequentially from WORK.DAT and the information that is to be retained is placed in a new file named WORK.TMP. After the program has finished building the new file WORK.TMP, the KILL and NAME commands, discussed in Appendix A, are used to delete the old WORK.DAT and rename WORK.TMP as WORK.DAT:

```
10 REM  *** EMPLOYEE$ = Employee name
20 REM  *** WAGE = Rate per hour
30 REM  *** HOURS = Total hours worked
40 REM  *** RETIRED$ = Retired employee's name
50 INPUT "Who has retired"; RETIRED$
60 OPEN "I", 1, "B:WORK.DAT"
70 OPEN "O", 2, "B:WORK.TMP"
80 FOR EMPLOYEE = 1 TO 6
90      INPUT #1, EMPLOYEE$, WAGE, HOURS
100      IF EMPLOYEE$ = RETIRED$ THEN 120
110      WRITE #2, EMPLOYEE$, WAGE, HOURS
120 NEXT EMPLOYEE
130 CLOSE 1,2
140 KILL "B:WORK.DAT"
150 NAME "B:WORK.TMP" AS "B:WORK.DAT"
160 PRINT "THE INFORMATION ON "; RETIRED$; " HAS BEEN REMOVED."
170 END


RUN
Who has retired? RICK MACDONALD
THE INFORMATION ON RICK MACDONALD HAS BEEN REMOVED.
```

- **Line 50:** Inputs from the keyboard the name of the person who has retired.
- **Line 60:** Opens file WORK.DAT for "I"nput to the program on channel 1.
- **Line 70:** Opens the new file WORK.TMP for "O"utput from the program on channel 2.
- **Lines 80-120:** This loop checks the names in the file to find the retiree's name. If the names match, the retiree's data is ignored because line 110 is skipped. Otherwise, the data is written to WORK.TMP.
- **Line 130:** Closes both files.
- **Line 140:** Erases the file WORK.DAT from the diskette.
- **Line 150:** Renames the file WORK.TMP as WORK.DAT.
- **Line 160:** Prints out a completion message.

This program works well in this limited example, but the technique it uses is not always practical. The FOR...NEXT loop between lines 80 and 120 prevents the program from attempting to read past the end of the data file. This method was used because the length of the file WORK.DAT was known. Otherwise, a loop using a GOTO statement must be used to ensure that the entire file is read. The file will then be read sequentially until the program comes to the file's end. At this point an INPUT PAST END error will occur, and the program will be halted. If this occurs, files will be left open and important data may be lost. To prevent this error, the EOF (end of file) function is used in conjunction with a WHILE...WEND loop as explained in the next section.

Review

5. Write a program which will access the data in the file CALENDAR.DAT and update it so that it stores only months containing a letter R.

6. Sneezy and Bashful are getting old. Write a program which will update DWARF.DAT by letting these two retire and removing them from the file.

EOF

When the computer stores a sequential file, it places a character called an end of file (eof) marker at the end of the file. The EOF function determines when, in reading a file, the eof marker has been reached. Its form is:

$$EOF (<channel>)$$

The function returns a value of (–1) when the end of the file has been reached; otherwise, a value of 0 is returned. This function is very useful when used in conjunction with a WHILE...WEND loop. For example, the following loop will continue to execute until the end of the file opened on channel 1 is reached:

```
100 WHILE EOF (1) = 0
        •
        •
139 WEND
```

Program 10.5

This program is a revision of Program 10.4, which allows the file WORK.DAT to be of any length:

```
10 REM   *** EMP$ = Employee name
20 REM   *** WAGE = Rate per hour
30 REM   *** HOURS = Total hours worked
40 REM   *** RET$ = Retired employee's name
50 REM   *** FLAG = Indicator to test for data
60 FLAG = 0
70 INPUT "Who has retired"; RET$
80 OPEN "I", 1, "B:WORK.DAT"
90 OPEN "O", 2, "B:WORK.TMP"
100 WHILE EOF(1) = 0
110       INPUT #1, EMP$, WAGE, HOURS
120       IF EMP$ = RET$ THEN FLAG = -1
                     ELSE WRITE #2, EMP$, WAGE, HOURS
130 WEND
140 CLOSE 1,2
150 IF FLAG = 0 THEN PRINT "There is no "; RET$;" on the payroll":
                 KILL "B:WORK.TMP" : GOTO 190
160 KILL "B:WORK.DAT"
170 NAME "B:WORK.TMP" AS "B:WORK.DAT"
180 PRINT "THE INFORMATION ON "; RET$; " HAS BEEN REMOVED."
190 END
```

```
RUN
Who has retired? SANDRA THOMAS
There is no SANDRA THOMAS on the payroll
```

Program 10.5 demonstrates two major improvements over Program 10.4. First, the program informs the user if a name has been entered that is not in the file, using the variable FLAG as an indicator. If the name is in the file, FLAG becomes −1; if not, it remains 0 and the new file WORK.TMP is killed and WORK.DAT is left unchanged. Second, the EOF function and a WHILE...WEND loop are utilized to read the entire file. This technique is recommended for reading most sequential files since it avoids the possibility of attempting to read beyond the end of a file.

Review

7. Rewrite the answers for Review Problems 5 and 6 to incorporate WHILE...WEND loops with the EOF function.

LINE INPUT and PRINT#

In transferring data from a file to a program, INPUT# recognizes commas placed in the file by WRITE# as data separators. Therefore, these statements can not be used when the data contains embedded commas. This is only a problem when dealing with strings. For example, N$ = "BOB, JILL, AND JUDY WENT TO A PARTY." can not be placed in a file by WRITE# since the string contains commas. Rather than using commas to separate data, PRINT# places a carriage return character after each item of data to separate it from the next. The carriage return character is sent to the file each time the ENTER key is pressed. Since commas are not used to separate data in the PRINT# statement, commas may be contained within strings. The form of the PRINT# statement is:

PRINT# <channel>, <string variable>

A program which uses the PRINT# statement to transfer data to a file cannot use the standard INPUT statement since it recognizes commas as data separators. Instead, the LINE INPUT statement must be used because it recognizes a carriage return rather than a comma. Its form is:

LINE INPUT <string variable>

The LINE INPUT statement does not supply a question mark to prompt the user as does the INPUT statement so if one is desired it must be included in quotation marks. For example,

90 LINE INPUT "?"; A$

will print a question mark each time A$ is to be input.

Program 10.6

This program can be used to build a series of files containing form letters used by a company. Each file has a name corresponding to the type of letter it contains:

```
10 REM  *** LETTER$ = Form letter
20 REM  *** LENGTH = Number of lines in the letter
30 REM  *** TEXT$ = Input text
40 INPUT "Which letter will this be"; LETTER$
50 LETTER$ = "B:" + LETTER$ + ".DAT"
60 OPEN "O", 1, LETTER$
70 INPUT "How many lines will this be"; LENGTH
80 FOR L = 1 TO LENGTH
90      LINE INPUT "?"; TEXT$
100     PRINT #1, TEXT$
110 NEXT L
120 CLOSE 1
130 END
```

```
RUN
Which letter will this be? REJECT
How many lines will this be? 6
?       Thank you for your manuscript, "Belling the Mouse".  It
?was very good, but we already have over two hundred works with
?that title.  We are sorry, but your material does not fill our
?current needs.
?
?                                     Happy Book Publishers
```

- **Line 40:** Assigns a value to LETTER$ which is the name of the file in which the letter will be stored.
- **Line 50:** Uses the string addition function to join the drive prefix and extension on to the file name.
- **Line 60:** Opens an "O"utput file on channel 1 whose name is stored in LETTER$.
- **Line 70:** Inputs the number of lines in the letter.
- **Line 80:** Initiates a loop which will be repeated once for each line of the letter.
- **Line 90:** Accepts each line of the letter as input from the keyboard and places a carriage return character at the end of the line when the RETURN key is pressed. Notice that a question mark is printed at the beginning of each line to prompt the user. The question mark is not sent to the file.
- **Line 100:** Transfers data input for TEXT$ to the file open on channel 1.
- **Line 110:** Ends the loop started at line 80.
- **Line 120:** Closes the file open on channel 1.

LINE INPUT#

The INPUT# statement cannot be used to read data from a file that has embedded commas, because it recognizes commas as data separators. LINE INPUT# recognizes the carriage return characters placed by PRINT# as data as separators and is therefore used to transfer data from a file written using PRINT#. Its form is:

LINE INPUT#<channel>, <string variable>

It is important not to confuse the use of LINE INPUT# and PRINT# with INPUT# and WRITE#.

___

Program 10.7   This program will read one of several form letters stored in diskette files and personalize it for mailing to different people:

```
10 REM   *** LETTER$ = Form letter
20 REM   *** N = Number of recipients of the letter
30 REM   *** TEXT$ = Input text
40 INPUT "Which letter will this be"; LETTER$
50 LETTER$ = "B:" + LETTER$ + ".DAT"
60 INPUT "How many recipients"; N
70 DIM RECIPIENT$(N)
80 FOR I = 1 TO N
90       PRINT "Recipient #"; I;
100      INPUT RECIPIENT$(I)
110 NEXT I
120 REM  *** Produce Letter
130 FOR L = 1 TO N
140      PRINT
150      OPEN "I", 1, LETTER$
160      PRINT "Dear "; RECIPIENT$(L); ":"
170      WHILE EOF(1) = 0
180          LINE INPUT #1, L$
190          PRINT L$;
200      WEND
210      CLOSE 1
220      PRINT
230 NEXT L
240 END

RUN
Which letter will this be? REJECT
How many recipients? 2
Recipient # 1 ? Mr. Steinbeck
Recipient # 2 ? Mr. Shakespear
```

```
Dear Mr. Steinbeck:
     Thank you for your manuscript, "Belling the Mouse".  It
was very good, but we already have over two hundred works with
that title.  We are sorry, but you material does not fill our
current needs.
                              Happy Book Publishers

Dear Mr. Shakespear:
     Thank you for your manuscript, "Belling the Mouse".  It
was very good, but we already have over two hundred works with
that title.  We are sorry, but you material does not fill our
current needs.
                              Happy Book Publishers
```

- **Lines 40-50:** Assign the name of the file to be OPENed.
- **Lines 60-70:** Assign a dimension value for the array RECIPIENT$( ).
- **Lines 80-110:** Assign values to the elements of the array RECIPIENT$( ).
- **Line 130:** Initiates a loop which will repeat once for each recipient.
- **Line 150:** OPENs the letter file as input on channel 1.
- **Line 160:** Prints a greeting.
- **Line 170:** Uses a WHILE statement to test for the end of file (EOF) condition so that an attempt will not be made to read beyond the end of the file.
- **Line 180:** Reads in a line of the letter from the file to the program.

- **Line 190:** Prints the line of the letter.
- **Line 200:** Completes the WHILE loop.
- **Line 210:** CLOSEs the file open on channel 1.
- **Line 230:** Completes the loop started on line 130.

End of Chapter Problem

A baseball team needs a program to keep track of the player's batting averages. The information about the players should be kept in a sequential access file. Besides creating the file, BATTING.AVG, the user should be able to add new players to the file, update their averages, and print out a chart of the players with their respective averages.

Algorithm

1. Choose which option the user wishes to perform (create, append, update, print or exit).

2. Perform the required routine(s):
   a. Create File:
   > Find out number of players
   > Open the file
   > Enter the player information
   > Write the information to the file
   > Close the file

   b. Append File:
   > Find out number of new players
   > Open the file
   > Enter the player information
   > Write the information to the file
   > Close the file

   c. Update File:
   > Find out whose record to update
   > Open Files
   > Search for the correct player
   > Update the player's information
   > Write information to a temporary file
   > Close files
   > Erase old file / Rename temporary file

   d. Print File:
   > Open file
   > Print headings
   > Read file
   > Print player's information
   > Close file

   e. Exit:
   > Leave the program.

Input:

Player name	: N$
At Bats	: AB
Hits	: HITS
Number of Players	: NUM

Name to Search For	: CHECK$
New At Bats	: ADD
New Hits	: MORE

Output:

Player Name	: N$
At Bats	: AB
Hits	: HITS
Batting Avg	: AVG

Program 10.8

```
10 CLS : LOCATE 9,1
20 PRINT "1: Create File"
30 PRINT "2: Append File"
40 PRINT "3: Update File"
50 PRINT "4: Print File"
60 PRINT "5: Exit Program"
70 PRINT  : INPUT "Enter Selection:"; CHOICE
80 IF CHOICE < 1 OR CHOICE > 5 THEN BEEP : GOTO 10
90 ON CHOICE GOSUB 200, 300, 500, 700, 900
100 CLOSE : GOTO 10
200 REM
210 REM
220 REM  ****    Create File    ****
230 OPEN "O", 1, "B:BATTING.AVG"
240 INPUT "Enter Number of Players"; NUM
250 GOSUB 420
260 RETURN
300 REM
310 REM
320 REM  ****    Append File    ****
330 OPEN "A", 1, "B:BATTING.AVG"
340 INPUT "Enter Number of NEW Players"; NUM
350 GOSUB 420
360 RETURN
400 REM
410 REM
420 REM  ****    Write to Disk    ****
430 FOR I = 1 TO NUM
440     INPUT "Enter Name, At Bats, Hits"; N$, AB, HITS
450     AVG = HITS / AB
460     WRITE #1, N$, AB, HITS, AVG
470     PRINT
480 NEXT I
490 RETURN
500 REM
510 REM
520 REM  ****    Update File    ****
530 FLAG = 0
540 INPUT "Enter Name, additional At Bats, Hits"; CHECK$, ADD, MORE
550 OPEN "I", 1, "B:BATTING.AVG"
560 OPEN "O", 2, "B:BATTING.TMP"
570 WHILE EOF(1) = 0
580     INPUT #1, N$, AB, HITS, AVG
590     IF N$ <> CHECK$ THEN 640
600     FLAG = -1
610     AB = AB + ADD
```

```
620       HITS = HITS + MORE
630       AVG = HITS / AB
640       WRITE #2, N$, AB, HITS, AVG
650 WEND
660 CLOSE
670 IF FLAG = O THEN KILL "B:BATTING.TMP"
                ELSE KILL "B:BATTING.AVG":
                NAME "B:BATTING.TMP" AS "B:BATTING.AVG"
680 RETURN
700 REM
710 REM
720 REM   ****   Print File   ****
730 OPEN "I", 1, "B:BATTING.AVG"
740 CLS
750 PRINT "Name", "At Bats", "Hits", "Average" : PRINT
760 WHILE EOF(1) = 0
770       INPUT #1, N$, AB, HITS, AVG
780       PRINT N$, AB, HITS,: PRINT USING "#.###"; AVG
790 WEND
800 FOR I = 1 TO 2500 : NEXT I
810 RETURN
900 REM
910 REM
920 REM   ****   Exit Program   ****
930 CLS : END


RUN

1: Create File
2: Append File
3: Update File
4: Print File
5: Exit Program

Enter Selection:? 1
Enter Number of Players? 3
Enter Name, At Bats, Hits? MIKE,12,3

Enter Name, At Bats, Hits? BOB,16,5

Enter Name, At Bats, Hits? JOHN,23,3


1: Create File
2: Append File
3: Update File
4: Print File
5: Exit Program

Enter Selection:? 4

Name            At Bats         Hits            Average

MIKE            12              3               0.250
BOB             16              5               0.313
JOHN            23              3               0.130


Enter Selection:? 5
```

- **Lines 10-60:** Display the program menu.
- **Lines 70-80:** Accept the user's choice. If the number input is not within accepted range, the user is alerted and a new input requested.
- **Line 90:** Once a valid selection has been made, control of the program is sent to that subroutine.
- **Line 100:** Upon returning from a subroutine, all files are closed and the menu appears on the screen. Notice that the CLOSE statement without any channel numbers will close all open files.
- **Lines 200-260:** ✳✳✳ Create File ✳✳✳
  The file is opened for sequential "O"utput from the beginning of the file. The number of players (NUM) has been entered and control is passed to the subroutine WRITE TO DISK.
- **Lines 300-360:** ✳✳✳ Append File ✳✳✳
  The file is opened so that new information may be "A"ppended at the end of the file. The number of new players (NUM) is entered and control is passed to the subroutine WRITE TO DISK.
- **Lines 400-490:** ✳✳✳ Write To Disk ✳✳✳
  A loop is initiated to repeat NUM number of times. Within the loop, the players' names (N$), at bats (AB) and hits (HITS) are input, for which their batting averages are calculated. All this information is written to the file BATTING.AVG.
- **Lines 500-680:** ✳✳✳ Update File ✳✳✳
  The FLAG variable is used to check if the player entered is actually in the file. This will determine how the files are handled at the end of the routine. Two files are used in this routine. The data file BATTTING.AVG and a temporary file BATTING.TMP, which is a duplicate of BATTING.AVG. with the exception that the updated information is also stored. There are three data items which need to be updated: at bats, hits, and average. When a valid name is input, these data items are updated and the corrected information is written to the file BATTING.TMP from the program. When the end of file marker has been reached, the program checks to see if a valid name was entered (FLAG = −1). If an invalid name was entered, we erase BATTING.TMP because no data was updated. However, if a valid name was entered, the file BATTING.AVG will be erased, and the updated file, BATTING.TMP will be renamed accordingly.
- **Lines 700-810:** ✳✳✳ Print File ✳✳✳
  After the file has been opened for "I"nput, a heading is printed on a clear screen. A WHILE...WEND loop is used to read in the data from the file and display it.
- **Lines 900-930:** ✳✳✳ Exit Program ✳✳✳
  Clear the screen and exit the program.

EXERCISES

1. Store 50 random numbers between 0 and 20 in a sequential file. Use a second program to retrieve the numbers, add them and print their sum.

2. Store in a sequential file the names and prices of five different desserts served at MADGE'S DINER. With a second program, add two additional desserts. Have a third program retrieve and print the information.

3. Store ten different first names of friends in a sequential file. A second program is to print all the names in the file which begin with the letters D, E, F, G and H or a message if none is found.

4. (a) Two persons, JACK and JUDY, measured the Farenheit temperature (F) outside on February 12 at various times (T) during a ten-hour period. Their results are recorded here. Set up two sequential files, one for each person's data, naming each file after that person.

Jack		Judy	
T	F	T	F
0.0	18.1	1.0	20.9
2.1	24.0	1.9	23.3
3.8	27.2	3.5	26.1
6.0	29.3	6.0	28.8
8.0	26.6	8.2	26.2
9.0	16.1	10.0	16.0

(b) Write a program that will merge the two files into one sequential file named MERGE.DAT. The times should be sequentially in order. However, when a value of (T) occurs both in JACK and JUDY, the average of the two values of (F) should be placed in MERGE.DAT.

(c) Retrieve and print the contents of MERGE.DAT.

5. (a) Create a sequential payroll file called PAY.DAT that stores each of ten person's names (last name first), his or her hourly pay rate, the number of dependents and deductions for medical and life insurance for each week. Supply appropriate data.
(b) Write a program in which you supply the number of hours (H) each person worked during the week. Then using PAY.DAT prepare a payroll data sheet which lists the name, hours worked, gross pay, three deductions, and net pay for each employee. Assume a tax rate of 25%, with 2% being subtracted from this rate for each dependent.

6. (a) Establish a sequential file named SEQ.DAT which contains the members of the following sequence: 1001, 1002, 1003,...1128.

   (b) Write a program to retrieve any member of the sequence from SEQ.DAT and print it when its place in the sequence (i.e. third number, eigth number, etc.) is input.

7. (a) Write a program that will create a sequential file FRAT.DAT which contains the names, fraternities, and ages of thirty college students.

   (b) Write a program that will access FRAT.DAT and create a sequential file THETA.DAT which contains the names and ages of only students who live in THETA DELTA.

   (c) Modify the above program to create another sequential file THETA20.DAT which accesses THETA.DAT and stores only the people in THETA DELTA who are twenty years old.

8. There are twenty seats (numbered 1-20) in a classroom which will be used to administer the College Board Examination. The computer is to select seats randomly for each student taking the examination and store the student's name in a sequential file named SEATS.DAT.

   (a) Write a program that will create and zero (place a blank space in for each name) the sequential file SEATS.DAT.

   (b) Write a program that will randomly assign a seat to each of twenty students whose names are in a data statement and then store the name in SEATS.DAT with the appropriate seat number. Make sure no repeats occur.

   (c) List the contents of the file SEATS.DAT.

9. The Drama Club has decided to use the computer to print out tickets for a play it will perform in the school's auditorium. To reserve a seat a student runs a program called DRAMA.BAS, and types in the name and the row and seat number he or she would like. There are ten rows with five seats to a row. His or her ticket will appear as below. Have the program open a file named SHOW.DAT which stores the seat assignments. Make sure that a seat may not be chosen more than once.

   > DRAMA CLUB SHOW
   > CHRISTOPHER DINGLE HAS
   > RESERVED ROW 4
   > SEAT 3 FOR
   > JULY 4, 1985

10. (a) Write a program for the WE SELL IT SOFTWARE STORE, which saves the titles of twenty popular programs in a sequential file named SEQ.DAT.

    (b) Write a second program that asks the user for a software title, and then determines if the WE SELL IT SOFTWARE STORE carries that program.

Advanced Exercise

The following exercise requires the development of a detailed algorithm. The program should not be written until all details of the algorithm have been worked out.

11. The school's new coin collecting club needs a program to keep track of its ten members and their five most valuable coins.

    (a) Establish a sequential file named COIN.DAT. It should contain each member's name followed by a brief description of five of his or her most valuable coins. If a member has fewer than five coins, then blanks should be used.

    (b) Write a program, UPDATE.BAS, which performs the following functions:

    1. Allows the descriptions of each member's coins to be changed as he or she trades with club members.
    2. Changes the names and coin descriptions of members who are either joining or leaving the club.
    3. Produces a print-out of all members names and coin descriptions.

11

RANDOM ACCESS FILES

OPEN

FIELD

LSET

RSET

PUT

GET

LOC

A random-access file is structured like drawers in a filing cabinet, each holding a block of data that may be accessed individually. This system has several advantages over sequential files. To read the last line of data in a sequential file, you must read every line of data preceding it in sequence. However, any line of data in a random-access file can be read without reading the others. Updating a random-access file is easier than updating a sequential file since the contents of one line of data can be changed without accessing the rest. Unlike a sequential file, which is opened for a specific mode, a random-access file can be both written to and read from in the same mode.

In a random-access file each "drawer", called a record, consists of space reserved to store information. The length of the records in a file (i.e., the amount of information each can hold) is specified when a random-access file is created, and is the same for all the records within a given file. When the system is initialized, the computer assumes the maximum length of a record to be 128 characters unless otherwise instructed. The user may define records to be of any length up to the maximum specified at start up. A single record may contain many pieces of data, as long as they do not require more space than the specified size of the record.

To utilize the potential offered by random-access files, it is necessary to understand how the computer stores information. For file processing, the computer could have been designed to put each small item of information on the disk as soon as that information was made available. However, since accessing the disk is time-consuming, it is more efficient to transfer information to the disk in complete records. This requires the computer to have temporary storage space, called a buffer, where information is stored until a record is complete.

With sequential files the user has no control over the interaction between the buffer and the disk. Instead, the computer automatically determines when the buffer is full and then transfers its contents to the disk. Random-access files, however, give the user complete control over both the structure of the buffer's contents and its transfer to the disk.

The process of transferring data between a program and a random-access file involves the following series of steps:

1. Using the OPEN statement, the file is created, opened, and a buffer made ready to receive data.
2. Using the FIELD statement, the buffer is partitioned to fit the structure of each record.
3. Data is transferred from the program to the buffer using the LSET and RSET commands.
4. Data is transferred from the buffer to the file using the PUT command.
5. To retrieve data from the file for use in the program, the GET command is used.

Each of these steps is presented separately and should be read carefully to understand how each step interacts with the others.

OPEN

Like sequential files, random-access files use the OPEN statement. The format for opening random-access files is:

OPEN "R", <channel>, "<file name>", <record length>

where mode "R" stands for a random-access file, and the record length is the total number of characters in the record. By using the "R" mode, the computer creates a temporary storage area called a buffer whose size is the same as the record length. The buffer is an area in memory where a record is stored before it is written to the disk file. For example,

20 OPEN "R", 3, "KAZOO.DAT", 50

will open a file named KAZOO.DAT for random-access on channel 3, with each record in the file containing fifty characters, and will assign it a buffer.

Converting Numbers to Strings

Unlike sequential files, random-access files store all information as strings. This requires numerical data to be converted to strings before being stored. The functions MKI$( ), MKS$( ) and MKD$( ) perform this operation. They will convert an integer, single precision or double precision number, respectively, into a string variable.

Function	Operation
N$ = MKI$(N%)	Converts an integer (N%) into a two character string (N$).
N$ = MKS$(N!)	Converts a single precision number (N!) into a four character string (N$).
N$ = MKD$(N#)	Converts a double-precision number (N#) into an eight character string (N$).

FIELD

After the OPEN statement assigns a buffer to the file, the FIELD statement is used to organize the buffer so that data can be sent through it from the program to the file and from the file to the program. The FIELD statement partitions the buffer into regions which hold a string and are referenced by specific string variables. The simplest form of the FIELD statement is:

FIELD <channel>, <length> AS <string variable>

For example,

10 OPEN "R", 2, "KAZOO.DAT", 50
20 FIELD 2, 50 AS A$

After the file has been opened at line 10, the FIELD statement at line 20 reserves fifty characters in the buffer for the string variable A$. It is possible to partition the buffer to hold more than one string. The statement

20 FIELD 2, 20 AS A$, 30 AS B$

will reserve the first twenty characters of the buffer for the contents of A$ and the last thirty characters for the contents of B$. To better visualize how data is stored in the buffer, it is a good practice to diagram the buffer as illustrated below.

128 Character Buffer

A$	B$	
20	30	Unused

LSET and RSET

The FIELD statement reserves a certain number of spaces for string variables in a buffer, but it does not transfer the strings to the buffer. To do this, it is necessary to use the LSET and RSET commands. The form for both is:

LSET <string variable> = <string to be transferred to buffer>

or

RSET <string variable> = <string to be transferred to buffer>

Besides transferring strings to the buffer, these commands also change the strings to make sure they fit the space allotted in the FIELD statement. For example, if the field contains 24 characters and N1$ contains 15 characters, 9 blank characters have to be added to bring the total to 24. If N1$ contains more than 24 characters, it must be truncated to 24. These operations are performed by either the LSET or RSET statements.

The LSET statement left-justifies a string by adding needed blank characters to the right end. If N1$ contains 15 characters, LSET will add 9 blank characters on the right. RSET justifies by adding the 9 blank characters on the left. Both LSET and RSET will truncate excess characters from the right end of a string which is larger than the space specified in the FIELD statement. Since most programmers would rather add blanks at the end instead of the beginning of a string, LSET is used more frequently than RSET.

For example:

20 FIELD 1, 24 AS N1$
30 LSET N1$ = "24 CHARACTERS!!"

128 Character Buffer

N1$	
24	Unused

or

20 FIELD 1, 24 AS N1$
30 RSET N1$ = "24 CHARACTERS!!"

128 Character Buffer

N1$	
24	Unused

In the first example, the contents of N1$ are transferred into the buffer with its information left-justified, which means that 9 spaces are added to the right end of the string. In the second example, the contents of N1$ are transferred into the buffer with its information right- justified, with 9 spaces added to the left end of the string.

Program 11.1   This program demonstrates how LSET and RSET change strings assigned to them:

```
10 OPEN "R", 1, "B:SAMPLE.DAT", 30
20 FIELD 1, 5 AS A$, 10 AS B$, 5 AS C$, 10 AS D$
30 LSET A$ = "ABCDEFG"
40 LSET B$ = "ABCDEFG"
50 RSET C$ = "ABCDEFG"
60 RSET D$ = "ABCDEFG"
70 PRINT "THIS IS HOW THE 30 CHARACTERS APPEAR IN THE"
80 PRINT "BUFFER, EXCLUDING THE PARENTHESES"
90 PRINT TAB(3); "A$"; TAB(12); "B$"; TAB(22); "C$"; TAB(31); "D$"
100 PRINT "("; A$; ") ("; B$; ") ("; C$; ") ("; D$; ")"
110 CLOSE 1
120 END

RUN
THIS IS HOW THE 30 CHARACTERS APPEAR IN THE
BUFFER, EXCLUDING THE PARENTHESES
   A$        B$         C$        D$
(ABCDE) (ABCDEFG   ) (ABCDE) (   ABCDEFG)
```

- **Line 10:** Opens a random-access file named "SAMPLE.DAT" using channel 1. A buffer is set up to match the record length of 30 characters.
- **Line 20:** The 30 character buffer is divided into 4 sections to hold the variables A$, B$, C$ and D$. Their respective lengths are 5, 10, 5 and 10 characters each.

128 Character Buffer

A$	B$	C$	D$	
5	10	5	10	Unused

- **Line 30:** LSET is used to place a string left justified into the portion of the buffer referenced by A$.
- **Line 40:** LSET is used to place a string left justified into the portion of the buffer referenced by B$.

- **Line 50:** RSET is used to place a string right justified into the portion of the buffer referenced by C$.
- **Line 60:** RSET is used to place a string right justified into the portion of the buffer referenced by D$.
- **Lines 70-90:** Displays headings.
- **Line 100:** Prints the strings stored in A$, B$, C$ and D$.
- **Line 110:** Breaks the line of communication from the program to the file.

Notice that the FIELD statement at line 20 has set aside 5 characters for A$, but since the string in line 30 is longer than that, LSET has truncated the last two characters. Since 10 characters were set aside for B$, the LSET statement in line 40 has added 3 spaces to the right of the string to make it 10 characters long. As only 5 spaces were allocated to C$, the RSET command in line 50 truncated the excess characters from the right. The RSET command in line 60 has added 3 spaces to the left of B$ so that it fills up the space allotted by the FIELD statement.

Review

1. Write a program to set up a random-access file called MAILING.LST. The buffer should be divided into 5 areas as follows:

Variable		Meaning	Maximum Length
N$	=	Name	(20 characters left-justified)
ADDRESS$	=	Street Address	(25 characters left-justified
CITY$	=	City	(20 characters left-justified)
STATE$	=	State	(20 characters left-justified)
ZIP$	=	Zip Code	(9 characters right-justified)

PUT

The LSET and RSET commands transfer information from the program to the buffer, but do not transfer the contents of the buffer to the file. The PUT statement transfers data from the buffer to a record in the file. Each record is numbered sequentially, from one to the number of records in the file.

The form of the PUT statement is

PUT <channel>, <record number>

where channel represents the channel specified in the OPEN statement and record number refers to the position in the file where the record will be stored. If the record number is not specified, the data is transferred to the record immediately following the last record accessed by the program. For example,

20 PUT 2, 4

instructs the computer to transfer the contents of the buffer into the fourth record of the file open on channel 2. If the next PUT statement executed does not specify a record number, the data in the buffer is transferred to the fifth record.

Keyboard Input   When an INPUT statement is employed to input data to a program from the keyboard, it is necessary to use variable names different from those used in the FIELD statement. Otherwise, the computer would confuse the data stored in the program with the data stored in the buffer if the same variable names were used. The data assigned to the INPUT variables will be assigned to the FIELD statement variables by LSET and RSET. Study Program 11.2 carefully since it demonstrates this proper use of variable names.

Program 11.2   This program creates the file ADDRESS.DAT and will allow the names and addresses for five people to be placed in the file:

```
10 REM PERSON$, P$ = Name (15 characters)
20 REM ADDRESS$, A$ = Address (25 characters)
30 OPEN "R", 1, "B:ADDRESS.DAT", 40
40 FIELD 1, 15 AS PERSON$, 25 AS ADDRESS$
50 FOR X = 1 TO 5
60     INPUT "Name"; P$
70     INPUT "Address"; A$
80     LSET PERSON$ = P$
90     LSET ADDRESS$ = A$
100    PUT 1, X
110 NEXT X
120 PRINT "File creation completed"
130 CLOSE 1
140 END

RUN
Name? BIDWELL
Address? 62 MAIN STREET
Name? PRESLEY
Address? 111 WEBSTER LANE
Name? CRANE
Address? 1212 MOCKINGBIRD LANE
Name? TIBBETTS
Address? 14 PALISADES PARKWAY
Name? PORTER
Address? 10 GRAVEL DRIVE
File creation completed
```

- **Line 30:** Opens the random-access file ADDRESS.DAT on channel 1 with a record length of 40 characters.
- **Line 40:** Partitions the 40 character buffer into 2 sections, one 15 characters referenced by PERSON$, and another 25 characters referenced by ADDRESS$.

128 Character Buffer

PERSON$	ADDRESS$	
15	25	Unused

- **Line 50:** Initiates a loop which will execute five times to transfer 5 sets of names and addresses from the program to the file.
- **Lines 60-70:** Accept the user's input from the keyboard for name (P$) and address (A$).

- **Lines 80-90:** Place the information input in lines 60-70 left-justified into the buffer. Notice that the variable names used in the INPUT statements are not the same as those described in the FIELD statement. This is necessary so that the data is transferred correctly into the buffer from the program.
- **Line 100:** Takes the record placed in the buffer in lines 80-90 and writes it from the buffer to the file at position X.
- **Line 110:** Ends the loop started in line 50.
- **Line 120:** Prints a message that file creation is now complete.
- **Line 130:** Closes the file open on channel 1.

Review

2. Modify the program from Review 1 so that it takes the record stored in the buffer and transfers it to a disk file. Write the program so that a variable number of names may be entered.

GET

The GET statement performs the opposite function of the PUT statement. It is used to transfer information in a record from a file to the buffer. Again, a FIELD statement must be employed in order to partition the buffer. The form of the GET statement is:

GET <channel>, <record number>

Like the PUT statement, the GET statement transfers data into the buffer from the record following the last record accessed if no record number is specified. For example,

20 GET 3, 12

transfers the contents of record number 12 to the buffer associated with channel 3. If no record number is placed in the next GET statement, the information from record number 13 will be placed into the buffer from the file.

Program 11.3

This program retrieves and prints the name and address of any person stored in the file ADDRESS.DAT.

```
10 REM PERSON$, P$ = Name (15 characters)
20 REM ADDRESS$, A$ = Address (25 characters)
30 REM RECORD = Record Number
40 REM
50 PRINT "Enter a negative number to stop the program"
60 OPEN "R", 2, "B:ADDRESS.DAT", 40
70 FIELD 2, 15 AS PERSON$, 25 AS ADDRESS$
80 INPUT "WHICH RECORD"; RECORD
90      IF RECORD <= 0 THEN 150
100     GET 2, RECORD
110     PRINT PERSON$
120     PRINT ADDRESS$
130     PRINT
140 GOTO 80
150 PRINT "File accessing completed"
160 CLOSE 2
170 END
```

```
RUN
Enter a negative number to stop the program
WHICH RECORD? 4
TIBBETTS
14 PALISADES PARKWAY

WHICH RECORD? 2
PRESLEY
111 WEBSTER LANE

WHICH RECORD? -1
File accessing completed
```

- **Line 60:** Opens the random-access file ADDRESS.DAT on channel 2 with a record length of 40 characters.
- **Line 70:** Paritions the 40 character buffer into 2 sections, one 15 characters referenced by PERSON$, and another 25 characters referenced by ADDRESS$.

128 Character Buffer

PERSON$	ADDRESS$	
15	25	Unused

- **Line 80:** Asks the user for the record number associated with the information needed from the file.
- **Line 90:** If the input value is less than 0, the program branches to the CLOSE statement.
- **Line 100:** Transfers the contents of the record at position RECORD to the buffer.
- **Lines 110-120:** Print out the name and address.
- **Line 140:** Branches back to line 80 in order to retrieve and print another record.
- **Line 150:** Prints a message that file accessing is complete.
- **Line 160:** Cuts off communication between the program to the file.

Review

3. Write a program using the random access file MAILING.LST created in Review 1. Have the user input a number to select the record the computer will GET. Print the data from this record or the message "No Data Found".

Converting Strings Into Numbers

When converted numeric data is retrieved from a random-access file as a string, it may be converted back to numeric data using the following functions:

Function	Operation
N% = CVI (N$)	Converts a two-character string (N$) into an integer (N%).
N! = CVS(N$)	Converts a four-character string (N$) into a single-precision number (N!).
N# = CVD(N$)	Converts an eight-character string (N$) into a double-precision number (N#).

LOC   The LOC function returns the record number used in the last GET or PUT executed on a particular channel. The statement

$$N = LOC(3)$$

assigns the variable N the record number used in the last GET or PUT operation performed on channel 3. The LOC function will return zero until a GET or PUT is executed.

If a GET statement attempts to read a record past the end of a file, the buffer associated with that file is filled with null characters (ASCII code 0). This information can be used to determine the number of records in a random-access file. Proceeding sequentially, all of the records in a file can be read and counted until null records are found.

Program 11.4   This program shows how LOC can be used to find the end of a random-access file.

```
10 REM PERSON$ = Name (15 characters)
20 REM ADDRESS$ = Address (25 characters)
30 REM
40 OPEN "R", 3, "B:ADDRESS.DAT", 40
50 FIELD 3, 15 AS PERSON$, 25 AS ADDRESS$
60 GET 3
70 TEST$ = PERSON$ + ADDRESS$
80 IF TEST$ = STRING$(40,0) THEN 100
90 GOTO 60
100 PRINT "THERE ARE"; LOC (3) - 1; "RECORDS IN THE FILE"
110 CLOSE 3
120 END

RUN
THERE ARE 5 RECORDS IN THE FILE
```

- **Line 40:** Opens a random-access file named ADDRESS.DAT using channel 3. The record length is 40 characters.
- **Line 50:** Partitions the 40 character buffer into 2 sections, one 15 characters referenced by PERSON$, and another 25 characters referenced by ADDRESS$.

128 Character Buffer

PERSON$	ADDRESS$	
15	25	Unused

- **Line 60:** Transfers a record from the file to the buffer starting with the first record and moving sequentially.
- **Line 70:** Uses string addition to create a string as long as the buffer.
- **Line 80:** Tests to see if the string in TEST$ is equivalent to a string of 40 null (ASCII code 0) characters which will determine the end-of-file location.
- **Line 90:** GETs another record if the end-of-file has not been reached.
- **Line 100:** Uses the LOC function to determine the number of records when end-of-file is reached.
- **Line 110:** Closes the file open on channel 3.

**Accessing
Multiple Files**

Program 11.5

It is possible to work with two or more random-access files simultaneously within a single program. The random-access file HOBBY.DAT is created in this program to store the hobbies of people whose names are stored in ADDRESS.DAT (previously created by Program 11.2). It is important not to confuse the variables associated with each file. Note how the channel numbers are used to keep the information in each file separate within the program:

```
10 REM PERSON$ = Name (15 characters)
20 REM ADDRESS$ = Address (25 characters)
30 REM HOBBY$, H$ = Hobby (10 characters)
40 REM
50 OPEN "R", 1, "B:ADDRESS.DAT", 40
60 OPEN "R", 2, "B:HOBBY.DAT", 10
70 FIELD 1, 15 AS PERSON$, 25 AS ADDRESS$
80 FIELD 2, 10 AS HOBBY$
90 RECORD = RECORD + 1
100 GET 1, RECORD
110 TEST$ = PERSON$ + ADDRESS$
120 IF TEST$ = STRING$(40,0) THEN 170
130 PRINT PERSON$; "'S HOBBY IS ";:INPUT H$
140 LSET HOBBY$ = H$
150 PUT 2, RECORD
160 GOTO 90
170 CLOSE
180 END

RUN
BIDWELL          'S HOBBY IS ? MUSIC
PRESLEY          'S HOBBY IS ? COMPUTERS
CRANE            'S HOBBY IS ? COOKING
TIBBETTS         'S HOBBY IS ? TRAVEL
PORTER           'S HOBBY IS ? DRIVING
```

- **Line 50:** Opens a random-access file named ADDRESS.DAT using channel 1. The record length is 40 characters.
- **Line 60:** Opens another random-access file, HOBBY.DAT. It uses channel 2 and has a record length of 10 characters.
- **Line 70:** Partitions the buffer for channel 1 into two segments. One is 15 characters referenced by PERSON$ and the other 25 characters referenced by ADDRESS$.

128 Character Buffer

PERSON$	ADDRESS$	
15	25	Unused

- **Line 80:** Partitions the buffer for channel 2 into one segment, which is 10 characters referenced by HOBBY$.

128 Character Buffer

HOBBY$	
10	Unused

- **Line 90:** Increments the record location counter.
- **Line 100:** Transfers a record into the buffer open on channel 1 from the file ADDRESS.DAT.
- **Line 110:** Uses string addition to create a character string (TEST$) which is as long as the buffer.
- **Line 120:** Tests for end-of-file, a string of null (CHR$(0)) characters as long as the buffer.
- **Line 130:** Uses the name of the person located in the buffer to prompt the user to INPUT that person's hobby (H$).
- **Line 140:** Uses LSET to transfer H$ into the buffer for channel 2, referenced by HOBBY$.
- **Line 150:** Takes the information from the buffer for channel 2 and transfers it into the file assigned to channel 2, HOBBY.DAT.
- **Line 160:** Branches back to get another record if end-of-file has not been reached.
- **Line 170:** Since a channel is not specified, all files are closed.

End of Chapter Problem

This program is an updated version of Program 10.8. It will illustrate the advantages of random access files over sequential access files.

A baseball team needs a program to keep track of the player's batting averages. The information about the players should be kept in a random-access file. Besides creating the file, BATTING2.AVG, the program should be able to add new players to the file, update their averages, or print out a chart of the players with their respective averages. The players' uniform numbers will correspond to their record numbers in the file.

Algorithm:
1. Choose which option the user wishes to perform (create, append, update, print or exit).

2. Perform the required routine(s).

      a. Create File:
            Find out number of players
            Open the file
            Initialize the file
            Partition the buffer
            Enter the player information
            Load player data into the buffer
            Write the information to the file
            Close the file

      b. Append File:
            Find out number of new players
            Open the file
            Partition the buffer
            Enter the player information
            Load player data into the buffer
            Write the information to the file
            Close the file

   c. Update File:
> Find out whose record to update
> Open file
> Partition the buffer
> Search for the correct player
> Update the player information
> Load updated information into the buffer
> Write information to the file
> Close file

   d. Print File:
> Open file
> Print headings
> Load information into the buffer
> Print player information
> Close file

   e. Exit:
> Leave the program

3. Since Create File and Append File perform similar activities, they both call Input Routine to enter the player information and calculate the batting average. Then, Conversion Routine is called by Input Routine.

4. Input Routine and Update File both call Conversion Routine which converts numeric information into strings, places that data into the buffer and PUTs it in the file.

Input:

Check String	: CHECK$
Player Number	: NUM
Player Name	: N$
At Bats	: AB
Hits	: HITS
Number of Players	: LOOP
Name to Search For	: CHECK$
New at Bats	: ADD
New Hits	: MORE

Output:

Player Number	: NUM
Player Name	: N$
At Bats	: AB
Hits	: HITS
Batting Avg	: AVG

Program 11.6

```
10 CLS : LOCATE 9,1
20 PRINT "1: Create File"
30 PRINT "2: Append File"
40 PRINT "3: Update File"
50 PRINT "4: Print File"
60 PRINT "5: Exit Program"
70 PRINT  : INPUT "Enter Selection:"; CHOICE
80 IF CHOICE < 1 OR CHOICE > 5 THEN BEEP : GOTO 10
90 OPEN "R", 1, "B:BATTING2.AVG", 29
100 FIELD 1, 1 AS CHECK$, 20 AS PLAYER$, 2 AS AB$,
    2 AS HIT$, 4 AS AVG$
110 ON CHOICE GOSUB 200, 300, 500, 700, 1100
120 CLOSE : GOTO 10
200 REM
210 REM
220 REM ****    Create File    ****
230 INPUT "Enter Number of Players"; LOOP
240 GOSUB 1000
250 GOSUB 400
260 RETURN
300 REM
310 REM
320 REM ****    Append File    ****
330 INPUT "Enter Number of NEW Players"; LOOP
340 GOSUB 400
350 RETURN
400 REM
410 REM
420 REM ****    Input Routine    ****
430 FOR I = 1 TO LOOP
440     INPUT "Number, Name, At Bats, Hits"; NUM, N$, AB, HITS
450     AVG = HITS / AB
460     C$ = "*" : GOSUB 900
470     PRINT
480 NEXT I
490 RETURN
500 REM
510 REM
520 REM ****    Update File    ****
530 INPUT "Enter Player Number"; NUM
540 GET 1, NUM
550 IF PLAYER$ = STRING$(20,0) THEN PRINT "NOT FOUND" : GOTO 630
560 N$ = PLAYER$
570 INPUT "Enter Additional At Bats, Hits"; AB, HITS
580 AB = AB + CVI(AB$)
590 HITS = HITS + CVI(HIT$)
600 AVG = HITS / AB
610 GOSUB 900
620 PRINT PLAYER$; "updated"
630 INPUT "Another Y/N"; YES$
640 IF YES$ = "Y" OR YES$ = "y" THEN 530
650 RETURN
```

```
700 REM
710 REM
720 REM   ****    Print File    ****
730 CLS
740 PRINT "Name", "At Bats", "Hits", "Average" : PRINT
750 FOR I = 1 TO 100
760     GET 1, I
770     IF CHECK$ = "#" THEN 790
780     PRINT PLAYER$, CVI(AB$), CVI(HIT$), CVS(AVG$)
790 NEXT I
800 FOR I = 1 TO 2500 : NEXT I : REM  ***   delay
810 RETURN
900 REM
910 REM
920 REM   ****    Conversion Routine    ****
930 RSET AB$ = MKI$(AB)
940 RSET HIT$ = MKI$(HITS)
950 RSET AVG$ = MKS$(AVG)
960 LSET PLAYER$ = N$
970 LSET CHECK$ = C$
980 PUT 1, NUM
990 RETURN
1000 REM
1010 REM
1020 REM   ****    Initialize file    ****
1030 FOR I = 1 TO 100
1040     C$ = "#"
1050     LSET CHECK$ = C$
1060     PUT 1, I
1070 NEXT I
1080 RETURN
1100 REM
1110 REM
1120 REM   ****    Exit Program    ****
1130 CLS
1140 END
```

```
RUN
1: Create File
2: Append File
3: Update File
4: Print File
5: Exit Program

Enter Selection:? 1
Enter Number of Players? 3
Enter Number, Name, At Bats, Hits? 2, MIKE, 12, 5

Enter Number, Name, At Bats, Hits? 5, BOB, 16, 9

Enter Number, Name, At Bats, Hits? 1, PAUL, 15, 3

Enter Selection:? 5
```

- **Lines 10-70:** Display the menu and ask the user to input a selection.
- **Line 80:** If an invalid selection number is input, the user is alerted by a BEEP and must choose again.
- **Line 90:** Opens a random-access file named BATTING2.AVG, which has a record size of 29 characters and uses channel 1.
- **Line 100:** Partitions the buffer into 5 segments, a 1 character string named CHECK$, a 20 character string named PLAYER$, a 2 character

string named AB$, another 2 character string named HIT$ and finally, a 4 character string named AVG$.

128 Character Buffer

√$	PLAYER$	AB$	HIT$	AVG$	
1	20	2	2	4	Unused

- **Line 110:** Branches to another section of the program based upon the user's input.
- **Line 120:** Terminates communication between the program and file.
- **Lines 200-260:** ∗∗∗ Create File ∗∗∗
  The user is asked to input the number of players on the team. The program then branches to the subroutine INITIALIZE FILE which then loads the CHECK$ field with pound signs. Upon return from this routine, the program branches to the subroutine INPUT ROUTINE which transfers the player records to the file.
- **Lines 300-350:** ∗∗∗ Append File ∗∗∗
  This routine asks the user to input the number of new players and then branches to the subroutine INPUT ROUTINE, which writes the player records to the file.
- **Lines 400-490:** ∗∗∗ Input Routine ∗∗∗
  This routine initiates a loop to be executed LOOP times. Within the loop, information about the player is entered and a batting average calculated. The check variable C$ is set to an asterisk (∗) to note that a valid record will be stored. The program then branches to the subroutine CONVERSION ROUTINE. The loop continues after returning from this routine.
- **Lines 500-650:** ∗∗∗ Update File ∗∗∗
  In order to update the file, the program first checks to see if the requested record exists. If it does not, a new record is created. Then, the user is asked to input the new information from the keyboard. The program now branches to the subroutine CONVERSION ROUTINE. Note how the CVI function is used to convert the string variables to numerics so that the information may be updated in lines 580 and 590.
- **Lines 700-810:** ∗∗∗ Print File ∗∗∗
  After the screen is cleared and headings printed, a loop is initiated which executes 100 times (the maximum number of records in the file). When the record is brought into the buffer from the file in line 760, it is then checked to see if it is, in fact, a valid record (CHECK$ <> "#"). If the record is valid, an output line is then produced. If the record is not valid, that record is skipped and the loop continues.
- **Lines 900-990:** ∗∗∗ Conversion Routine ∗∗∗
  In lines 930-950, the MKI and MKS functions are used to convert the numeric variables to character strings so that RSET can load this information into the buffer. The LSET statements are used to load PLAYER$ and CHECK$ into the buffer. This information is then PUT into the file from the buffer via channel 1.
- **Lines 1000-1080:** ∗∗∗ Initialize File ∗∗∗
  This routine loads a pound sign into the field CHECK$ in the buffer. If the computer checks a record and finds a "#" in the CHECK$ field, then it realizes that the record stores no data.
- **Lines 1100-1140:** Exit the program.

EXERCISES

1. Store the 26 letters of the alphabet in a random-access file named LETTER.DAT. Have a program pick five random numbers from 1 to 26 and use these numbers to put together a five letter "word" made up from the letters stored in LETTER.DAT.

2. Store titles of ten books in a random-access file named BOOK.DAT. Use this file to make a sequential file for all the titles beginning with letters from N to Z, inclusive.

3. (a) Create a random-access file named ACCOUNTS.DAT that will contain the customer name and current balance for twenty-five savings accounts:

   Name? FRED ZIFFEL
   Starting balance? 500.00
   Account number 1 assigned.

   Name? JILL MONTANA
   Starting balance? 700.00
   Account number 2 assigned.

   Name? PETER JONES
   Starting balance? 400.00
   Account number 3 assigned.

   (b) Write a program that will update the file ACCOUNTS.DAT whenever an individual makes a deposit or withdrawal:

   RUN
   Enter a negative number to stop.
   Account? 1
   Deposit (D) or withdrawal (W)? W
   Amount? 600
   Transaction recorded
   Account? 3
   Deposit (D) or withdrawal (W)? D
   Amount? 50
   Transaction recorded
   Account? –99

(c) Write a program using the file ACCOUNTS.DAT that sends letters of warning to the holders of all overdrawn accounts or of congratulations to those with accounts containing $500 or more informing them that they will be receiving a toaster in the mail.

> Dear FRED ZIFFEL:
>   It has come to our attention that your account
> is overdrawn by $100. Please make a deposit for
> at least that amount immediately.
>   Thank you
>   THE BANK

> Dear JILL MONTANA:
>   You have an exceptionally large account.
> You will be receiving a toaster in the mail
> as an award.
>   Thank you
>   THE BANK

4. (a) Create a random-access file named CARS.DAT to record how many full-sized, mid-sized and compact cars a dealer sells each month for a twelve month period.

   (b) Write a program that will retrieve information from the file CARS.DAT for a specific month and then print a bar graph comparing the sales of the three sizes of cars. Entering a negative number should halt the program.

   > Which month <1–12> ? 12
   >
   > Full-sized:***************
   > Mid-sized:***************
   > Compact:********************
   >
   > Which month <1–12> ? –99

5. (a) Write a program that will create a random-access file FRAT.DAT which contains the names, fraternities and ages of thirty college students.

   (b) Write a program that will access FRAT.DAT and create a sequential file SIGMA.DAT which contains the names and ages of students who live in SIGMA CHI.

   (c) Write a program that accesses the file FRAT.DAT and randomly selects twenty-five students for seats in a classroom of five rows, five seats in a row. Have the computer print a seating plan for the class, placing each student's name at the correct seat location.

6. (a) Establish a random-access file named SAYING.DAT which contains wise sayings. Each sage remark is to consist of up to 128 characters. The number of such utterances is to be determined by the user.

   (b) Write the program required to retrieve and print any one of the wise sayings in SAYING.DAT.

7. (a) Write a program that creates a random-access file named SEN-TENCE.DAT, which contains 25 words.

   (b) Write another program to pick 5 random numbers (between 1-25) and have the program print out a 'sentence' consisting of the five words from the random records chosen from the file SENTENCE.DAT. Place spaces between the five words and add a period to the end.

Advanced Exercises

Each of the following exercises requires the development of a detailed algorithm. The program should not be written until all details of the algorithm have been worked out.

8. The computer is to be used to store information on charge account customers at the Buy Low Department Store in a random access file named CHARGE.DAT. The information on each customer is to be stored in a single record with the record number serving as the customer's charge account number.

   Write a program that creates a file CHARGE.DAT in which the name, street address, city, state, zip code and total unpaid balance for each customer is stored. Have the program perform each of the following functions:

   1. Updates the balances by adding to the unpaid balance when sales are made and subtracting when bills are paid.
   2. Sends a bill to each customer at the end of the month. If the total due exceeds $800.00, the message YOUR ACCOUNT EXCEEDS YOUR CHARGE LIMIT, PAY IMMEDIATELY is printed at the bottom of the bill.
   3. Closes the account of a customer who has paid his or her balance and moved away. (Hint: Place all blanks in the record.)
   4. Opens an account for a new customer using the first empty record.

9. (a) Write a program that will create a random-access file named SAVINGS.DAT that can be used by a bank to store information about ten depositors. Each depositor's name, social security number, complete address (number and street, city, state, and zip code), and account balance are to be included.

   (b) Have the program allow any of the information, including the balance of the account, to be changed or updated.

   ```
   RUN
   DEPOSITOR'S ACCOUNT NUMBER? 2
   NAME: MARK WALTER
            (1) CHANGE NAME
            (2) CHANGE SOCIAL SECURITY NUMBER
            (3) CHANGE ADDRESS
            (4) CHANGE BALANCE
   OPTION? 4
   OLD BALANCE: 155.63
   NEW BALANCE? 183.76
   ```

   (c) The bank gives its depositors 1/2% interest per month compounded monthly. Add a routine to the above program that can be run at the end of each month to add 1/2% to the balance of each account.

12

SEARCHING AND SORTING

SWAP

SWAP

SWAP

SWAP

SWAP

SWAP

SWAP

*T*his chapter explains techniques for searching and sorting data. Since the topics in this chapter involve considerable use of material covered earlier, it should not be read until that material is understood thoroughly.

Bubble Sort

When working with a large amount of data it is usually advisable to sort it first. A list of names might be sorted into alphabetical order, or a list of numbers might be sorted into ascending or descending order. One of the most fundamental sorting techniques is the bubble sort. In a bubble sort the computer starts at the bottom of a list, then proceeds sequentially to the top, comparing each item in the list with the one above it. If two elements are not in their proper order, they are interchanged. In this way the name that comes first alphabetically in the list is "bubbled" to the top of the list. For example, given the initial list

```
Lester      —Top
Diane
Bruce
Susan
Eli         —Bottom
```

the computer would start at the bottom comparing the names Susan and Eli. Because Eli comes alphabetically before Susan, the computer switches the names and the list becomes:

```
Lester
Diane
Bruce
Eli
Susan
```

Next, Bruce and Eli are compared. Because Bruce comes before Eli, no change is made. Then Diane and Bruce are compared and interchanged, so the list becomes:

```
Lester
Bruce
Diane
Eli
Susan
```

Bruce and Lester are then compared and interchanged. The order of the names in the list now becomes:

> Bruce
> Lester
> Diane
> Eli
> Susan

Bruce, the name that comes first alphabetically, is now at the top. Now the computer starts over at the bottom and the name that comes next alphabetically is "bubbled" up to its proper position. After this procedure has been repeated for as many names as are on the list, the order becomes:

> Bruce   —Top
> Diane
> Eli
> Lester
> Susan   —Bottom

The algorithm below is for a bubble sort which takes a subscripted array of data containing N elements and sorts it so that it ends up structured in increasing order.

Initial Conditions:
N = number of elements in the array N$( )
N$( ) = subscripted array

Step 1   FOR I = 1 TO N – 1
Step 2   FOR J = N TO I + 1 STEP – 1
Step 3   IF N$(J) < N$(J – 1) THEN TEMP$ = N$(J):
                                N$(J) = N$(J – 1):
                                N$(J – 1) = TEMP$

Step 4   NEXT J
Step 5   NEXT I

The outer loop repeats the whole process N − 1 times because the maximum number of iterations for the process is one less than the number (N) of items in the unsorted list. The inner loop starts initially at the bottom of the list (N) and proceeds sequentially to the top. This loop becomes smaller after each iteration of the bubble process because as the names are moved into their proper positions, they need not be checked again. This is accomplished by using the end condition (I + 1) in conjunction with STEP –1, where I is the current value of the outer loop variable. During the execution of this loop, the computer compares each element with the previous element. If they are not in the correct order, the data from the array are interchanged, thus putting them into the correct order. And so, elements not in proper order are moved up or down the list into their correct positions.

Notice how data is switched in Step 3 when N$(J) < N$(J − 1). First, TEMP$ is assigned the value of N$(J), then N$(J) is assigned the value of N$(J − 1) and finally N$(J − 1) is assigned the value of TEMP$. TEMP$ is needed to hold the value of N$(J) while the switch is being made, otherwise the value would be erased. This can be demonstrated using the first switch made in the list of names between Susan and Eli.

First:

N$(5) = Eli
N$(4) = Susan

N$(4) N$(5)

| SUSAN | ELI |

then

TEMP$ = N$(5)

N$(4) N$(5) TEMP$

| SUSAN | ELI | ELI |

then

N$(5) = N$(4)

N$(4) N$(5) TEMP$

| SUSAN | SUSAN | ELI |

and finally,

N$(4) = TEMP$

N$(4) N$(5) TEMP$

| ELI | SUSAN | ELI |

and the switch is complete.

Program 12.1   This program is a bubble sort used to sort a list of 5 names into alphabetical order:

```
10 CLS
20 DIM N$(5)
30 N = 5
40 REM  Read names into array
50 FOR I=1 TO N
60    READ N$(I)
70 NEXT I
80 TITLE$ = "Unsorted Data"
90 X = 3 : Y = 10
100 GOSUB 230
110 REM Bubble sort routine
120 REM
130 REM
140 FOR I = 1 TO N-1
150    FOR J = N TO I+1 STEP -1
160       IF N$(J) < N$(J-1) THEN TEMP$ = N$(J) :
                                   N$(J) = N$(J-1) :
                                   N$(J-1) = TEMP$
170    NEXT J
180 NEXT I
190 X = 11 : Y = 10
200 TITLE$ = "Sorted Data"
210 GOSUB 230
220 GOTO 330
230 REM
240 REM  Output the data
250 REM
260 LOCATE X,Y
270 PRINT TITLE$ : PRINT
280 FOR I=1 TO N
290    PRINT TAB(Y); "Element #";I;" : ";N$(I)
300 NEXT I
310 RETURN
320 DATA LESTER, DIANE, BRUCE, SUSAN, ELI
330 END

RUN

        Unsorted Data

        Element # 1   : LESTER
        Element # 2   : DIANE
        Element # 3   : BRUCE
        Element # 4   : SUSAN
        Element # 5   : ELI

        Sorted Data

        Element # 1   : BRUCE
        Element # 2   : DIANE
        Element # 3   : ELI
        Element # 4   : LESTER
        Element # 5   : SUSAN
```

- **Lines 50-70:** A FOR...NEXT loop used to read in the unsorted array N$( ).
- **Line 90:** Assigns position value.
- **Lines 140-180:** A pair of nested loops where the sorting takes place. Notice how if the value of N$(J) is less than the value of N$(J − 1), the two values are switched by employing a temporary holding variable TEMP$.
- **Line 190:** Assigns position value.
- **Lines 240-310:** A subroutine which displays the array N$( ) first as an unsorted array when called from line 100 and then as a sorted array when called from line 210.

Review

1. Write a program that will accept as INPUT a list of twenty numbers and then sort them into descending order.

Making the Bubble Sort More Efficient

Efficiency is the cornerstone of a properly structured, well written program. There are several ways to make the bubble sort in Program 12.1 more efficient. One method is to employ a WHILE...WEND loop instead of a FOR...NEXT loop to avoid unnecessary iterations. It is possible that a list will be properly sorted after only a few passes, but using FOR...NEXT the computer continues to scan the list even though no swaps are made. If a WHILE...WEND loop and a flag are used, the computer will only scan a properly sorted list once and then terminate.

SWAP

Rather than employ the swapping routine used in line 160 of Program 12.1, it is simpler and more efficient to use the SWAP statement. For example,

160 TEMP$ = N$(J) : N$(J) = N$(J − 1) : N$(J − 1) = TEMP$

can be replaced by

160 SWAP N$(J), N$(J − 1)

Employing the two techniques mentioned above, the sort routine of Program 12.1 would look like this:

```
120 L$ = "UNORDERED" : I = 1
130 WHILE L$ <> "ORDERED"
140      L$ = "ORDERED"
150      FOR J = N TO I+1 STEP -1
160          IF N$(J) < N$(J-1) THEN L$ = "UNORDERED":
                                      SWAP N$(J), N$(J-1)
165      NEXT J
170      I = I + 1
180 WEND
```

Notice how L$ is used to determine when the list is properly sorted. The SWAP statement is not available on the Models I and III computers.

Review

2. Rewrite the program from Review 1 employing a WHILE...WEND loop and the SWAP statement.

Binary Search

A binary search is one of the fastest and easiest methods for searching a previously sorted list in order to find an item of data. It can be thought of as the "divide and conquer" approach to searching. In general, a list of data is divided in half. Then the half that contains the item being searched for is determined with the process repeated on that half. More specifically, the computer starts by comparing the item in the middle of the list with the item being searched for. If the two match, the search is complete. If the middle element is greater than the item being searched for, then the desired item is in the first half of the list; if not, it is in the second half. The appropriate half is then in turn divided in half and the middle element of that sublist is compared with the item being searched for. This process is repeated until the exact position of the desired item is determined. For example, to find the location of the letter I in the alphabet (a previously sorted list) the computer starts by finding the middle letter of the alphabet.

$$1\ 2\ 3\ 4\ 5\ 6\ 7\ 8\ 9\ 10\ 11\ 12\ 13\ 14\ 15\ 16\ 17\ 18\ 19\ 20\ 21\ 22\ 23\ 24\ 25\ 26$$
$$A\ B\ C\ D\ E\ F\ G\ H\ I\ J\ K\ L\ M\ N\ O\ P\ Q\ R\ S\ T\ U\ V\ W\ X\ Y\ Z$$

Strictly speaking, there is no middle letter in the alphabet because it contains an even number of letters. The index of the middle of any list of data is found with the formula

$$M = INT((L + H) / 2)$$

where L is the index of the lowest element of the section being examined and H is the index of the highest element. On the first pass through the alphabet, the index of the lowest element is 1 (A) and the index of the highest element is 26 (Z). Therefore, the index of the middle element of the alphabet is

$$INT ((1 + 26) / 2) = INT(13.5) = 13$$

which corresponds to the letter M. Since M comes after I, the computer continues its search in the first half of the alphabet.

The index of the middle element of the first half of the alphabet is

$$INT ((1 + 12) / 2) = INT(6.5) = 6$$

which corresponds to the letter F. Since F comes before I, the computer continues its search in the second half of the current section. The index of the middle element of this new section is

$$INT ((7 + 12) / 2) = INT(9.5) = 9$$

which corresponds to the letter I, the desired letter, so the search is over. The algorithm for a binary search is given below:

Initial Conditions:
L = index of first element in list (usually 1)
N = number of elements in the array N$( )
N$ = element to search for

Step 1   L = 1
Step 2   H = N
Step 3   M = INT ((L + H) / 2)
Step 4   IF N$ = N$(M) THEN PRINT N$; " in position"; M: END
Step 5   IF N$ > N$(M) THEN L = M + 1 ELSE H = M − 1
Step 6   IF L > H THEN PRINT "Not on list" : END
Step 7   GOTO 3

Program 12.2   This program demonstrates the use of a binary search. When a person's name is entered, the program displays that person's name and telephone number or a message if the name is not on the list:

```
10 DIM N$(20), T$(20)
20 FOR X = 1 TO 20
30    READ N$(X),T$(X)
40 NEXT X
50 INPUT "Enter name to be found"; C$
60 FLAG$ = "NOT FOUND"
70 L = 1 : H = 20
80 WHILE FLAG$ = "NOT FOUND"
90    M = INT((L + H) / 2)
100   IF C$ = N$(M) THEN FLAG$ = "FOUND" : GOTO 130
110   IF C$ > N$(M) THEN L = M + 1
                     ELSE H = M - 1
120    IF L > H THEN FLAG$ = "NOT ON LIST"
130 WEND
140 IF FLAG$ = "NOT ON LIST" THEN PRINT "Not on list"
                            ELSE PRINT N$(M), T$(M)
160 DATA ABBOTT,555-1234,BIDWELL,555-7821,CARRINGTON,555-1654
170 DATA DAVIDSON,555-9892,DEMPSEY,555-1243,DINGLE,555-1423
180 DATA EVERHEART,555-1423,FAIRCHILD,555-9999,FARRIS,555-6666
190 DATA GOLDBERG,555-2634,HARRISON,555-1267,JONES,555-1256
200 DATA KEMP,555-2434,NOONAN,555-2434,PETERS,555-1765
210 DATA PETERSON,555-1298,ROBERT,555-9821,ROBERTS,555-8765
220 DATA TIBBETTS,555-0742,TRANE,555-0000
999 END

RUN
Enter name to be found? FAIRCHILD
FAIRCHILD      555-9999

RUN
Enter name to be found? FRANKLIN
Not on list
```

- **Lines 20-40:** Read in the names N$( ) and telephone numbers T$( ) of 20 individuals.
- **Line 50:** Asks the user to enter a name.
- **Line 60:** FLAG$, used in the WHILE...WEND loop, is assigned the value "NOT FOUND".
- **Line 70:** Initializes the lowest L and highest H elements to be searched at 1 and 20 respectively.
- **Line 80:** Begins a loop which searchs through a list until the requested name is found or it can be determined that it is not on the list.
- **Line 90:** Calculates the midpoint of the list to be searched by taking the sum of the high and low element values and dividing by 2.

- **Line 100:** If the name at the midpoint of the current section of the list is equal to the requested name, the flag is set to "FOUND".
- **Line 110:** If the requested name is alphabetically greater than the name at the midpoint; the lower limit is raised to one point above the current midpoint; otherwise, the upper limit is lowered to one below the current midpoint.
- **Line 120:** If the lower limit is greater than the upper limit, then the name in question cannot be on the list if the list is sorted alphabetically. The flag is set to "NOT ON LIST" so that the loop can terminate.
- **Line 130:** Ends the loop initiated in line 80.
- **Line 140:** Checks to see if the loop ended with FLAG$ = "NOT ON LIST". If so, an appropriate message is displayed; otherwise, the requested name and phone number are displayed.

Review

3. Write a program that will store the letters of the alphabet, in order, in a subscripted string variable. The program should accept a letter of the alphabet as input, and print a number corresponding to that letter's location in the subscripted variable.

EXERCISES

1. (a) You have just been hired to help produce a new dictionary. Write a program to create the sequential file WORDS.DAT. The file is to contain twenty-five words in random order.

   (b) Write a program to sort the contents of the file WORDS.DAT into alphabetical order. The program should also print the sorted list.

2. (a) Write a program to create the sequential file PEOPLE.DAT. The file is to contain the first names and ages of fifteen people.

   (b) Write a program to sort the contents of PEOPLE.DAT alphabetically. For example, given the list:

Rob	20
Don	19
Lester	21

   the program should change it to:

Don	19
Lester	21
Rob	20

   Note the ages have been moved also.

   (c) Write a program to sort the contents of PEOPLE.DAT by age. For example, given the above initial list, the computer should change it to:

Don	19
Rob	20
Lester	21

3. (a) Create a sequential file named PHONE.DAT that contains a list of telephone numbers. The area codes are not to be included.

(b) Write a program to sort the contents of PHONE.DAT by exchange only. For example, given the list:

676-2004
609-4444
676-5112
867-5309
932-6840
867-1441

the computer should change it to:

609-4444
676-2004
676-5112
867-1441
867-5309
932-6840

4. Write a program that sorts the data shown below by name and associated telephone number into alphabetical order by last name. For example, the first three names of the sorted list should be:

JOHN ADAMS   555-1640
BOB ATKINS   555-1964
PHIL COLLINS   555-6498

900   DATA   LARRY PELHAM, 555-1234
910   DATA   PHIL COLLINS, 555-6498
920   DATA   LAWRENCE RUSSELL, 555-5285
930   DATA   ALICIA OSTRIKER, 555-4788
940   DATA   JOHN ADAMS, 555-1640
950   DATA   DEBORAH PALEY, 555-7749
960   DATA   LAURIE JOHNSON, 555-0012
970   DATA   GARY WALLACE, 555-1537
980   DATA   BOB ATKINS, 555-1964
990   DATA   DAVID NAUGHTON, 555-5487

5. Rewrite the answer to problem 1 using a random-access file. Instead of storing the contents of the file in a subscripted variable and sorting it out in memory, the program should exchange the contents of each record in the file directly. Is this approach faster or slower than the first solution to the problem? Why?

6. Write a program that will use a binary search to find the age of a person whose name is in the sorted file PEOPLE.DAT created in Exercise 2.

7. (a) Create a random-access file named EMPLOYEE.DAT that contains the last names, ages, social security numbers, salaries and years of service for each of a company's twenty employees. The information on each employee should be in a separate record.

(b) Write a program to create a sequential file named SALARY.DAT that contains only the order in which the records in EMPLOYEE.DAT should be recalled to produce a list of the employees in ascending order based on salary.

8. (a) Using a binary search, search the file EMPLOYEE.DAT (created in Exercise 7) using SALARY.DAT as an index for the name of the employee making a particular salary. For the purposes of this problem, assume that no two persons in the file are making the same salary.

(b) Rewrite the answer to part (a), allowing for the possibility that there might be two or more persons in the file making the same salary.

Advanced Exercise

The following exercise requires the development of a detailed algorithm. The program should not be written until all details of the algorithm have been worked out.

9. A small but rapidly growing electronic company wants a computerized phone directory of its employees. The computer should allow the company's phone operator to input an employee's name and output his or her phone number or input the number and output the name. Two random-access files should be used; the first, NAME.DAT, to store the names in alphabetical order along with their corresponding phone numbers, and the second, NUMBER.DAT, to store the phone numbers in ascending order along with their corresponding names.

One program should be written that will perform the following four functions. In each case a binary search should be used to locate the appropriate records in the two files.

1. Allow data to be input for a new employee by shifting records in the files to make room for the new data.
2. Allow data to be eliminated for an employee who leaves the company by shifting records so that the employees record no longer exists.
3. Display an employee's phone number when his or her name is entered.
4. Display an employee's name when his or her phone number is entered.

Note that after functions 1 (add data) or 2 (delete data) are performed no empty records should exist. Each file should contain all its data in properly ordered records.

It should be apparent that as the files grow longer, inserting and deleting information will require moving more and more records, especially when records are inserted or deleted early in the file. To avoid this, the records can be linked into what is called a "linked-list". In this case, each record contains a "pointer" to the next record so that only pointers are changed when an insertion or deletion is made rather than moving records. A more advanced text should be consulted for an explanation of this technique.

APPENDIX
A

BASIC
COMMANDS

SAVE

LOAD

KILL

FILES

RENUM

MERGE

NAME

CHAIN

COMMON

SYSTEM

Program and File Names

Every program and file on a disk is identified by a unique name. The general format for a program or file name is:

<name> . <extension>

The name may be from one to eight characters long, the first character of which must be a letter. The extension, which is optional, may be from one to three characters, starting with a letter. It is useful to standardize extensions by employing .BAS for BASIC programs and .DAT for files. This allows the user to easily distinguish between programs and files. Only the following characters are allowed as part of a name or extension.

A,B, ... Z
0,1, ... 9
( ) { }
@ # $ % &
– _ ~ !

The following examples are valid program or file names:

MAIL.BAS
CODES.DAT
POTATOES

SAVE

The SAVE command is used to store a program on a disk. Its form is:

SAVE "<disk drive>:<program name>"

For example,

SAVE "B:MYPROG.BAS"

will save the program currently in memory on the disk in drive B and give it the name MYPROG.BAS. If no disk drive is specified the computer assumes the default drive (usually drive A). Note that the program name must be enclosed in quotation marks. If no extension is specified, .BAS is assumed.

If a P option is specified, the program will be saved in a coded format on the disk. For example,

SAVE "B:MYPROG.BAS",P

While the program will still run, any attempt to list or edit it will result in an "illegal function call" message. It is not possible to unprotect a program.

LOAD

Programs previously saved on a disk may be recalled using the LOAD command. For example,

LOAD "B:MYPROG.BAS"

will load MYPROG.BAS into memory from the disk in drive B.

KILL

Unwanted programs and files currently stored on a disk can be removed using the KILL command. Its form is:

KILL "<program or file name>"

The command

KILL "B:MYPROG.BAS"

will delete MYPROG.BAS from the disk in drive B.

FILES

The FILES command displays the directory of a disk. For example,

FILES

will display the directory of the disk in the default drive (usually drive A).

FILES "B:"

will display the directory of the disk in drive B.

RENUM

The RENUM command is used to renumber the line numbers of a program currently in the computer's memory. Its form is:

RENUM <newline> , <startline> , <increment>

Newline is the new line number of the first line of the program to be renumbered. When not specified, the computer will assume 10. Startline is the line number of the original program where renumbering is to begin. When not specified, renumbering begins with the first line in the program and then renumbers the entire program. Increment specifies the difference between successive renumbered program lines. If omitted, the computer assumes 10. For example, the command:

RENUM 100,,20

will renumber the entire program currently in memory, so that the first line number is 100, the second 120, the third 140, and so on. Note that startline was not specified in this example. The RENUM command will also change the line numbers used within statements so that they correspond with the new line numbers.

MERGE

The MERGE command is used to combine a program in memory with one that has been previously stored on a disk. Its form is:

MERGE "<program name>"

For example,

MERGE "B:ADDENDUM.BAS"

will combine the program in memory with the program ADDENDUM.BAS on the disk in drive B. If any line numbers in the program in memory match line numbers in the program from the disk, the lines in memory will be replaced by those from the disk.

Programs are usually stored on a disk in a coded format which will not allow them to be merged with a program in memory. To be merged, the program on disk must be stored in ASCII format. This is accomplished with the command:

SAVE "B:MYPROG.BAS",A

NAME

The NAME command is used to change the name of a program or file stored in a disk. Its form is

NAME "<old name>" AS "<new name>

For example,

NAME "B:CAT.BAS" AS "B:HARRY.BAS"

will give the program CAT.BAS on the disk in drive B the new name HARRY.BAS.

CHAIN and COMMON

The CHAIN command enables a program in memory to pass control to another. Its form is:

CHAIN "<program name>", <line>, ALL

"Program name" is the name of the program to be chained to. Line is the line number where execution will start. If not specified, execution will start at the first line of the program. Specifying the ALL option instructs the computer to pass the values of all the variables used by the first program to the chained program. To use the value of a variable from the first program in the second, the variable must be given the same name in both programs.

50 CHAIN "B:MYPROG.BAS",60,ALL

passes program execution to line 60 of MYPROG.BAS stored on the disk in drive B and passes the values of all variables.

50 CHAIN "B:MYPROG.BAS",, ALL

passes program execution to the first line of MYPROG.BAS and passes the values of all variables.

If the ALL option is not specified, the COMMON statement may be used to pass the values of selected variables to the chained program. The COMMON statement must be executed before a CHAIN statement. Its form is:

COMMON <variable list>

For example,

20 COMMON Q, Z( ), R$

will cause CHAIN to pass only the values of variables Q, Z( ) and R$ to the second program. Note the format used to specify the subscripted variable Z. Z( ) must be dimensioned in the original program.

SYSTEM   When running BASIC, the SYSTEM command is used to return control to the disk operating system (DOS).

APPENDIX B

DISK OPERATING SYSTEM

BASIC

COPY

DIR

RENAME

ERASE

FORMAT

DISKCOPY

**Starting
the System**

To start the computer in the disk operating mode, place a copy of the DOS disk in drive A (the left hand drive if two are available) and then turn on the computer. After a few seconds, the computer will respond by asking a series of questions.

> Current date is Tue 1-01-1980
> Enter new date:

Enter the date in the form requested (e.g. 6-22-1985)

> Current time is 0:00:15.72
> Enter new time:

Enter the time in the form requested (e.g. 14:32:10). Note that the computer uses a 24 hour clock. The computer will now respond

> The IBM Personal Computer DOS
> Version 2.10 (c) Copyright IBM Corp

BASIC

If the user wishes to leave the DOS and work with BASIC, the command BASIC is used. Its simplest form is

> BASIC
> or
> BASICA

BASIC instructs the computer to load the standard Disk BASIC supplied with the DOS. BASICA instructs the computer to load the optional Advanced BASIC if available. A more complete form of the BASIC command is:

> BASIC/F:<files>/S:<buffer size>/M:<max workspace>

or

> BASICA/F:<files>/S:<buffer size>/M:<max workspace>

/F:<files> sets the maximum number of files that may be opened simultaneously by one program (up to 15). If the option is not specified, the computer will allow three files to be opened simultaneously.
/S:<buffer size> sets the maximum allowable record length for use with random-access files, up to 32767 characters. If not specified, records may

be up to 128 characters long.

/**M:**<**max workspace**> sets the maximum amount of memory that can be used for programs and data by BASIC, up to 65536 bytes. If not specified, BASIC uses all the available memory up to 65536 bytes. For example,

BASICA/F:5/S:512

will allow five files to be opened simultaneously and random-access files to have a maximum record length of 512 characters.

COPY

The COPY command is used to duplicate a file or program. Its simplest form is:

COPY <original>

For example,

COPY PAYROLL.DAT SAFETY.DAT

will cause the computer to make an exact copy of PAYROLL.TXT and place it in a new file named SAFETY.TXT on the same disk. Note the space between the two file names.

COPY B:MYPROG.BAS A:

will make an exact copy of the program MYPROG.BAS on the disk in drive B and place it on the disk in drive A, naming it also MYPROG.BAS.

The copy command can also be used to append two or more files. This is done by specifying two or more source files separated by plus signs (+). For example,

COPY FILE1.DAT + FILE2.DAT FILE3.DAT

will place the contents of both FILE1.DAT and FILE2.DAT in FILE3.DAT. If a duplicate file is not specified, the appended file will be placed in the first file mentioned. For example,

COPY FILE1.DAT + FILE2.DAT

will place the combined contents of both FILE1.DAT and FILE2.DAT in FILE1.DAT.

DIR

To produce a catalog of a disk, type

DIR <drive>

which will list the directory of the disk in the specified drive (A or B). For example.

DIR A:

will list the directory of the disk on drive A.

RENAME

It is possible to change the name of files and programs using the RENAME command. Its form is

RENAME <old name> <new name>

For example,

RENAME B:PAYROLL.BAS B:SALARY.BAS

will give the program PAYROLL.BAS on the disk in drive B the new name SALARY.BAS.

ERASE

The ERASE command is used to remove unwanted files and programs from a disk. For example,

ERASE B:OLDFILE.DAT

will remove the file OLDFILE.DAT from the disk in drive B.

FORMAT

New disks must be initialized, or "formatted" before the computer can use them. The form of the FORMAT is:

FORMAT <drive>:

For example,

FORMAT B:

will cause the computer to respond with the instructions:

Insert new diskette for drive B:
and strike any key when ready.

After the disk has been inserted, the computer will format the disk and print a status report when finished.

DISKCOPY

The DISKCOPY command is used to copy an entire disk at one time. Its form is:

DISKCOPY <original disk>: <backup>:

For example,

DISKCOPY A: B:

will copy the contents of the disk in drive A onto the disk in Drive B. For systems with only one drive follow the computer's instructions after typing DISKCOPY. If the disk being copied to has not been previously formatted, DISKCOPY will format it automatically.

GLOSSARY

algorithm: a precise, step-by-step description of a method for solving a problem.

accumulator: a variable that changes its value each time its assignment statement is repeated, thus collecting a total. The change in its value may vary each time it is repeated.

array: subscripted set of variables that stores related values.

assign: to give a variable a value.

BASIC: a popular computer language. It is an acronym for Beginner's All-Purpose Symbolic Instruction Code.

branch: a change in the direction of the flow of instructions in a program.

bug: an error in either the design or the coding of a program.

character string: a sequence of letters, number and/or special characters such as punctuation marks.

code: the instructions that make up a program.

coding: the process of writing "code," or instructions, that the computer can understand.

command: an instruction to the computer in a language the computer understands.

conditional branch: a change in the flow of the program from one part to another based on a comparison.

constant: a variable value that remains unchanged throughout a program.

counter: a variable that changes its value by a specific amount each time it is repeated, therefore keeping a count of the occurrences of an event.

cursor: a special symbol used by the computer to show where the next character will be printed on the screen.

debugging: the process of finding and removing "bugs", or errors, in a program.

edit: to make changes in a program.

execute: to carry out the commands and instructions of a program.

E notation: called scientific notation, a way of expressing very large or very small numbers by indicating the number or places to the left or right the decimal point should be moved.

exponent: a number indicating how many times a number should be multiplied by itself, i.e., $2^2 = 2 * 2$, $2^3 = 2 * 2 * 2$.

flag: when a condition equals this specified value, the program branches to a different section of the program. Usually used with the IF . . . THEN statement.

format: the way in which instructions are laid out.

home: the starting position of the cursor at the top left hand corner of the screen.

immediate mode: the mode in which the computer executes commands and instructions immediately when the RETURN key is pressed.

initialize: to assign a variable a value equal to the value it must have at the beginning of a program or subroutine.

input: the act of entering data into the computer.

integer: a whole number or the whole number part of a mixed number.

line number: the number in front of each line of code that is used to place each line of instructions in its order of execution within the program.

loop: a section of a program designed to be executed repeatedly.

nested loop: a loop placed entirely within another loop.

numeric variable: a variable that is assigned number values.

order of operations: the order in which the computer will carry out math operations beginning with exponents, then multiplication and division, and finally addition and subtraction.

output: data or information displayed by the computer on a device such as the screen or a printer.

program: a series of instructions that tells the computer what operations to carry out and in what order to perform them.

program line: one line of code in a program. Each line is preceded by a line number.

random number: a number picked by chance.

reserved word: a word, such as PRINT or FOR, that is part of the language of the computer and therefore cannot be used as part of a variable name.

scrolling: the upward and downward movement of output on the computer's display screen.

statement: all the elements that combined carry out an instruction, i.e., a PRINT instruction can be followed by quotation marks, variable names, semicolons, commas, etc., to make an entire PRINT statement.

string: a sequence of letters, numbers and/or special characters such as punctuation marks.

string variable: a variable that has a string as its value.

structured program: a program that is designed so that its parts and how they work are obvious to anyone reading the program.

subroutine: a section of a program that executes a specific task and is called by a GOSUB and exited by a RETURN.

subscript: the number used to identify each of the individual variables that make up an array.

subscripted variable: one of the numbered variables that make up an array.

syntax: the correct rules, or "grammar", with which a programming language is used.

variable: a name used to represent a value that is stored in the memory of the computer. This value can be changed.

Summary of BASIC Instructions

ABS: a mathematical function that returns the absolute value of a number.

AND: used in IF...THEN statements when more than one condition is to be checked.

ASC: a function that returns the ASCII code corresponding to the specified character.

ATN: a mathematical function that returns the principle arctangent of an angle measured in radians.

AUTO: a command that automatically prints a new line number each time ENTER is pressed.

BASIC: puts the computer in BASIC from DOS.

BEEP: causes the speaker to beep.

CHAIN: passes program control and variables to the specified program.

CHR$: a function that returns a character corresponding to the specified ASCII code.

CIRCLE: draws a circle (or elipse) on the display.

CLEAR: a command used to free space in the computer's memory taken up by unneeded variables.

CLOSE: closes all disk files on the specified channel(s).

CLS: clears the screen and returns the cursor to it's home position.

COLOR: sets the foreground, background and border colors.

COMMON: allows variables to be passed to a CHAINed program.

CONT: causes execution of a program to resume after it has been interrupted by CTRL-C, STOP or END.

COPY: copies the specified program(s) onto the specified drive.

COS: a mathematical function that returns the cosine of an angle measured in radians.

CVI, CVS, CVD: convert string variables into integer, single precision, and double precision, respectively.

DATA: used to signify a list of data that is part of a program.

DEF FN: creates a user defined function.

DELETE: a command that deletes the specified line(s) from a program in memory.

DIM: used to reserve space for subscripted variables.

DIR: a DOS command used to produce a list of files stored on a disk.

DISKCOPY: a DOS command used to make an exact copy of an entire disk.

END: halts execution of a program.

EOF: indicates if the end-of-file has been reached in a sequential file.

ERASE: a DOS command that erases a file from a disk; also a BASIC statement that removes a previously DIMed array from memory.

ERL: returns the line number in which the last error occurred.

ERR: returns the error code of the last error that occurred.

EXP: a mathematical function that returns the value of the number e ($\sim$2.71828) raised to the specified power.

FIELD: partitions the buffer used for a random access data file.

FILES: a BASIC command used to produce a list of files stored on a disk.

FOR...TO...STEP, NEXT: used to define the beginning, increment and end of a loop which executes a pre-defined number of times.

FORMAT: formats a disk in the specified drive.

GET: places a record from a random access file into a buffer.

GOSUB: instructs the computer to branch to a subroutine starting at the specified line number.

GOTO: instructs the computer to branch to a specified line in a program.

IF...THEN...ELSE: instructs the computer to take one of two actions depending on whether a condition is true or false.

INKEY$: used to input a single character from the keyboard without pressing ENTER.

INPUT#: assigns data from a sequential disk file to a variable.

INT: a mathematical function that returns the integer portion of a floating point number.

KILL: a BASIC command for deleting files from the specified disk.

LEFT$: a function that returns a specified number of characters from the left end of a string.

LEN: a function that returns the number of characters in a string.

LINE: a graphics statement that draws a line on the screen.

LINE INPUT: allows commas to be ignored when reading data from the keyboard.

LINE INPUT#: allows commas to be ignored when reading data from a disk file.

LIST: displays the lines of a program in memory.

LOAD: a command for recalling a program previously stored on a disk.

LOC: returns the number of the last record accessed from a random access file on the specified channel.

LOCATE: positions the cursor at the specified vertical and horizontal coordinates.

LOG: a mathematical function that returns the natural logarithm of a number.

LSET: positions data in a file buffer, left-justifying the string and padding any blank positions with spaces.

MERGE: joins the program lines from an ASCII file to the program stored in memory.

MID$: a function that returns a specified number of characters from the middle of a string.

MKD$, MKI$, MKS$: converts a double precision, integer or single precision variable, respectively, to a string to be output to a random access file.

MODE: used to switch display modes.

NAME: a BASIC command that allows a previously named file to be renamed.

NEW: removes the program currently in memory so that a new one may be entered.

ON ERROR GOTO: causes program execution to branch to the specified line when an error occurs.

ON...GOSUB: causes program execution to branch to one of several subroutines depending on the value of an expression.

ON...GOTO: causes program execution to branch to one of several program lines depending on the value of an expression.

OPEN: prepares the specified disk file to be accessed. If the specified file does not exist, it is created.

OPTION BASE: sets the minimum value for array subscripts (must be 0 or 1).

OR: used in an IF...THEN statement to check if any of several conditions are true.

PAINT: paints a section of the screen with the specified color.

POINT: returns the color of the screen at the specified coordinates.

PRESET: draws a point on the screen at the specified coordinates in the specified color. If no color is specified, the background color is used.

PRINT: causes the computer to display information on the screen.

PRINT#: writes data to a sequential file, allowing data to contain imbedded commas.

PRINT USING: displays data in a user defined format.

PSET: draws a point on the screen at the specified coordinates in the selected color.

PUT: writes a record from a buffer to a random access disk file.

RANDOMIZE TIMER: causes the random number sequence generated to be different each time the program is RUN.

READ: takes data from a data statement and assigns it to the specified variable.

REM: signifies what follows is a comment by the programmer, not a command to be executed by the computer.

RENAME: a DOS command that allows a previously named program to be renamed.

RENUM: allows a program stored in memory to be renumbered with a fixed interval between program lines.

RESTORE: allows DATA in a program to be read again starting at the beginning of the data.

RESUME: sends program execution back to the point where the error occured after the error is trapped.

RETURN: used at the end of a subroutine, it sends the program back to the point where the subroutine was called from.

RIGHT$: a function that returns a specified number of characters from the right end of a string.

RND: a function that returns a random number greater than or equal to zero but less than one.

RSET: positions data in a file buffer, right-justifying the string and padding any blank positions with spaces.

RUN: starts program execution.

SAVE: stores the program in memory on the specified disk using a specified filename.

SCREEN: sets the screen to the specified display mode with the specified color.

SGN: a mathematical function that returns the signum of the specified number.

SIN: a mathematical function that returns the sine of an angle measured in radians.

SOUND: produces a tone from the speaker.

SQR: a mathematical function that returns the positive square root of the specified number.

STOP: halts program execution.

SWAP: switches the values of two variables.

SYSTEM: causes the computer to leave BASIC and enter DOS.

TAB: moves the cursor to the right a specified number of spaces.

TAN: a mathematical function that returns the tangent of an angle measured in radians.

TROFF: turns trace mode off.

TRON: turns trace mode on. Trace displays the sequence of line numbers a program follows as it is being executed.

VAL: a function that returns the numeric value of the first set of numerical characters in a string.

WHILE...WEND: executes a loop while a given condition is true.

WRITE#: writes data from a program to a sequential file.

REVIEW ANSWERS

CHAPTER ONE

1.   1. Phone travel agent to make reservations.
          2. Pack luggage.
          3. Go to the aiport
              a) check baggage
              b) get ticket
              c) board plane.
          4. Arrive at Charles De Gaulle Airport.
          5. Take a taxi to the hotel.
          6. Check in at the hotel.

2.   1. Make up a guest list.
          2. Write out invitations.
          3. Send out invitations.
          4. Arrange for entertainment.
          5. Go to the store for food and party favors.
          6. Prepare the food.
          7. Decorate the room for the party.
          8. Welcome guests to the party.

6.
```
PRINT 2 + 5
 7

PRINT 6 - 3
  3

PRINT 5 * 3
  15

PRINT 5 / 3
  1.666667
```

7.
```
PRINT "I AM 6 FEET TALL"
I AM 6 FEET TALL
```

8.
```
PRLNT "LOOK MA! NO HANDS"
Syntax error
```

9.
```
PRINT "LOOK MA! NO HANDS"
```

10.
```
RUN
MY COMPUTER IS
A CHIP OFF THE OLD
BLOCK
```

11.
```
RUN
 1368
 351
```

12.   RUN
       12 COOKIES MAKE A DOZEN

13.   RUN
        8 EQUALS 8
       40 + 20 = 60

14.   10 PRINT "BRUCE PRESLEY"
       20 END

15.   10 PRINT "BRUCE PRESLEY"
       15 PRINT "THE COMPUTER IS FAST"
       20 END

20.   10 PRINT "BRUCE PRESLEY"
       20 END

21.   10 PRINT "BRUCE PRESLEY"
       15 PRINT "THE COMPUTER IS POWERFUL"
       20 END

23.   10 PRINT "25 + 15 =" 25 + 15
       20 END

CHAPTER TWO

1.   10 B = 45
       20 C = 15
       30 PRINT B - C
       40 END

2.   RUN
        30

3.   10 B = 64
       20 A = 32
       30 C = A + B
       40 PRINT C
       50 END

4.   RUN
       GO FOR BROKE

5.   10 A$ = "COMPUTER"
       20 B = 64
       30 PRINT A$
       40 PRINT B
       50 END

6.   10 X = 25
       20 Y = 50
       30 PRINT "THE PRODUCT OF" X "AND" Y "IS" X * Y
       40 PRINT X "*" Y "=" X * Y
       50 END

7.   10 INPUT A
       20 INPUT B
       30 PRINT A "+" B "=" A + B
       40 PRINT A "*" B "=" A * B
       50 END

8.
```
10  INPUT A$
20  PRINT "HELLO " A$
30  END
```

9.
```
10  INPUT "WHAT IS YOUR NAME";Y$
20  INPUT "WHAT IS YOUR FRIEND'S NAME";F$
30  PRINT F$ " IS A FRIEND OF " Y$
40  END
```

10.
```
10  PRINT "BRUCE PRESLEY"
20  GOTO 10
30  END
```

11.
```
*****
*****
*****
*****
*****
*****
*****
*****
*****
*****
*****
*****
*****
*****
*****
*****
*****
*****
*****
*****

Break in 10
```

12.
```
10  INPUT "WHAT IS N";N
20  PRINT "12 + " N "=" N + 12
30  PRINT "12 * " N "=" N * 12
40  GOTO 10
50  END
```

13.
```
10  INPUT "WHAT IS YOUR NAME";Y$
20  INPUT "WHAT IS YOUR FRIEND'S NAME";F$
30  PRINT F$ " IS A FRIEND OF " Y$
40  GOTO 10
50  END
```

14.
```
10  READ X, Y
20  PRINT X "-" Y "=" X - Y
30  DATA 5, 3
40  END
```

15.
```
10  READ X$, Y$
20  PRINT "A " X$ " IS MY FAVORITE SNACK."
25  PRINT "A " Y$ " IS MY FAVORITE DRINK."
30  DATA HAMBURGER, COKE
40  END
```

16.
```
10  PRINT "MY FAVORITE TEAMS:"
20  READ T$
30  PRINT T$
40  GOTO 20
50  DATA BOSTON RED SOX, NEW ENGLAND PATRIOTS, NEW YORK GIANTS
60  END
```

17.
```
10 READ X, X
20 PRINT X
30 GOTO 10
40 DATA 1, 2, 3, 4, 5
50 DATA 6, 7, 8, 9, 10
60 END
```

18.
```
RUN
SECRET AGENT FILE

Syntax error in 60

60 DATA JAMES BOND, 007, MAXWELL SMART, 86, MRS. SMART, 99
```

CHAPTER THREE

1.
```
10 INPUT "ENTER PASSWORD PLEASE";P$
20 IF P$ = "AVIATRIX" THEN 50
30 PRINT "SORRY CHARLIE"
40 GOTO 10
50 PRINT "YOU'RE THE BOSS"
60 END
```

2.
```
10 INPUT "TYPE A NUMBER";N
20 IF N > 25 THEN 60
30 IF N < 25 THEN 80
40 PRINT "JUST RIGHT"
50 GOTO 100
60 PRINT "TOO LARGE"
70 GOTO 10
80 PRINT "TOO SMALL"
90 GOTO 10
100 END
```

3.
```
10 INPUT "ENTER FIRST NUMBER";F
20 INPUT "ENTER SECOND NUMBER";S
30 IF F > S THEN 70
40 PRINT S
50 PRINT F
60 GOTO 90
70 PRINT F
80 PRINT S
90 END
```

4.
```
10 INPUT "ENTER A LAST NAME";N1$
20 INPUT "ENTER ANOTHER NAME";N2$
30 IF N2$ < N1$ THEN 70
40 PRINT N1$
50 PRINT N2$
60 GOTO 90
70 PRINT N2$
80 PRINT N1$
90 INPUT "TWO MORE NAMES TO COMPARE";A$
100 IF A$ = "NO" THEN 120
110 GOTO 10
120 PRINT "BYE."
130 END
```

5.
```
10 INPUT "WHAT IS YOUR AVERAGE";A
20 IF A => 90 THEN PRINT "HIGH HONORS"
              ELSE IF A > 80 THEN PRINT "HONORS"
                            ELSE IF A >=60   THEN PRINT "PASSING"
30 IF A < 60 THEN PRINT "FAILING"
40 END
```

6.
```
10 I = 1
20 PRINT "ENTER NUMBER";I;
30 INPUT N
40 T = T + N
50 I = I + 1
60 IF I > 5 THEN 70 ELSE 20
70 PRINT "THE SUM OF THE FIVE NUMBERS IS";T
80 END
```

7.
```
10 FOR X = 1 TO 25
20    T = T + X
30 NEXT X
40 PRINT T
50 END
```

8.
```
10 FOR X = 20 TO 10 STEP -2
20    PRINT X;
30 NEXT X
40 END
```

9.
```
10 INPUT "STEP VALUE";N
20 FOR X = 8 TO 20 STEP N
30    PRINT X;
40 NEXT X
50 END
```

10.
```
10 READ N$, H, R
15 IF N$ = "ZZZ" THEN 90
20 S = H * R
30 PRINT N$;"'S SALARY FOR THIS WEEK IS";S
40 GOTO 10
50 DATA FRED FLINTSTONE, 40, 7.50
60 DATA ED NORTON, 40, 6.75
70  DATA BARNEY RUBBLE, 60, 7.75
80 DATA ZZZ, 0, 0
90 END
```

11.
```
10 CLS
20 PRINT TAB(40);"*"
30 FOR X = 1 TO 5
40 PRINT TAB(40 - X);"*"; TAB(40 + X);"*"
50 NEXT
60 PRINT TAB(40 - X);"* * * * * * *"
70 END
```

12.
```
10 PRINT "ITEM"; TAB(20);"QUANTITY"; TAB(40);"PRICE"; TAB(60);
   "TOTAL VALUE"
15 FOR X = 1 TO 4
20    READ I$, Q, P
30    PRINT I$; TAB(19);Q; TAB(39);P; TAB(59);Q * P
40 NEXT X
100 REM Name Quantity Price
110 DATA Grand Piano, 4, 12795.95
120 DATA Bass Fiddle, 7, 784.95
130 DATA Electric Guitar, 15, 398.95
140 DATA Mandolin, 6, 235.95
```

13.
```
10 CLS
20 FOR L = 1 TO 4
30    READ Y, X
40    LOCATE Y, X
50    PRINT "*";
60 NEXT L
70 DATA 2,1
80 DATA 23, 1
90 DATA 2, 80
100 DATA 23, 80
110 END
```

CHAPTER FOUR

1.

a.	3	b.	70
c.	10	d.	33
e.	41	f.	2
g.	9	h.	15

2.
```
10 INPUT "TYPE A NUMBER";A
20 INPUT "TYPE ANOTHER NUMBER";B
30 C = (A + B ) * 2
40 PRINT C
50 END
```

3.

a.	12.5	b.	3.142857
c.	.7083333	d.	18.5
e.	3.666667		

4.

a.	199	b.	3
c.	-4	d.	0
e.	-1		

5.
```
10 FOR X = 1 TO 10
20    R = INT(100 * RND + 1)
30    PRINT R,
40 NEXT X
50 END
```

6.
```
10 R = INT(25 * RND + 1)
20 X = INT (25 * RND + 1)
30 PRINT R;"+";X;"=";R + X
40 END
```

7.
```
10 FOR X = 1 TO 15
20    R = INT(11 * RND + 10)
30    PRINT R;
40 NEXT X
50 END
```

8.
```
10 R = INT(26 * RND + 25)
20 X = INT(25 * RND + 1)
30 PRINT R;"-";X;"=";R - X
40 END
```

9.

a.	.014	b.	432100
c.	456231000	d.	.005
e.	6708700	f.	.000067896

10.
```
RUN
 .005
 123400
 1.984E-05
ALL DATA READ
```

11.
```
10 INPUT "WHAT NUMBER IS TO BE ROUNDED";N
20 N1 =INT(10 * N + .5)
30 N1 = N1 / 10
40 PRINT N;"TO THE NEAREST TENTH IS";N1
50 END
```

CHAPTER FIVE

1.
```
10 FOR O = 1 TO 3
20     PRINT "OUTER LOOP =";O
30     FOR I = 1 TO 4
40        PRINT "INNER =";I;" ";
50     NEXT I
60     PRINT
70 NEXT O
80 END
```

2.
```
RUN
+**********+
+**********+
+**********+
+**********+
+**********+
+**********+
+**********+
+**********+
+**********+
+**********+
```

3.
```
5 RANDOMIZE TIMER
10 FOR X = 1 TO 10
20     L(X) = INT(100 * RND + 1)
30 NEXT X
40 FOR X = 1 TO 9 STEP 2
50     PRINT "L(";X;") =";L(X); TAB(25);"L(";X+1;") =";L(X+1)
60 NEXT X
70 END
```

4.
```
10 FOR X = 1 TO 3
20     INPUT "ENTER A NUMBER";N(X)
30 NEXT X
40 FOR X = 3 TO 1 STEP -1
50     PRINT N(X)
60 NEXT X
70 END
```

5.
```
5 RANDOMIZE TIMER
10 FOR X = 1 TO 7
20     INPUT "ENTER A WORD";W$(X)
30 NEXT X
40 FOR X = 1 TO 4
50     R = INT(7 * RND + 1)
60     PRINT W$(R);" ";
70 NEXT X
80 END
```

6.
```
5 RANDOMIZE TIMER
7 DIM L(15)
10 FOR X = 1 TO 15
20     L(X) = INT(100 * RND + 1)
30 NEXT X
40 FOR X = 1 TO 15
50     PRINT L(X)
60 NEXT X
70 FOR X = 1 TO 15
80     PRINT L(X);
90 NEXT X
100 END
```

7.
```
10 DIM X$(5, 3)
20 FOR I = 1 TO 5
30     FOR J = 1 TO 3
40         READ X$(I,J)
50     NEXT J
60 NEXT I
70 FOR J = 1 TO 3
80     FOR I = 1 TO 5
90         PRINT X$(I, J);"   ";
100     NEXT I
110     PRINT
120 NEXT J
130 DATA A, B, C, D, E, F, G, H, I, J, K, L, M, N, O
140 END
```

CHAPTER SIX

1.
```
10 INPUT"NAME";A$
20 PRINT A$
30 IF A$ = "DONALD" THEN GOSUB 60 : GOTO 80
40 PRINT
50 GOTO 10
60 PRINT "------"
70 RETURN
80 END
```

2.
```
10 RANDOMIZE TIMER
20 FOR X = 1 TO 5
30     S = INT(4 * RND + 1)
40     V = INT(13 * RND + 1)
50     FOR D = 1 TO V
60         READ C$
70     NEXT D
80     PRINT "CARD";X;"IS THE ";C$;" OF ";
90     ON S GOSUB 150, 160, 170, 180
100     PRINT S$
110     RESTORE
120 NEXT X
130 DATA ACE, 2, 3, 4, 5, 6, 7, 8, 9, 10, KING, QUEEN, JACK
140 GOTO 190
150 S$ = "CLUBS" : RETURN
160 S$ = "DIAMONDS" : RETURN
170 S$ = "HEARTS" : RETURN
180 S$ = "SPADES" : RETURN
190 END
```

3.
```
10  INPUT "Enter A";A
20  ON A + 1 GOTO 40, 50, 60, 70
30  GOTO 10
40  PRINT "ENGLAND" : GOTO 80
50  PRINT "FLORIDA" : GOTO 80
60  PRINT "NEW YORK" : GOTO 80
70  PRINT "CALIFORNIA" :GOTO 80
80  END
```

4.
```
10  FOR J = 0 TO 10
20     A = J / 2
30     IF A = INT(J / 2) THEN 50
40     PRINT A
50  NEXT J
60  END
```

5.
```
10  REM Program to PRINT the 5 times table
20  FOR I = 1 TO 12
30     J = I * 5
40     PRINT I;"* 5 =";J
50  NEXT I
60  END
```

6.
```
[10][20][30][40][50] 15      16
[60][20][30][40][50] 63      32
[60][20][30][40][50] 64      32
[60][70][80]
```

CHAPTER SEVEN

1.
a.	1011100		d.	1111111
b.	1101		e.	100011
c.	111		f.	111111

2.
a.	39		d.	57
b.	19		e.	42
c.	10		f.	21

3.
```
10  INPUT "A LETTER FROM THE ALPHABET, PLEASE";L$
20  IF LEN(L$) <> 1 THEN 10
30  L =ASC(L$)
40  IF L < 65 OR L > 90 THEN 100
50  T = L + 2
60  IF T > 90 THEN T = T - 26
70  PRINT "THE ASCII OF '";L$;"' IS";L
80  PRINT "TWO LETTERS AFTER ";L$;" IS '";CHR$(T);"'"
90  GOTO 10
100 END
```

4a.
```
RUN
PESTICIDE
```

b.
```
RUN
LEFT
RIGHT
LEFT
RIGHT
RIGHT
```

5.
```
10 INPUT I$
20 X = 1
30 WHILE X < = LEN(I$) AND F = 0
40    V = ASC(MID$(I$, X, 1))
50    IF V < 48 OR V > 57 THEN F = 1 : GOTO 70
60    X = X + 1
70 WEND
80 IF F = 0 THEN PRINT "THE INPUT WAS NUMERIC"
              ELSE PRINT "THE INPUT WAS ALPHANUMERIC"
90 END
```

6.
```
10 CLS
15 PRINT "NAME"; TAB(15);"HOURS"; TAB(29);"RATE"; TAB(45);
       "GROSS PAY"; TAB(61);"NET PAY"
20 DIM N$(5), R(5), H(5), G(5), N(5)
30 FOR X = 1 TO 5
40    READ N$(X), H(X), R(X)
50    G(X) = R(X) * H(X)
60    N(X) = G(X) - G(X) * .25
70 PRINT N$(X); TAB(14);H(X),
75 PRINT USING"$##.##           ";R(X), : PRINT USING
   "$###.##         "; G(X), N(X)
80 NEXT X
90 DATA MIKE, 25, 10, CAROL, 37, 9, JOHN, 26, 6, HEIDI, 35, 7,
       MAGGIE, 15, 5
100 END
```

CHAPTER EIGHT

1.
```
10 SCREEN 0, 1
20 COLOR 8, 2
30 PRINT "OLD GLORY IS MADE UP OF"
40 COLOR 4
50 PRINT TAB(11);"RED"
60 COLOR 7
70 PRINT TAB(11);"WHITE"
80 COLOR 8
90 PRINT TAB(7);"AND ";
100 COLOR 1
110 PRINT "BLUE ";
120 COLOR 8
130 PRINT "STRIPES."
140 END
```

2a.
```
Color text screen:
light blue flashing characters
cyan background
blue border
```

b.
```
Medium resolution graphics:
magenta background
palette 1
```

3.
```
10 CLS
20 RANDOMIZE TIMER
30 SCREEN 1, 0
40 COLOR 0, 1
50 FOR S = 1 TO 500
60    X = INT(319 * RND + 1)
70    Y = INT(199 * RND + 1)
80    PSET(X, Y), 3
90 NEXT S
```

```
100 LOCATE 24, 10
110 PRINT "STARRY STARRY NIGHT";
120 END
```

4.
```
10 RANDOMIZE TIMER
20 CLS
30 SCREEN 1,0
40 COLOR 0,1
50 FOR I = 1 TO 6
60      X = INT(RND * 260)
70      Y = INT(RND * 160)
80      C = INT(RND * 3) + 1
90      LINE (X,Y) - (X+60,Y+30), C, BF
100 NEXT I
110 END
```

5.
```
10 R = 10
20 X = 159
30 Y = 99
40 SCREEN 1,0
50 COLOR 0,1
60 FOR I = 1 TO 10
70     FOR J = 1 TO 3
80         CIRCLE (X,Y), R, J,,,.5
90         R = R + 4
100    NEXT J
120 NEXT I
130 END
```

6.
```
10 REM Set up a constant for PI
20 PI = 3.14159
30 REM Put computer into graphics mode
40 SCREEN 1,0 : COLOR 0,1
50 REM Draw the outline of the face
60 CIRCLE (150,90),140,3,,,.5
70 PAINT (150,90),1,3
80 REM Draw the nose
90 CIRCLE (150,80),35,3,,,7
100 PAINT (150,80),2,3
110 REM Draw the eyes
120 CIRCLE (99,60),15,3
130 PAINT (99,60),2,3
140 CIRCLE (199,60),15,3
150 PAINT (199,60),2,3
160 CIRCLE (99,60),2,3
170 PAINT (99,60),0,3
180 CIRCLE (199,60),2,3
190 PAINT (199,60),0,3
200 REM Draw the mouth
210 CIRCLE (150,130),50,3,-PI,-2*PI,.4
220 PAINT (150,145),2,3
230 END
```

CHAPTER NINE

1.   x = -2

2.
```
10 INPUT "Enter a number";N
15 IF N = 999 THEN 40
20 IF SGN(N) = 1 THEN PRINT "The sign of";N;"is positive"
       ELSE IF SGN(N) =-1 THEN PRINT "The sign of";N;"is negative"
       ELSE PRINT "The sign of 0 is considered positive"
30 GOTO 10
40 END
```

3.
```
10 DEF FN DEG(R) = (R / 3.141592654# * 180)
20 DEF FN RAD(D) = (D * 3.141592654# / 180)
30 INPUT "DEGREES";D
40 PRINT "That is";FN RAD(D);"radians."
50 PRINT
60 INPUT "RADIANS";R
70 PRINT "That is";FN DEG(R);"degrees."
80 END
```

CHAPTER TEN

1.
```
10 OPEN "O", 1, "MONTHS.DAT"
20 FOR X = 1 TO 12
30     READ M$
40     WRITE#1, M$
50 NEXT X
60 DATA JANUARY, FEBURARY, MARCH, APRIL, MAY, JUNE
70 DATA JULY, AUGUST, SEPTEMBER, OCTOBER, NOVEMBER, DECEMBER
80 CLOSE 1
90 END
```

2.
```
10 OPEN "O", 1, "DWARF.DAT"
20 FOR X = 1 TO 7
30     READ N, N$
40     WRITE#1, N, N$
50 NEXT X
60 DATA 1, DOPEY, 2, SLEEPY, 3, SNEEZY, 4, GRUMPY, 5, HAPPY,
        6, BASHFUL, 7, DOC
70 CLOSE 1
80 END
```

3.
```
10 OPEN "I", 1, "MONTHS.DAT"
20 FOR X = 1 TO 6
30     INPUT#1, M$
40     PRINT M$
50 NEXT X
60 CLOSE 1
70 END
```

4.
```
10 OPEN "I", 1, "DWARF.DAT"
15 PRINT TAB(2);"NUMBER", "NAME"
17 PRINT TAB(2);"------", "----"
20 FOR X = 1 TO 7
30     INPUT#1, N, N$
40     PRINT N, N$
50 NEXT X
60 CLOSE 1
70 END
```

5.
```
10 OPEN "I", 1, "MONTHS.DAT"
20 OPEN "O", 2, "MONTHS.TEMP"
30 FOR X = 1 TO 12
40     INPUT#1, M$
50     L = LEN(M$)
60     I = 1
70     IF MID$(M$,I,1) = "R" THEN WRITE#2, M$ : GOTO 100
80     I = I + 1
90     IF I < L THEN 70
100 NEXT X
110 CLOSE 1, 2
```

```
     120 KILL "MONTHS.DAT"
     130 NAME "MONTHS.TEMP" AS "MONTHS.DAT"
     140 END

6.   10 OPEN "I", 1, "DWARF.DAT"
     20 OPEN "O", 2, "DWARF.TEMP"
     30 FOR X = 1 TO 7
     40     INPUT#1, N, N$
     50     IF N <> 3 AND N <> 6 THEN WRITE#2, N, N$
     60 NEXT X
     70 CLOSE 1, 2
     80 KILL "DWARF.DAT"
     90 NAME "DWARF.TEMP" AS "DWARF.DAT"
     100 END

7a.  10 OPEN "I", 1, "MONTHS.DAT"
     20 OPEN "O", 2, "MONTHS.TEMP"
     30 WHILE EOF(1) = 0
     40     INPUT#1, M$
     50     L = LEN(M$)
     60     I = 1
     70     IF MID$(M$,I,1) = "R" THEN WRITE#2, M$ : GOTO 100
     80     I = I + 1
     90     IF I < L THEN 70
     100 WEND
     110 CLOSE 1, 2
     120 KILL "MONTHS.DAT"
     130 NAME "MONTHS.TEMP" AS "MONTHS.DAT"
     140 END

b.   10 OPEN "I", 1, "DWARF.DAT"
     20 OPEN "O", 2, "DWARF.TEMP"
     30 WHILE EOF(1) = 0
     40     INPUT#1, N, N$
     50     IF N <> 3 AND N<> 6 THEN WRITE#2, N, N$
     60 WEND
     70 CLOSE 1, 2
     80 KILL "DWARF.DAT"
     90 NAME "DWARF.TEMP" AS "DWARF.DAT"
     100 END
```

CHAPTER ELEVEN

```
1.   10 OPEN "R", 1, "MAILING.LST", 94
     20 FIELD 1, 20 AS N$, 25 AS ADDRESS$, 20 AS CITY$, 20 AS STATE$,
               9 AS ZIP$
     30 INPUT "NAME";N1$
     40 LSET N$ = N1$
     50 INPUT "ADDRESS";A$
     60 LSET ADDRESS$ = A$
     70 INPUT "CITY";C$
     80 LSET CITY$ = S$
     90 INPUT "STATE";S$
     100 LSET STATE$ = S$
     110 INPUT "ZIPCODE";Z$
     120 LSET ZIP$ = Z$
     130 CLOSE 1
     140 END
```

2.
```
10 OPEN "R", 1, "MAILING.LST", 94
20 FIELD 1, 20 AS N$, 25 AS ADDRESS$, 20 AS CITY$, 20 AS STATE$,
        9 AS ZIP$
30 PRINT "ENTER A BLANK LINE TO END"
40 INPUT "NAME";N1$
50 IF N1$ = "" THEN 170
60 LSET N$ = N1$
70 INPUT "ADDRESS";A$
80 LSET ADDRESS$ = A$
90 INPUT "CITY";C$
100 LSET CITY$ = S$
110 INPUT "STATE";S$
120 LSET STATE$ = S$
130 INPUT "ZIPCODE";Z$
140 LSET ZIP$ = Z$
150 PUT 1
160 GOTO 40
170 CLOSE 1
180 END
```

3.
```
10 OPEN "R", 1, "MAILING.LST", 94
20 FIELD 1, 20 AS N$, 25 AS ADDRESS$, 20 AS CITY$, 20 AS STATE$,
        9 AS ZIP$
30 PRINT "ENTER ZERO TO EXIT"
40 INPUT "ENTER RECORD NUMBER"; N
50 IF N = 0 THEN 140
60 GET 1, N
70 IF N$ = STRING$(20, 0)  THEN PRINT "NO DATA FOUND" : GOTO 40
80 PRINT N$
90 PRINT ADDRESS$
100 PRINT CITY$
110 PRINT STATE$
120 PRINT ZIP$
130 GOTO 40
140 CLOSE 1
150 END
```

CHAPTER TWELVE

1.
```
10 DIM N(20)
20 FOR X = 1 TO 20
30    PRINT "ENTER NUMBER";X;
40    INPUT N(X)
50 NEXT X
60 FOR I = 1 TO 19
70    FOR J = 20 TO I + 1 STEP -1
80        IF N(J) > N(J - 1) THEN TEMP = N(J) : N(J) = N(J-1)
                                : N(J - 1) = TEMP
90    NEXT J
100 NEXT I
110 FOR X = 1 TO 20
120    PRINT N(X)
130 NEXT X
140 END
```

2.
```
10 DIM N(20)
20 FOR X = 1 TO 20
30    PRINT "ENTER NUMBER";X;
40    INPUT N(X)
50 NEXT X
60 L$ = "UNORDERED" : I = 1
70 WHILE L$ <> "ORDERED"
80       L$ = "ORDERED"
90      FOR J = 20 TO I + 1 STEP -1
100         IF N(J) < N(J - 1) THEN 120
110         SWAP N(J), N(J - 1) : L$ = "UNORDERED"
120      NEXT J
130      I = I + 1
140 WEND
150 FOR X = 1 TO 20
160    PRINT N(X)
170 NEXT X
180 END
```

3.
```
10 OPTION BASE 1
20 DIM A$(26)
30 FOR X = 1 TO 26
40    A$(X) = CHR$(X + 64)
50 NEXT X
60 PRINT "Enter a blank line to exit."
70 INPUT "Enter a letter";L$
80 IF L$ = "" THEN 200
90 IF LEN(L$) < > 1 OR ASC(L$) < 65 OR ASC(L$) > 90 THEN 70
100 FLAG$ = "NOT FOUND"
110 L = 1 : H = 26
120 WHILE FLAG$ = "NOT FOUND"
130      M = INT((L + H) / 2)
140      IF L$ = A$(M) THEN FLAG$ = "FOUND" : GOTO 170
150      IF L$ > A$(M) THEN L = M + 1
                      ELSE H = M - 1
160      IF L > H THEN FLAG$ = "NOT ON LIST"
170 WEND
180 IF FLAG$ = "NOT ON LIST " THEN PRINT "Not on list"
                      ELSE PRINT "A$(";M;") = ";L$
190 GOTO 70
200 END
```

ANSWERS
To Odd Numbered Exercises

CHAPTER ONE

1.
```
a) PRINT 5 + 6          b) PRINT 33 - 16
   11                      17

c) PRINT 13 * 3         d) PRINT 239 * 27
   39                      6453

e) PRINT 250 / 5        f) PRINT 999 / 11
   50                      90.81818
```

3.
```
10 PRINT "************"
20 PRINT "*          *"
30 PRINT "*          *"
40 PRINT "*          *"
50 PRINT "************"
60 END
```

5.
```
10 CLS
20 PRINT "    *****    "
30 PRINT "   *     *   "
40 PRINT "  * o   o *  "
50 PRINT " *    +    * "
60 PRINT "  *  \_/  *  "
70 PRINT "   *     *   "
80 PRINT "    *****    "
90 END
```

7.
```
10 PRINT 275 "*" 39 "=" 275 * 39
20 PRINT 275 "/" 39 "=" 275 / 39
30 END
```

9.
```
10 PRINT "BIOLOGY LAB"
20 PRINT "GERBILS:" 5
30 PRINT "MICE:" 6
40 PRINT "BIRDS:" 3
50 END
```

11.
```
10 PRINT "****************************"
20 PRINT "*                          *"
30 PRINT "*          BIG SALE        *"
40 PRINT "*                          *"
50 PRINT "*    ORANGE JUICE   $1.99  *"
60 PRINT "*    MILK / QUART   $ .89  *"
70 PRINT "*                          *"
80 PRINT "****************************"
90 END
```

CHAPTER TWO

1. The value of B
   19

3. ```
   10 READ A, B
   20 PRINT "The sum is";A + B
   30 GOTO 10
   40 DATA 12, 8, 3, 11
   50 END
   ```

5. ```
   10 INPUT "Price, total number of loaves";P,N
   20 PRINT "Total spent = $"; P * N
   30 END
   ```

7. ```
   10 INPUT X, Y
   20 PRINT "X =";X, "Y =";Y, "X * Y =";X * Y
   30 GOTO 10
   40 END
   ```

9. ```
   RUN
    123              234
    435      456765
   ```

11. ```
    RUN
    abcdxyz
    abcd 7
    7 xyz
    -4 xyz
    ```

13. ```
    10 PRINT" X", " Y", " 12X + 7Y"
    20 READ X, Y
    30 PRINT X, Y, 12 * X + 7 * Y
    40 GOTO 20
    50 DATA 3, 2, 7, 9, 12, -4
    60 END
    ```

15. ```
    10 INPUT "Enter length, width, and height of room";L, W, H
    20 V = L * W * H
    30 PRINT
    50 PRINT "The room's volume is";V;"cubic meters."
    60 END
    ```

17. ```
    10 INPUT"Enter height, width, length and presence <in cm.>";
       H, W, L, P
    20 T = H * W * L * P
    30 PRINT
    40 PRINT"                              4"
    50 PRINT "The tesseract is";T;"cm."
    60 END
    ```

19. ```
    10 INPUT "How many books have you borrowed that are late";B
    20 INPUT "How many days late are they";D
    30 F = B * D * .1
    40 PRINT "Your fine is $";F
    50 END
    ```
    ```

21.
```
10 INPUT "What is the player's name";P$
20 PRINT "What is ";P$;"'s wage";
30 INPUT W
40 T = W * .44
50 PRINT P$;" Would keep $";W - T
60 PRINT "He would pay $";T;"in taxes."
70 END
```

23.
```
10 INPUT "What is the base";B
20 INPUT "What is the altitude";A
30 PRINT
40 PRINT "The area is";A * B * .5
50 END
```

25.
```
10 READ S1, G1, S2, G2, S3, G3, S4, G4, S5, G5
20 S = S1 + S2 + S3+ S4 + S5
30 G = G1 + G2 + G3+ G4 + G5
40 T = S + G
50 PRINT "Smith's total vote was";S
60 PRINT "His total percentage was"; 100 * S / T
70 PRINT
80 PRINT "Jones's total vote was";G
90 PRINT "His total percentage was"; 100 * G / T
100 DATA 528, 210, 313, 721, 1003, 822, 413, 1107, 516, 1700
110 END
```

27.
```
10 READ A, B, C, D, E, N
20 V = (A + B + C + D + E) / N
30 PRINT "THE AVERAGE IS";V
40 GOTO 10
50 DATA 2, 7, 15, 13, 0, 4
60 DATA 8, 5, 2, 3, 0, 4
70 DATA 12, 19, 4, 0, 0, 3
80 DATA 15, 7, 19, 24, 37, 5
90 END
```

CHAPTER THREE

1.
```
10 INPUT A,B
20 IF A > B THEN 60
30 IF A < B THEN 80
40 PRINT A; "is equal to"; B
50 GOTO 999
60 PRINT A; "is greater than"; B
70 GOTO 999
80 PRINT A; "is less than"; B
999 END
```

3.
```
10  INPUT A$
15  IF A$ = "ZZZ" THEN 70
20  IF A$ = "BIGWOW" THEN 50
30  PRINT "??????"
40  GOTO 10
50  PRINT "!!!!!!"
60  GOTO 10
70  END
```

5.
```
RUN
 1
   2
     3
       4
                          1
                          2
                          3
                          4
```

7.
```
10  INPUT X
20  IF X < -24 OR X > 17 THEN 40
30  GOTO 10
40  PRINT "NOT BETWEEN"
50  END
```

9.
```
10  INPUT X
20  IF X > 25 AND X < 75 THEN 50
30  PRINT "NOT IN THE INTERVAL"
40  GOTO 60
50  PRINT "IN THE INTERVAL"
60  END
```

11.
```
10  A$ = "************"
20  FOR I = 1 TO 3
30      PRINT A$
40  NEXT I
50  END
```

13.
```
10  FOR I = 4 TO 84 STEP 10
20      PRINT I
30  NEXT I
40  END
```

15.
```
10  FOR I = 10 TO 97 STEP 3
20      PRINT I
30  NEXT I
40  END
```

17.
```
10 INPUT "Monster";A$
20 FOR I = 1 TO 6
30    READ C$, W$
40    IF A$ <> C$ THEN 70
50    PRINT C$; " can be killed with a "; W$
60    N$ = "FOUND"
70 NEXT I
80 IF N$ = "FOUND" THEN 999
90 PRINT A$; " not found"
100 DATA Lich, fire ball
110 DATA Mummy, flaming torch
120 DATA Werewolf, silver bullet
130 DATA Vampire, wooden stake
140 DATA Medusa, sharp sword
150 DATA Triffid, fire hose
999 END
```

19.
```
10 INPUT "How old are you";A
20 IF A > = 16 THEN PRINT "You are old enough to drive a car!"
                 : GOTO 30
                 ELSE PRINT "You must wait";16 - A;"years to drive a car."
30 END
```

21.
```
10 FOR I = 1 TO 10
20    READ N$, A
30    PRINT : PRINT "Dear ";N$;","
40    PRINT "      Thank you for your generous contribution"
50    PRINT "of";A;"dollars to my election campaign.  Maybe"
60    PRINT "next year we will have better luck!"
70    PRINT TAB(42); "Sincerely,"
80    PRINT : PRINT TAB(42); "Smiley R. Politico"
90    PRINT
100 NEXT I
110 DATA Rich Bryburry, 25000, Swindling Shwabb, 5000
120 DATA Semore Funds, 850, Bany Cramer, 75, Carol Tibbetts, 250
130 DATA Sherry French, 150, Sunny Waters, 200, Muriel Rogers, 100
140 DATA Karen Lemone, 25, Brave Sir Robin, 768
150 END
```

23.
```
10 FOR C = 1 TO 10
20    INPUT "What model did you buy";M
30    READ D
40    IF D = -1 THEN PRINT "Your car is fine!" : GOTO 70
50    IF D = M THEN PRINT "You got a lemon!" : GOTO 70
60    GOTO 30
70    RESTORE
80 NEXT C
90 DATA 102, 780, 119, 220, 189, 195, -1
100 END
```

25.
```
10 T = 10
20 PRINT TAB(T);"*"
30 FOR X = 1 TO 5
40    PRINT TAB(T - X);"*"; TAB(T + X);"*"
50 NEXT X
60 PRINT TAB(4);"*************"
70 END
```

27.
```
10 REM    C1 = Price / share when purchased
20 REM    C2 = Price / share when sold
30 REM    T1 = Total value of stock purchased
40 REM    T2 = Total value of stock sold
50 REM    P  = Profit
60 REM    N  = Number of shares of stock
70 FOR X = 1 TO 2
80    READ A$, N, C1, C2
90    T1 = N * C1
100   T2 = N * C2
110   P = T2 - T1
120   PRINT "For ";A$;", ";
130   IF P > 0 THEN PRINT "The profit was $";P
                ELSE PRINT "The loss was $"; -P
140 NEXT X
150 DATA C.T, 200, 85.58, 70.82
160 DATA A.A.S, 400, 35.60, 47.32
170 END
```

29.
```
1 REM A = Amount of money left
10 A = 200
20 INPUT "How much does the item cost";C
30 IF C = 0 THEN 90
40 A = A - 1.05 * C
50 IF A < 0 THEN PRINT "You don't have enough money" :
                     A = A + 1.05 * C
60 PRINT "Your total is now $";A
70 PRINT
80 GOTO 20
90 END
```

31.
```
10 INPUT "The amount of the loan"; L
20 INPUT "The length of the loan in years";Y
30 INPUT "Interest rate (in percent)";I
35 I = I / 100
40 M = Y * 12
50 P = (I * L) / ((1 - (1 + I) ^ (-M)))
60 PRINT "The monthly payment is $";P
70 PRINT "The total amount paid will be $";P * M
80 END
```

CHAPTER FOUR

1.
```
10 RANDOMIZE TIMER
20 FOR I = 1 TO 10
30    N = RND
40     IF N > .5 THEN PRINT N;
50 NEXT I
60 END
```

3.
```
10 INPUT N
20 IF N = INT(N) THEN PRINT N
30 GOTO 10
40 END
```

5.
```
10 RANDOMIZE TIMER
20 N = INT(4 * RND + 2)
30 D = INT(4 * RND + 1)
40 Q = INT(4 * RND)
50 F = .05 * N + .1 * D + .25 * Q : REM Total amount found
60 PRINT "You found $"; F
70 IF F >=1 THEN PRINT "You can buy lunch."
            ELSE PRINT "Sorry, you can't buy lunch."
80 END
```

7.
```
10 REM    A = Amount in bank
20 REM    I = Week number
30 A = 11
40 FOR I = 1 TO 4
50    PRINT "Week";I;", how many pennies do you have";
60    INPUT N
70    A = A + N
80    PRINT "Your total is now $"; A/100
90 NEXT I
100 END
```

9.

(A) 3^2^3	= 729	(B)	5 - 4^2	= -11
(C) 3 * (5 + 16)	= 63	(D)	5 + 3 * 6 / 2	= 14
(E) 640 / 10 / 2 * 5	= 160	(F)	5 + 3 * 4 - 1	= 16
(G) 2^3^2	= 64	(H)	2^(3^2)	= 512
(I) 64 / 4 * .5 + ((1 + 5) * 2^3) * 1 / (2 * 4)				= 14

11.
```
10 RANDOMIZE TIMER
20 FOR I = 1 TO 10
30    PRINT INT(18 * RND +8);
40 NEXT I
50 END
```

13a.
```
10 RANDOMIZE TIMER
20 CLS : LOCATE 1, 10
30 A = INT(10 * RND + 1)
40 B = INT(10 * RND + 1)
50 PRINT TAB(12);A;"*"B;"=";
60 INPUT C
70 IF C = A * B THEN 120
80 W = W + 1
90 IF W = 3 THEN PRINT "LEARN THE MULTIPLICATION TABLE" : GOTO 140
100 PRINT "You are wrong.  Try again."
110 GOTO 50
120 PRINT TAB(12);
130 PRINT "Correct"
140 END
```

b.
```
5 RANDOMIZE TIMER
10 CLS : LOCATE 1, 10
20 FOR I = 1 TO 5
25     W = 0 : REM Reset to give 3 chances for each question
30     A = INT(10 * RND + 1)
40     B = INT(10 * RND + 1)
50     PRINT TAB(12);A;"*";B;"=";
60     INPUT C
70     IF C = A * B THEN 120
80     W = W + 1
90     IF W = 3 THEN PRINT "LEARN THE MULTIPLICATION TABLE" :
                    GOTO 150
100    PRINT "You are wrong.  Try again."
105    F = 1 : REM Indicate that a wrong response was given
110    GOTO 50
120    PRINT TAB(12); "Correct"
130 NEXT I
140 IF F = 0 THEN PRINT "NICE GOING"
150 END
```

15.
```
10 RANDOMIZE TIMER
20 FOR I = 1 TO 1000
30     N = INT(9 * RND + 1)
40     IF N / 2 = INT (N / 2) THEN E = E + 1   ELSE O = O + 1
50 NEXT I
60 PRINT "There were";O;"odd integers."
70 PRINT "There were";E;"even integers."
80 END
```

17.
```
10 Y = 1985 : B = 1000
20 PRINT "Date",, "Balance"
30 Y = Y + 1
40 B = B * 1.05
50 PRINT "Jan 1,";Y,,"$";INT(100 * B + .5) / 100
60 IF B > 2000 THEN GOTO 80
70 GOTO 30
80 END
```

19a.
```
5 RANDOMIZE TIMER
10 FOR X = 1 TO 20
20     R = INT(101 * RND)
30     PRINT R;
40 NEXT X
50 END
```

b.
```
5 RANDOMIZE TIMER
10 FOR X = 1 TO 12
20     R = INT(26 * RND)
30     PRINT R;
40 NEXT X
50 FOR X = 1 TO 8
60     R = INT(101 * RND)
70     PRINT R;
80 NEXT X
90 END
```

21.
```
10 CLS
20 FOR P = 1 TO 10
30     READ Y, X
40     LOCATE Y, X
50     PRINT"*"
60     READ X
70     LOCATE Y, X
80     PRINT"*"
90 NEXT P
100 DATA 7, 20, 20, 8, 23, 17, 9, 24, 16, 10, 25, 15, 11, 25, 15
110 DATA 12, 25, 15, 13, 25, 15, 14, 24, 16, 15, 23, 17, 16, 20, 20
120 END
```

CHAPTER FIVE

1.
```
10 FOR C = 1 TO 8
20     FOR R = 1 TO 30
30         PRINT"*";
40     NEXT R
50     PRINT
60 NEXT C
70 END
```

3.
```
5 DIM L$(15)
10 FOR I = 1 TO 15
20     INPUT "Enter a single letter";L$(I)
30 NEXT I
35 PRINT
40 FOR I = 15 TO 1 STEP -1
50     PRINT L$(I);
60 NEXT I
70 END
```

5a.
```
RUN
 1                5
 1                6
 2                5
 2                6
 3                5
 3                6
```

b.
```
RUN
   10
   10
   10
   12
   12
   11
   14
   13
   11
```

c.
```
RUN
  45                89                35
```

7.
```
The output looks like:
B4 =  1  But B(4) =  86
 14
 125             111
```

9.
```
5 PRINT " A", " B", " C"
6 PRINT "-------------------------------"
10 FOR I = 3 TO 30
20     FOR J = I + 1 TO 40 : REM add one so no duplicates
30         FOR K = J + 1 TO 50
40             IF K * K = J * J + I * I THEN PRINT I, J, K
50         NEXT K
60     NEXT J
70 NEXT I
80 END
```

11.
```
10 DIM N(20)
20 RANDOMIZE TIMER
30 FOR I = 1 TO 20
40     N(I) = INT(90 * RND + 10)
50 NEXT I
60 PRINT    "odd integers:";
70 FOR I = 1 TO 20
80     IF N(I) / 2 <> INT(N(I) / 2) THEN PRINT N(I);
90 NEXT I
100 PRINT : PRINT "Even integers:";
110 FOR I = 1 TO 20
120     IF N(I) / 2 = INT(N(I) / 2) THEN PRINT N(I);
130 NEXT I
140 END
```

13.
```
10 DIM N(100)
20 RANDOMIZE TIMER : R = INT(100 * RND + 1)
30 FOR X = 1 TO 100
40     INPUT "Guess";G
50     IF G = R THEN 150
60     FOR Z = 1 TO X - 1
70         IF N(Z) = G THEN 130
80     NEXT Z
90     N(X) = G
100    IF G > R THEN PRINT "Lower" : GOTO 120
110    PRINT "Higher"
120 NEXT X
130 PRINT "Wake up! You guessed that number before!"
140 GOTO 40
150 PRINT "Correct"
160 END
```

15.
```
10 REM    P() = Number of times each roll occurs
20 REM    D1  = Die #1
30 REM    D2  = Die #2
40 DIM P(12)
50 RANDOMIZE TIMER
60 FOR I = 1 TO 1000
70     D1 = INT(6 * RND + 1)
80     D2 = INT(6 * RND + 1)
90     P(D1 + D2) = P(D1 + D2) + 1
100 NEXT I
110 PRINT "Point Total", "Times Appearing"
120 FOR I = 2 TO 12
130     PRINT TAB(5);I, TAB(22);P(I)
140 NEXT I
150 END
```

17a.
```
10 DIM N$(5,6)
20 INPUT "What day and time would you like";D,T
30 IF D < 1 OR D > 5 OR T < 1 OR T > 6 THEN 20
40 IF N$(D,T) <> "" THEN PRINT "That time is taken" : GOTO 20
```

```
50 INPUT "What is your name";N$(D,T)
60 PRINT "Thank you so very much."
70 GOTO 20
80 END
```

b.
```
10 DIM N$(5,6)
20 INPUT "Are you the doctor";A$
30 IF A$ = "YES" THEN 100
40 INPUT "What day and time would you like";D,T
50 IF D < 1 OR D > 5 OR T < 1 OR T > 6 THEN 40
60 IF N$(D,T) <> "" THEN PRINT "That time is taken" : GOTO 40
70 INPUT "What is your name"; N$(D,T)
80 PRINT "Thank you so very much."
90 GOTO 20
100 INPUT "Which day";D
110 IF D < 1 OR D > 5 THEN 100
120 PRINT
130 PRINT  "Schedule for day";D
140 PRINT "Time", "Patient"
150 FOR T = 1 TO 6
160    PRINT T,
170    IF N$(D,T) = "" THEN PRINT "Sanka Break" : GOTO 190
180    PRINT N$(D,T)
190 NEXT T
200 GOTO 20
210 END
```

CHAPTER SIX

1.
```
RUN
-6              6
```

3.
```
10 INPUT "One, two, three, four";X
20 IF X < > 1 AND X < > 2 AND X < > 3 AND X < > 4 THEN 10
30 ON X GOTO 40, 60, 80, 100
40 PRINT "NEVER LEAVE DISKS ON TOP OF A MONITOR"
50 GOTO 110
60 PRINT "UNPLUG YOUR COMPUTER DURING A LIGHTNING STORM"
70 GOTO 110
80 PRINT "OPEN THE DRIVE DOOR BEFORE POWERING OFF"
90 GOTO 110
100 PRINT "OPENING THE CASE WILL VOID YOUR WARRANTY"
110 END
```

5.
```
10 FOR Q = 1 TO 4
20    READ A, B, C
30    GOSUB 110
40    IF L = 1 THEN GOTO 80
50    R = A * B / 2
60    PRINT "Area";R, "Perimeter = "; A + B + C
70    GOTO 90
80    PRINT "Not a right triangle"
90 NEXT Q
100 GOTO 190
110 L = 0
120 IF A + B <= C THEN 160
130 IF A + C <= B THEN 160
140 IF B + C <= A THEN 160
150 IF INT(A^2 + B^2) = INT(C^2) THEN 170
160 L = 1
170 RETURN
180 DATA 3, 4, 5, 3, 1, 1, 2, 2, 2, 12,5, 13
190 END
```

7.
```
10 PRINT "Withdraw (1), Deposit (2), Calculate Interest (3) or Exit (4)"
20 INPUT "Selection";D
30 IF D < 1 OR D > 4 THEN 20
40 IF D = 4 THEN 220
50 ON D GOSUB 90,120, 150
60 B = INT (100 * B + .5) / 100
70 PRINT "Your balance now stands at";B;"dollars."
80 GOTO 20
90 INPUT "How much would you like to withdraw";A
100 IF A > = 0 AND B - A > 0 THEN B = B - A : RETURN
110 GOTO 90
120 INPUT "How much would you like to deposit";A
130 IF A > = O THEN B = B + A : RETURN
140 GOTO 120
150 INPUT "How many months since last calculation"; M
160 Q = M / 3
170 IF Q < 1 THEN PRINT "Too soon" : RETURN
180 FOR C = 1 TO Q
190     B = B + .0575 / 4 * B
200 NEXT C
210 RETURN
220 END
```

9.
```
10 INPUT "Enter the lengths of each side of the triangle";A, B, C
20 GOSUB 100
30 PRINT "Area =";A1
40 PRINT : GOTO 10
100 REM Subroutine to calculate area using Hero's formula
110 S = (A + B + C) / 2
120 A1 = SQR(S * (S - A) * (S - B) * (S - C))
130 RETURN
140 END
```

11.
```
10 ON ERROR GOTO 100
20 INPUT "A, B, C"; A, B, C
30 D = SQR(B^2 - 4 * A * C)
40 R1 = (-B + D) / (2 * A) : R2 = (-B - D) / (2 * A)
50 PRINT "The roots are";R1;"and ";R2
60 GOTO 20
100 IF ERR = 5 THEN PRINT "ROOTS ARE IMAGINARY" : RESUME 20
110 PRINT "Unexpected error encountered" : RESUME 20
120 END
```

CHAPTER SEVEN

1.
```
10 INPUT "A$";A$
20 FOR I = 1 TO LEN(A$)
30     PRINT ASC(MID$(A$,I,1));
40 NEXT
50 END
```

3.
```
10 FOR Q = 1 TO 15
20     READ X
30     PRINT CHR$(X);
40     NEXT Q
50 DATA 65, 83, 67, 73, 73, 32, 68, 73
60 DATA 68, 32, 84, 72, 73, 83, 33
70 END
```

5.
```
1 REM A$ = Original string
2 REM L$, M$, R$ = Left , Mid, Right strings of original
3 REM
4 REM
10 A$ = "THREE!@#$%STRING@#$%FUNCTIONS"
20 L$ = LEFT$(A$,5) : REM Sets L$ = "THREE"
30 M$ = MID$(A$,11,6) : REM Sets M$ = "STRING"
40 R$ = RIGHT$(A$,9) :REM  Sets R$ = "FUNCTIONS"
50 PRINT L$; " ";M$;" ";R$
60 END
```

7.
```
10 REM N$ = The name being examined
20 REM A() = The number of occurrences of each letter
30 REM S = ASCII code for the letters in N$
40 REM F = 1 If there is a tie between letters else F = 0
50 ON ERROR GOTO 250
60 DIM A(26)
70 INPUT "Name";N$
80 FOR I = 1 TO LEN(N$)
90    S = ASC(MID$(N$,I,1))
100   A(S-65) = A(S-65) + 1
110 NEXT I
120 REM Now look for the most common letter
130 MOST = 1
140 FOR I = 0 TO 25
150    IF A(I) = MOST THEN F = 1
160    IF A(I) > MOST THEN MOST = A(I) : V = I : F = 0
170 NEXT I
180 REM Print the most common letter
190 IF F = 0 THEN PRINT CHR$(V+65);" is the most common letter in ";
                N$;", which is ASC(";V + 65;")": GOTO 240
200 PRINT "The following letters have equal occurrence : "
210 FOR I = 0 TO 25
220    IF A(I) = MOST THEN PRINT CHR$(I + 65);", ASC(";I + 65;")"
230 NEXT I
240 GOTO  280
250 PRINT "Enter UPPER CASE only with no spaces"
260 ERASE A
270 RESUME 60
280 END
```

9.
Binary	Decimal
1011	11
10100	20
1111	15
1110	14
1010011	83
110011	51
1011100	92
1101111	111
11000000	192
10000111	135

11.
```
10 A$ = "ABCDEFGHIJKL"
20 FOR X = 1 TO 12
30    PRINT MID$(A$,1,X)
40 NEXT X
50 END
```

13.
```
RUN
  87
  72
  55
  54
```

15.
```
10 RANDOMIZE TIMER
20 FOR X = 1 TO 15
30    R = INT(26 * RND + 65)
40    PRINT CHR$(R);
50 NEXT X
60 END
```

17.
```
10 RANDOMIZE TIMER
20 FOR X = 1 TO 100
30    R = INT( 95 * RND + 32)
40    A$ = A$ + CHR$(R)
50    IF (R > 64 AND R < 91) OR (R > 96 AND R < 123)
          THEN L = L + 1
          ELSE IF R > 47 AND R < 58 THEN N = N + 1
                                  ELSE S = S + 1
60 NEXT X
70 PRINT "There are :";L;"letters,"
80 PRINT TAB(12);N;"numbers, and"
90 PRINT TAB(12);S;"special characters."
100 PRINT : PRINT A$
110 END
```

19.
```
1 REM A = Height
2 REM B = Distance to indent at bottom
3 REM c = Where bottom edge ends
20 S$ = "TRIANGLE"
30 INPUT "A, B, and C";A, B, C
40 S$ = S$ + S$
50 IF LEN(S$) < (C + LEN("TRIANGLE")) THEN 40
60 FOR H = 1 TO A
70    P1 = (B / A) * H
80    P2 = (C / A) * H
90    IF P1 < 1 THEN P1 = P1 + 1
100   PRINT TAB(P1);MID$(S$,P1,ABS(P2-P1))
110 NEXT H
120 END
```

CHAPTER EIGHT

1.
```
10 SCREEN 1,0 : COLOR 0,0
20 LINE (38,19) - (108,48), 2, BF
30 END
```

3.
```
10 SCREEN 1,0 : COLOR 0,1
20 LINE (140,0) - (140,199), 1
30 LINE (0,80) - (319,80), 3
40 END
```

5.
```
10 SCREEN 0,1 : COLOR 16,7,4
20 CLS
30 LOCATE 5,38
40 PRINT "Today Only!!"
50 PRINT TAB(38);"Uncle Bill's"
60 PRINT TAB(38);"WHAMBURGERS"
70 PRINT TAB(39);"Only $0.79"
80 END
```

7.
```
10 SCREEN 1,0 : COLOR 0,1
20 RANDOMIZE TIMER
30 DIM COUNT(10)
40 FOR I = 1 TO 100
50    X = INT(RND * 10 + 1)
60    FOR J = 1 TO 10
70       IF X = J THEN COUNT(J) = COUNT(J) + 1
80    NEXT J
90 NEXT I
100 HUE = 1 : WIDE = 16 : START = 16
110 LOCATE 24,1 : T = 2
120 FOR I = 1 TO 10
130    LINE (START,182) - (START + WIDE,182 - (COUNT(I)*10)),
              HUE, BF
140    HUE = HUE + 1
150    IF HUE > 3 THEN HUE = 1
160    START = START + WIDE + 8
170    PRINT TAB(T); I;
180    T = T + 3
190 NEXT I
200 FOR DELAY = 1 TO 1000 : NEXT DELAY
210 END
```

9.
```
10 SCREEN 1,0 : COLOR 0,1
20 CLS
30 FOR J = 1 TO 4
40    READ N$(J)
50    FOR I = 1 TO 7
60       READ PIZZA
70       TOTAL = TOTAL + PIZZA
80    NEXT I
90    AVG(J) = INT(TOTAL / 7)
100 NEXT J
110 HUE = 1 : WIDE = 16 : START = 16
120 LOCATE 24,1 : T = 2
130 FOR I = 1 TO 4
140    LINE (START,182) - (START + WIDE,182 - (AVG(I)*3)),HUE,BF
150    HUE = HUE + 1
160    IF HUE > 3 THEN HUE = 1
170    START = START + WIDE + (LEN(N$(I))*8)
180    PRINT TAB(T); N$(I);
190    T = T + LEN(N$(I)) + 2
200 NEXT I
210 FOR DELAY = 1 TO 1000 : NEXT DELAY
220 DATA SMITH, 18, 12, 9, 10, 16, 22, 14
230 DATA MUNYAN, 12, 21, 19, 16, 28, 20, 22
240 DATA RICARDO, 18, 20, 14, 19, 11, 16, 23
250 DATA FAZIOLI, 23, 27, 18, 16, 21, 14, 24
260 END
```

11.
```
10 CLS
20 SCREEN 1, 0
25 COLOR 0, 1
30 LINE(20,20) - (20,160), 1
40 LINE - (80,160), 1
50 LINE - (80, 20), 1
60 LINE - (140, 20), 1
70 LINE - (140, 160), 1
80 LINE - (20,20), 1
90 END
```

CHAPTER NINE

1.
```
10 INPUT N
20 IF N = 999 THEN 50
30 IF N < 0 THEN PRINT "No negative numbers allowed" : GOTO 10
40 PRINT "N =";N; TAB(17);"square roots = + or -";SQR(N) : GOTO 1
50 END
```

3.
```
5 PRINT "X"; TAB(20);"COS(X)"; TAB(40);"SIN(X+90)
10 FOR X = 0 TO 360 STEP 10
20    Y = X + 90
30    R1 = X * 3.141592654# / 180
40    R2 = Y * 3.141592654# / 180
50    PRINT X; TAB(20);COS(R1); TAB(40);SIN(R2)
60 NEXT X
70 END
```

5.
```
5 REM This program returns the ABS of N
10 INPUT N
20 PRINT SGN(N) * N
30 END
```

7.
```
10 PRINT "Radians"; TAB(20);"Degrees"
20 FOR R = 0 TO 3 STEP .25
30    D = R * 180 / 3.141592654#
40    PRINT R; TAB(20);D
50 NEXT R
60 END
```

9.
```
10 INPUT "Enter angle"; N
20 N = N * 3.1415926535# / 180
30 C = COS(N)
40 S = SIN(N)
50 T = TAN(N)
60 IF C > S AND C > T THEN PRINT "COSINE =";C
                      ELSE IF S > T THEN PRINT "SIN =";S
                      ELSE PRINT "TANGENT =";T
70 END
```

11.
```
10 DEF FNF(X) = 9 * X^3 - 7 * X^2 + 4 * X - 1
20 INPUT "A,B";A,B
30 PRINT FNF(B) - FNF(A)
40 END
```

13.
```
10 PRINT " X"; TAB(20);"LN(X)"; TAB(40); "EXP(X)
20 PRINT STRING$(47,"-")
30 FOR X = 1 TO 15
40    PRINT X; TAB(20); LOG(X); TAB(40); EXP(X)
50 NEXT X
60 END
```

15.
```
RUN
  5              -4              3              4
```

17.
```
10 DEF FNA(X) = X^2 + 3 * X + 2
20 DEF FNB(X) = LOG(X^2 + 1) - X
30 DEF FNC(X) = ATN(SIN(X))
40 PRINT  TAB(2);"X"; TAB(16);"X^2 + 3X + 2"; TAB(40);
   "LOG(X^2 + 1) - X"; TAB(60);"ATN(SIN(X))"
50 FOR X = -10 TO 10
60    PRINT X; TAB(20);FNA(X); TAB(40);FNB(X); TAB(60);FNC(X)
70 NEXT X
80 END
```

19a.
```
10 PRINT " X"; TAB(12);"EXP(X)"; TAB(25);"LOG(EXP(X))"
20 FOR X = -5 TO 10
30    PRINT X; TAB(9); EXP(X); TAB(28); LOG(EXP(X))
40 NEXT X
50 END
```

b.
```
1 REM Note how the rounding error effects output.
10 PRINT " X"; TAB(12);"LOG(X)" ;TAB(25);"EXP(LOG(X))"
20 FOR X = 1 TO 151 STEP 10
30    PRINT X; TAB(11);LOG(X); TAB(28);EXP(LOG(X))
40 NEXT X
50 END
```

c. The functions EXP() and LOG() appear
to be the inverse of each other. Occasionally
values appear that differ slightly from the
value of the original number. This can be
attributed to the rounding error.
Therefore, EXP(LOG(n)) = LOG(EXP(n)), an
inverse relation.

21.
```
10 P = .5 : REM Initial investment
20 P = P * EXP(.08 * 10) : REM First ten years
30 FOR X = 11 TO 50 : REM The 11th to 50th year
40    P = P - .05 : REM The nickel withdrawn
50    P = P * EXP(.08 * 1)
60 NEXT X
70 P = INT(100 * P + .05) / 100
80 PRINT "After 50 years Dennis has $";P
90 END
```

CHAPTER TEN

1a.
```
10 RANDOMIZE TIMER
20 DIM R(50)
30 FOR X = 1 TO 50
40    R(X) = INT(21 * RND)
50 NEXT X
60 OPEN "O", 1, "RANUM.DAT"
70 REM
80 REM
90 REM
100 REM Now write to the file
110 FOR I = 1 TO 50
120    WRITE #1, R(I)
130 NEXT I
140 CLOSE 1
150 END
```

b.
```
1 REM R = The number read from the file
2 REM S = The sum of all R's
10 OPEN "I", 2, "RANUM.DAT"
20 FOR I = 1 TO 50
30    INPUT #2, R
40    S = S + R
50 NEXT I
60 CLOSE 2
70 PRINT "The sum is";S
80 END
```

3a.
```
10 OPEN "O", 1, "NAMES"
20 FOR N = 1 TO 10
30    INPUT "Name";N$
40    WRITE #1, N$
50 NEXT N
60 CLOSE 1
70 END
```

b.
```
1 REM X = Number of qualifying names found
2 REM N$ = The name found in the file 'NAMES'
10 X = 0
20 OPEN "I", 1, "NAMES"
30 FOR I = 1 TO 10
40    INPUT #1, N$
50    IF N$ > "C" AND N$ < "I" THEN PRINT N$ : X = X + 1
60 NEXT I
70 CLOSE 1
80 IF X = 0 THEN PRINT "None found"
90 END
```

5a.
```
1 REM N$ = Name
2 REM R = Hourly pay rate
3 REM D = Number of dependents
4 REM M = Medical insurance deduction
5 REM L = Life insurance deduction
10 OPEN "O", 1, "PAY.DAT"
20 FOR X = 1 TO 10
30    READ N$, R, D, M, L
40    WRITE #1, N$, R, D, M, L
50 NEXT X
60 CLOSE 1
70 REM
100 DATA MENACE DENNIS, 1, 0, 2, 1
110 DATA BEAVER LEAVITTO, 2.25, 0, 1, 1
120 DATA ISLAND GILLIGAN, 4.50, 0, 2, 1
130 DATA WILSON MISTER, 4.95, 2, 5, 3
140 DATA HOGAN COLONEL, 40, 2, 3, 3
150 DATA SCHULTZ SEARGENT, 30, 1, 1, 2
160 DATA KIRK JIM, 78.50, 1, 1, 1
170 DATA BUNNY BUGS, 12.45, 2, 5, 3
180 DATA SERLING ROD, 55.90, 2, 2, 1
190 DATA BOND JAMES, 9.25, 3, 0, 0
200 END
```

b.

```
10 REM   N$ = Name
11 REM R = Hourly pay rate
12 REM D = Number of dependents
13 REM M = Medical insurance deduction
14 REM L = Life insurance deduction
15 REM
20 DEF FNR(X) = INT(100 * X + .5) / 100 : REM Round to nearest cent
30 OPEN "I", 1, "PAY.DAT"
40 FOR X = 1 TO 10
50    INPUT #1, N$, R, D, M, L
60    READ H : REM Get hours worked
70    G = H * R : T = (25 - 2 * D) * G / 100
80    IF T < 0 THEN T = 0
90    P = G - T - M - L
100    PRINT N$
102    PRINT STRING$(LEN(N$), "-") : PRINT
110    PRINT "Hours worked:"; TAB(42); H
120    PRINT "Gross pay:"; TAB(41);"$";FNR(G)
130    PRINT "Tax:"; TAB(41);"$";FNR(T)
140    PRINT "Medical insurance:"; TAB(41);"$";FNR(M)
150    PRINT "Life insurance:"; TAB(41);"$";FNR(L)
160    PRINT "Net:"; TAB(41);"$";FNR(P)
170    PRINT
180 NEXT X
190 CLOSE 1
220 DATA 40, 37.1, 51, 48, 39.2, 18.6, 59.8, 45.3, 68.3, 41
230 END
```

7a.

```
1 REM N$() = Student names
2 REM F$() = Fraternity names
3 REM A() = Ages
10 DIM N$(30), F$(30), A(30)
20 FOR X = 1 TO 30
30    INPUT "Name";N$(X)
40    INPUT "Fraternity"; F$(X)
50    INPUT "Age"; A(X)
60 NEXT X
100 REM Now write to file
110 OPEN "O", 1, "FRAT.DAT"
120 FOR I = 1 TO 30
130 WRITE #1, N$(I), F$(I), A(I)
140 NEXT I
150 CLOSE 1
160 END
```

b.

```
1 REM N$ = STUDENT NAMES
2 REM F$ = FRATERNITY NAMES
3 REM A = AGES
10 OPEN "I", 1, "FRAT.DAT"
20 OPEN "O", 2, "THETA.DAT"
30 FOR X = 1 TO 30
40    INPUT #1, N$, F$, A
50    IF F$ = "THETA DELTA" THEN WRITE #2, N$, A
60 NEXT X
70 CLOSE 1, 2
80 END
```

c.
```
1 REM N$ = Student names
2 REM A = Ages
10 OPEN "I", 1, "THETA.DAT"
20 OPEN "O", 2, "THETA20.DAT"
30 WHILE EOF(1) = 0
40      INPUT #1, N$, A
50      IF A = 20 THEN WRITE #2, N$
60 WEND
70 CLOSE 1, 2
80 END
```

9.
```
10 REM    X = Row of person's seat
20 REM    Y = Column of person's seat
30 REM S$() = Person's name at seat X, Y
40 DIM S$(10, 5)
50 ON ERROR GOTO 270
60 OPEN "I", 1, "SHOW.DAT"
70 I = 1
80 WHILE  I < 50
90      INPUT #1, X, Y, S$(X,Y)
100      I = I + 1
110      IF EOF(1) = -1 THEN I = 99
120 WEND
130 IF I = 99 THEN 150
140 PRINT "I'm sorry, we have a packed house" : CLOSE 1 : GOTO 320
150 CLOSE 1
160 INPUT "Your name";F$
170 INPUT "What seat would you like <ROW, COLUMN>";X1, Y1
180 IF X1 < 1 OR X1 > 10 OR Y1 < 1 OR Y1 > 5 THEN 170
190 IF S$(X1, Y1) <> "" THEN PRINT "That seat is taken" : GOTO 170
200 PRINT "DRAMA CLUB SHOW"
210 PRINT F$;" has"
220 PRINT "reserved row";X1;"seat";Y1;"for"
230 PRINT "July 4, 1985" : PRINT
240 OPEN "A", 1, "SHOW.DAT" : REM Append new person to the list
250 WRITE #1, X1, Y1, F$
260 CLOSE 1 : GOTO 320
270 REM If error there may be no file
280 IF ERR <> 53 THEN PRINT "Unexpected error." : STOP
290 CLOSE 1 : OPEN "O", 1, "SHOW.DAT"
300 WRITE #1, 0, 0, B
310 CLOSE 1 : RESUME
320 END
```

CHAPTER ELEVEN

1a.
```
1 REM    L = ASCII of letter
2 REM    L$ = letter
3 REM
10 OPEN "R", 1, "LETTER.DAT"
20 FIELD 1, 1 AS L$
30 FOR L = ASC("A") TO ASC("Z")
40    LSET L$ = CHR$(L)
50     PUT 1
60 NEXT L
70 CLOSE 1
80 END
```

b.
```
10 RANDOMIZE TIMER
20 OPEN "R", 1, "LETTER.DAT"
30 FIELD 1, 1 AS L$
40 FOR L = 1 TO 5
50    GET 1, INT(RND * 26 + 1)
60    PRINT L$;
70 NEXT L
80 CLOSE 1
90 END
```

3a.
```
1 REM N$, N1$ = Name (20 characters)
2 REM B, B$ = Balance (4 characters)
3 REM A = Account number
4 REM
5 CLS
10 OPEN "R", 1, "ACCOUNTS.DAT", 24
20 FIELD 1, 20 AS N$, 4 AS B$
30 FOR A = 1 TO 25
40    INPUT "Name";N1$ : LSET N$ = N1$
50    INPUT "Starting balance";B : LSET B$ = MKS$(B)
60    PRINT "Account number";A;"assigned."
70    PUT 1, A
80    PRINT
90 NEXT A
100 CLOSE 1
110 END
```

b.
```
1 REM N$ = Name (20 Characters)
2 REM B$ = Balance (4 Characters)
3 REM A1 = Account Number
4 REM T$ = Transaction Flag
5 CLS
6 REM
10 OPEN"R", 1, "ACCOUNTS.DAT", 24
20 FIELD 1, 20 AS N$, 4 AS B$
30 PRINT "Enter a negative number to stop"
40 INPUT "Account";A1
50    IF A1 < = 0 THEN 140
60    GET 1, A1
70    IF N$ = STRING$(20,0) THEN PRINT "Invalid Account #"
                                   : GOTO 40
80    INPUT "Deposit (D) or withdrawal (W)";T$
90    INPUT"Amount"; A2
100   IF ASC(T$) = 87 THEN A2 = - A2
110   LSET B$ = MKS$(CVS(B$) + A2)
120   PUT 1, A1 : PRINT"Transaction recorded"
130 GOTO 40
140 CLOSE 1
150 END
```

c.
```
1 REM N$ = Name (20 characters)
2 REM B$ = Balance (4 characters)
3 REM A = Account number
5 CLS
10 OPEN "R", 1, "ACCOUNTS.DAT", 24
20 FIELD 1, 20 AS N$, 4 AS B$
30 FOR A = 1 TO 25
40    GET 1
50    IF CVS(B$) > = 0 THEN 140
60    PRINT
70    PRINT "Dear ";N$
80    PRINT "      It has come to our attention that your"
90    PRINT "account is overdrawn by $";-CVS(B$);". Please"
100   PRINT "make a deposit for at least that amount immediately."
110   PRINT : PRINT TAB(40); "Thank you"
120   PRINT : PRINT TAB(40); "THE BANK"
130   GOTO 210
140   IF CVS(B$) < 500 THEN 210
150   PRINT
160   PRINT "Dear ";N$
170   PRINT "      You have an exceptionally large account."
180   PRINT "You will be receiving a toaster in the mail as"
190   PRINT "an award."
200   PRINT : PRINT TAB(40); "THE BANK"
210 NEXT A
220 CLOSE 1
230 END
```

5a.
```
1 REM N$, N1$ = Name (20 characters)
2 REM F$, F1$ = Fraternity (20 Characters)
3 REM  A , A$ = Age (2 Characters)
4 REM  S       = Student Number
10 OPEN "R", 1, "FRAT.DAT", 42
20 FIELD 1, 20 AS N$, 20 AS F$, 2 AS A$
30 FOR S = 1 TO 30
40    INPUT "Name";N1$ : LSET N$ = N1$
50    INPUT "Fraternity";F1$ : LSET F$ = F1$
60    INPUT "Age";A : LSET A$ = MKI$(A)
70    PUT 1
80    PRINT
90 NEXT S
100 CLOSE 1
110 END
```

b.
```
1 REM N$ = Name (20 characters)
2 REM F$ = Fraternity (20 characters)
3 REM A$ = Age (2 characters)
4 REM S  = Student number
10 OPEN "R", 1, "FRAT.DAT", 42
20 FIELD 1, 20 AS N$, 20 AS F$, 2 AS N$
30 OPEN "O", 2, "SIGMA.DAT"
40 FOR S = 1 TO 30
50    GET 1
60    IF LEFT$(F$,9) = "SIGMA CHI" THEN WRITE #2, N$, CVI(A$)
70 NEXT S
80 CLOSE 1,2
90 END
```

c.

```
1 REM N$    = Name (20 characters)
2 REM F$    = Fraternity (20 characters)
3 REM A$    = Age (2 characters)
4 REM S1    = Student number
5 REM R,S   = Row, Seat
6 REM R()   = Previously picked student numbers
7 REM C$(,) = Classroom seating chart
10 RANDOMIZE TIMER
20 OPEN "R", 1, "FRAT.DAT", 42
30 FIELD 1, 20 AS N$, 20 AS F$, 2 AS A$
40 DIM R(24), C$(5,5)
50 FOR R = 1 TO 5
60     FOR S = 1 TO 5
70         S1 = INT (30 * RND + 1)
80         FOR P = 1 TO (R-1) * 5 + S - 1
90             IF S1 = R(P) THEN 70
100        NEXT P
110        R((R-1) * 5 + S - 1) = S1
120        GET 1, S1
130        C$(R,S) = LEFT$(N$,INSTR(N$, "  "))
140     NEXT S
150 NEXT R
160 CLOSE 1
170 FOR R = 1 TO 5
180     PRINT "Row";R;":";TAB(13);C$(R,1); TAB(26);C$(R,2);
190     PRINT TAB(39);C$(R,3); TAB(53);C$(R,4); TAB(68);C$(R,5)
200 PRINT
210 NEXT R
220 CLOSE 1
230 END
```

7a.

```
1 REM W$ = word (10 characters)
10 OPEN "R", 1, "SENTENCE.DAT", 10
20 FIELD 1, 10  AS W$
30 FOR X = 1 TO 25
40     READ W1$
45     LSET W$ = W1$
50     PUT 1
60 NEXT X
70 DATA THE, A, AN, DISK, IS
80 DATA MONITOR, FASTER, SLOWER, PRINTER, MODEM
90 DATA INTERFACE, BOOK, CAR, RAN, DRIVE
100 DATA BOY, JUMP, PLAY, WHEEL, GIRL
110 DATA CAT, DOG, HOUSE, LIGHT, STREET
120 CLOSE 1
130 END
```

b.
```
10 REM W$ =  Word (10 characters)
20 RANDOMIZE TIMER
30 I = 1
40 OPEN "R", 1, "SENTENCE.DAT", 10
50 FIELD 1, 10 AS W$
60 FOR X = 1 TO 5
70    R = (25 * RND + 1)
80    GET 1 , R
90    IF I = 11 THEN 140
100   IF MID$(W$,I,1) = " " THEN 140
110   W1$ = W1$ + MID$(W$,I,1)
120   I = I + 1
130   GOTO 90
140   I = 1 : PRINT W1$;" "; : W1$ = ""
150 NEXT X
160 CLOSE 1
170 END
```

CHAPTER TWELVE

1a.
```
1 REM W$ = Word
10 OPEN "O", 1, "WORDS.DAT"
20 FOR X = 1 TO 25
30    READ W$ : WRITE #1, W$
40 NEXT X
50 CLOSE 1
60 DATA AIRCRAFT, DOG, TERMINAL, HAT, JAGUAR
70 DATA PRINTER, LASER, VEHICLE, HARBOR, NETWORK
80 DATA DAY, EARTH, COMPUTER, RADIO, ALARM
90 DATA THEATHER, BOOK, ZOO, ROBOT, FILE
100 DATA JET, SIGN, LAKE, TRAIN, BOAT
110 END
```

b.
```
1 REM W$() = Word
10 DIM W$(25)
20 OPEN "I", 1, "WORDS.DAT"
30 FOR X = 1 TO 25
40    INPUT #1, W$(X)
50 NEXT X
60 CLOSE 1
70 L$ = "UNORDERED" : I = 1
80 WHILE L$ <> "ORDERED"
90     L$ = "ORDERED"
100    FOR X = 25 TO I + 1 STEP -1
110       IF W$(X) > W$(X - 1) THEN 130
120       SWAP W$(X), W$(X - 1) : L$ = "UNORDERED"
130    NEXT X
140    I = I + 1
150 WEND
160 CLS
170 OPEN "O", 1, "WORDS.TEMP"
180 FOR X = 1 TO 25
190    PRINT W$(X) : WRITE #1, W$(X)
200 NEXT X
210 CLOSE 1
220 END
```

3a.
```
10 REM PH$ = Phone number
20 OPEN "O", 1, "PHONE.DAT"
30 FOR X = 1 TO 6
40    READ PH$
50    WRITE #1, PH$
60 NEXT X
70 CLOSE 1
80 DATA 676-2004, 659-4444, 676-5112, 867-5309, 932-6840,
       867-1441
90 END
```

b.
```
10 OPEN "I", 1, "PHONE.DAT"
20 FOR X = 1 TO 6
30    INPUT #1, PH$(X)
40 NEXT X
50 L$ = "UNSORTED" : I = 1
60 WHILE L$ <> "SORTED"
70      L$ = "SORTED"
80      FOR X = 6 TO I + 1 STEP -1
90         IF LEFT$(PH$(X), 3) > LEFT$(PH$(X - 1), 3) THEN 110
100           SWAP PH$(X), PH$(X - 1) : L$ = "UNSORTED"
110        NEXT X
120      I = I + 1
130 WEND
140 CLOSE 1
150 OPEN "O", 1, "PHONE.DAT"
160 FOR X = 1 TO 6
170    PRINT PH$(X) : WRITE #1, PH$(X)
180 NEXT X
190 CLOSE 1
200 END
```

5a.
```
1 REM W1$ = Word (10 characters)
10 OPEN "R", 1, "WORDS.DAT", 10
20 FIELD 1, 10 AS W1$
30 FOR X = 1 TO 25
40    READ W$ : LSET W1$ =W$
50    PUT 1
60 NEXT X
70 CLOSE 1
80 DATA AIRCRAFT, DOG, TERMINAL, HAT, JAGUAR
90 DATA PRINTER, LASER, VEHICLE, HARBOR, NETWORK
100  DATA DAY, EARTH, COMPUTER, RADIO, ALARM
110 DATA THEATHER, BOOK, ZOO, ROBOT, FILE
120 DATA JET, SIGN, LAKE, TRAIN, BOAT
130 END
```

b.
```
10  REM W1$ = Word (10 characters)
20  DIM W$(25)
30  OPEN "R", 1, "WORDS.DAT", 10
40  FIELD 1, 10 AS W1$
50  L$ = "UNORDERED" : I = 1
60  WHILE L$ <> "ORDERED"
70      L$ = "ORDERED"
80      FOR X = 25 TO I + 1 STEP -1
90          GET 1, X
100         T$ = W1$
110         GET 1, X - 1
120         IF T$ > W1$ THEN 140
130         PUT 1,X : LSET W1$ = T$ : PUT 1,X-1: L$ = "UNORDERED"
140     NEXT X
150     I = I + 1
160 WEND
170 CLS
180 FOR X = 1 TO 25
190 GET 1, X
200     PRINT W1$
210 NEXT X
220 CLOSE 1
230 END
```

7a.
```
10  OPEN "R", 1, "EMPLOYEE.DAT", 39
20  FIELD 1, 20 AS N1$, 2 AS A1$, 11 AS SS1$, 4 AS S1$, 2 AS Y1$
30  FOR X = 1 TO 20
40      INPUT "Name";N$ : LSET N1$ = N$
50      INPUT "Age";A : LSET A1$ =   MKI$(A)
60      INPUT "Social Security number";SS$ : LSET SS1$ = SS$
70      INPUT "Salary";S : LSET S1$ = MKS$(S)
80      INPUT "Years of service";Y : LSET Y1$ =MKI$(Y)
90      PUT 1
100 NEXT X
110 CLOSE 1
120 END
```

b.
```
10  DIM S(20). E(20)
20  OPEN "R", 1, "EMPLOYEE.DAT", 39
30  FIELD 1, 20 AS N1$, 2 AS A1$, 11 AS SS1$, 4 AS S1$, 2 AS Y1$
40  FOR X = 1 TO 20
50      GET 1
60      S(X) = CVI(S1$)
70      E(X) = X
80  NEXT X
90  CLOSE 1
100 L$ = "UNSORTED" : I = 1
110 WHILE L$ <> "SORTED"
120     L$ = "SORTED"
130     FOR X = 20 TO I + 1 STEP -1
140         IF S(X) > S(X-1) THEN 160
150         SWAP E(X), E(X-1) : L$ = "UNSORTED"
160     NEXT X
170     I = I + 1
180 WEND
190 OPEN "O", 1, "SALARY.DAT"
200 FOR X = 1 TO 20
210     WRITE #1, E(X)
220 NEXT X
230 CLOSE 1
```

INDEX